THE COMPLETE IDIOT'S GUIDE TO

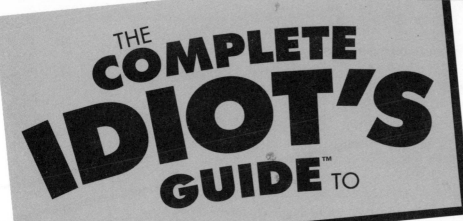

Curling

- ♦ **A complete introduction** to the game of curling
- ♦ **The rules**, shots, strategy, equipment, and techniques
- ♦ **Fun facts**—from your local club to national competitions

An Alpha Books/Prentice Hall Canada Copublication

Prentice Hall Canada Inc., Scarborough, Ontario

Rod Bolton & Ann Douglas

Canadian Cataloguing in Publication Data

Bolton, Rod

  The complete idiot's guide to curling

Includes bibliographical references and index.

ISBN 0-13-081815-1

1. Curling. I. Douglas, Ann, 1963- . II. Title.

GV845.B64 1998   796.964   C98-932028-6

© 1998 Prentice-Hall Canada Inc., Scarborough, Ontario
A Division of Simon & Schuster/A Viacom Company

Prentice-Hall, Inc., Upper Saddle River, New Jersey
Prentice-Hall International (UK) Limited, London
Prentice-Hall of Australia, Pty. Limited, Sydney
Prentice-Hall Hispanoamericana, S.A., Mexico City
Prentice-Hall of India Private Limited, New Delhi
Prentice-Hall of Japan, Inc., Tokyo
Simon & Schuster Southeast Asia Private Limited, Singapore
Editora Prentice-Hall do Brasil, Ltda., Rio de Janeiro

ISBN 0-13-081815-1

Director, Trade Group: Robert Harris
Copy Editor: Karen Rolfe
Assistant Editor: Joan Whitman
Production Editor: Lu Cormier
Production Coordinator: Shannon Potts
Art Direction: Mary Opper
Cover Design: Kyle Gell
Cover Photograph: Christopher Dew, The St. Clair Group
Page Layout: Gail Ferreira Ng-A-Kien

1 2 3 4 5   RRD   02 01 00 99 98

Printed and bound in the United States of America

Visit the Prentice Hall Canada Web site! Send us your comments, browse our catalogues, and more. www.phcanada.com

To all the curlers who curled with me over the years and who know only too well that I have seldom been able to put all this theory into practice; and to my loving wife who not only had to put up with my playing, but also had to put up with the postmortem afterward.

—R.B.

To my father for teaching me that there's more to playing than winning.

—A.D.

Contents

Introduction

You don't have to hang around a curling rink very long to discover that curling is a sport like no other. Curlers don't hip-check one another, nor do they use their brooms to hook or slash their competitors. If anything, they're surprisingly civil to one another, shaking hands before and after each game.

This is "The Spirit of Curling,"—a code of behavior followed by curlers around the world. You could show up in a rink on the other side of the world and expect to experience the same ideals of fair play that you're likely to encounter at the rink in your hometown.

We believe that it's more important to understand "The Spirit of Curling" than to master the various shots described in this book—although we do devote a fair bit of copy to strategy and skill. (Our editors would have been less than impressed if we handed in a 250-page book that merely reiterated, time and time again, the importance of being nice to your opponents. An important message, yes, but clearly the makings of a less-than-captivating book!)

Before we jump in and tell you exactly what we've got in store for you, we're going to tackle the question that's likely been burning in your mind: why on earth did it take two of us to write an Idiot's Guide?

Actually, there's a very simple reason why we collaborated on this project: one of us was an expert (at least when it comes to curling!) and the other was an Idiot. While Rod wrote this book from the vantage point of someone who has been curling since the pre-brush era (we'll get to that later on!), Ann wrote from the perspective of a total newbie: someone who didn't understand why rocks curled, what sweeping was supposed to accomplish, and how on earth the scoreboard worked.

Bottom line? We will have done our job if we've managed to convey the important facts about the sport (Rod's job) in a manner that even the most sports-challenged Idiot can understand (Ann's job).

Here's what you can expect to learn from this particular Expert–Idiot tag team:

In Part I, we describe the sport's long and proud history and then get into the specifics of the game: what equipment you need, who's on a team, and how the game is played.

In Part II, we move on to a detailed discussion of the fundamentals: the physics of the game, skill, and strategy.

In Part III, we focus on the importance of physical and mental fitness, and show you what it takes to have a winning team.

In Part IV, we zero in on bonspiels and other forms of competition that you may wish to experience as either a spectator or a participant.

The Appendices at the back of the book are crammed with all types of need-to-know information, including a glossary of curling terms, curling rules for both Canada and the United States, directories of curling organizations and suppliers; leads on the hottest Internet resources; recommended reading; and much more.

Like any other Complete Idiot's Guide, *The Complete Idiot's Guide to Curling* contains some other important elements designed to make for a more enjoyable—and more informative—read. Be sure to watch for the following sidebars as they appear in the text:

Rock Talk

This is where you'll find concise definitions of curling lingo.

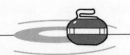

Tales from the Rink

This is where you'll find stories about curlers and curling.

From the Skip

This is where you'll find practical tips on improving your game.

This is where we'll pass along cautionary words and issue warnings.

We hope you'll enjoy reading this book as much as we enjoyed writing it.

Good curling!

Rod Bolton and Ann Douglas

Acknowledgments

We would like to take a moment to thank the large number of people who demonstrated "The Spirit of Curling" to us time and time again during the writing of this book. These people include Doug Anderson, marketing director for the United States Curling Association; Edieann Biesbrock-Didham of the United States Women's Curling Association; Steve Brown, coach of the U.S. Women's Olympic curling team; Dr. Bob Cowan, a living and breathing encyclopedia when it comes to the sport of curling; Marguerite Daubney, physiotherapist; Sarah Detomsi, physiotherapist; Wayne Gilmour, drawmaster for the Kingston Curling Club; Jim Henderson, the sales and marketing director for *Sweep! Curling's Magazine;* Colleen Jones, former Canadian curling champion and sportscaster extraordinaire; Danny Lamoreux, manager of the Ottawa Curling Club; Doug Maxwell, a journalist who has spent his career covering the world of curling and who continues to publish the *Canadian Curling News;* Dr. Vera Pezer, sports psychologist for the 1988 and 1992 Olympic curling teams; Warren Proctor, marketing director for the Canadian Curling Association; Marg Regts, curling enthusiast and bonspiel champ; Bill Tschirhard, national high-performance coach for the Canadian Curling Association; and the countless other curlers who wrote to us to share their wonderful curling stories.

We would also like to thank our research assistants Janice Kent and Barb Payne, for helping us to dig up such terrific material; and our families, for understanding why we spent so much time in front of our computers—during the height of curling season, no less!

Part I
Getting Started

If you've watched a game of curling at your friendly neighborhood rink, you already know that there's much more to the sport than most people realize. There's skill, there's strategy... and then there's the socializing after the game!

Over the next few chapters, we're going to give you a broad overview of the game—teaching you enough of the curling lingo to prevent you from embarrassing yourself in front of your skip. (Hey, your mother was right: first impressions do count!)

So sit back, get comfortable, and get ready to take a quick tour of the ice....

The Game

"Picture bowling if the pins belonged to both you and your opponents. Or horizontal darts on ice, with big Fisher Price™ tea kettles as pucks. Or maybe hockey and chess blended with billiards and croquet, then crossbred with a really good scrub of the kitchen floor."

That's how a news story on the MSNBC Web site described curling to a puzzled American public when the sport debuted as a medal sport at the 1998 Winter Olympics in Nagano, Japan.

While the 15,000 Americans who curl on a regular basis were quick to jump to the sport's defence, the majority of Americans seemed determined to treat curling as a sport with about as much credibility as snowboarding—and a whole lot less sex appeal.

Many Americans probably agreed with late-night talk-show host David Letterman when he jokingly urged the U.S. curling team to boost the sport's viewing appeal by throwing in a few punches now and again: "If you want the game to grow, go out and fight a little bit," he urged them.

While U.S. Olympic curler Myles Brundidge—a guest on the Letterman show—did his best to humor his host, admitting there were times when the sheer frustration of the

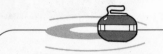

Tales from the Rink

Curling is enjoyed by 1.5 million men, women, and children in 33 countries. Approximately 80 percent of the world's curlers—1.2 million people—are Canadian.

game was enough to drive a curler to blows, in the end he managed to deliver resounding proof of what the American public had already decided: curling is a sport like no other.

The Ten Top Reasons Why Curling Is So Popular

On the off-chance that Letterman decides to invite curlers on his show again, someone should be prepared to explain the game's appeal in a manner that even Dave can understand. As a service to curlers everywhere, we are proud to present our "Top Ten Reasons Why Curling Is So Popular." We've even presented them in descending order, in true Letterman style, to make it easier for Dave:

10. You can find a curling rink anywhere.

While you can find curling rinks in large cities, the majority of the 1200 Canadian and 138 American curling clubs are found in small communities—towns and hamlets that often have little more in the way of amenities than a grocery store, a bank, and a convenience store. Curling isn't just a sport in these small towns, it's a way of life. Heck, it's practically a religious experience.

9. The game is relatively inexpensive to play.

While you can easily fork over $1000 or more per year for the privilege of batting around a few golf balls, a typical curling club membership can be had for between $100 and $200 per year. Since there's considerably less equipment to purchase than for golf—you don't, after all, need a bag full of brooms in order to play various shots!—curling tends to be an affordable sport.

8. It's played by people from all walks of life.

Because curling is relatively affordable, it attracts people from all types of occupations. The assembly line worker is every bit as likely to curl as the executive vice-president of the plant. Hey, they might even be on the same team.

This is how Jean Sonmor describes the camaraderie in her book *Burned by the Rock*: "In curling rinks you see vivacious stay-at-home grandmothers in intense conversation with slick male accountants. On the street, they inhabit different worlds but here, in the club, they are buddies."

Bottom line? Curling is one of life's great levelers.

7. It appeals to people of all ages.

It doesn't matter whether you're eight or eighty. Curling is one of the few sports that's open to people of all ages. As a result, most bonspiels boast at least one rink with two or more generations of curling enthusiasts from the same family. (Yes, it's true—the game does get in your genes.)

6. Sportsmanship counts— period.

The so-called "Spirit of Curling" dictates a level of decorum that is absent from most modern sports. Rather than distracting your opponents or doing anything that might prevent them from doing their best, you encourage them. And should you discover that you've inadvertently broken one of the rules of the game, you're honor-bound to report your infringement. While this code of conduct probably sounds like sheer lunacy to hockey and baseball players, to curlers around the world it makes perfect sense. After all, a true curler—one who understands the spirit of the sport—realizes that it's better to lose a game than to win unfairly.

5. There's a certain mystique to the game.

The fact that rocks curl is fascinating enough, but the fact that rocks curl different amounts at different speeds and on different parts of the ice means that the game is anything but boring.

What's more, it's quite common for the ice to change substantially during the course of a game. The pebble—curling-speak for the intentional roughing of the ice surface—gets worn in, and frost may build up near the outside edges of the sheet. The cycling of the refrigeration system may even change

Tales from the Rink

"Much of the tone and etiquette of the curling world seems to have originated in an earlier, more sedate world where it was not considered appropriate to go into paroxysms of delight when you win. One should be sensitive to the feelings of the loser, shake hands, commiserate, and buy the drinks. Only later, when you're alone, is it acceptable to dance around with delight."

—Jean Sonmor, *Burned by the Rock.*

Tales from the Rink

Former Canadian women's curling champion Colleen Jones acquired a healthy respect for the physics of curling when she decided to build a miniature rink in her own backyard. It didn't take her long to discover that there is more to making ice than meets the eye. The curling stone that she had carefully transported back from Scotland didn't just perform poorly—it wouldn't budge at all.

the speed of the ice—a real concern at some of the older rinks.

It's kind of like what happens to a baseball field when it rains—but in this case the curlers don't pick up their rocks and go home.

4. Anything can happen on the ice.

No matter how good your chances are or how well you played the day before, anything can happen when your team hits the ice. It's a lesson that the Canadian Olympic men's curling team learned the hard way in Nagano. After Canadian lead George Karrys was quoted in the media as saying that the 50th- to 60th-ranked teams in Canada could beat the best teams in Europe hands down, his team was slaughtered by the Swiss team 9–3. The moral of the story? The game ain't over until the full-figured curler sings.

3. You don't have to be a jock to enjoy the game.

Curling is a sport that is forgiving to the less-than-athletically inclined and has emerged as the sport of choice for many a phys-ed dropout. Still, despite the skewering that many Olympic curlers were forced to endure at the hands of the U.S. media, curling is not a sport for couch potatoes. Whether the non-curling majority chooses to believe it or not, sweeping is downright hard work that demands both physical conditioning and endurance. We kid you not.

2. It's a thinking person's game.

Curling has often been compared to chess, and it bears more than a passing resemblance to snooker as well. It's a game that relies more on strategy and skill than on speed or sheer brute force. Consequently, it's not unusual for team members to spend a considerable amount of time discussing strategy before attempting a particularly challenging shot. It's hearing the strategy that makes it so appealing to the large number of non-curlers who remain glued to their television sets throughout the championship season.

1. It's a social sport.

It's hard to imagine a sport that's more social than curling. While the powers-that-be in curling circles are trying to tone down the sport's reputation as the game of party animals, the social aspects of curling are largely responsible for its extraordinary popularity. Curling is a great way to meet people, particularly in rural Canada where a membership in the local curling club is right up there with other necessities of life like food and shelter.

In his book *The Joy of Curling: A Celebration*, Ed Lukowich describes the bond that emerges between those who share the game of curling: "No matter where I travel, the intensity on the ice is matched by a goodwill off the ice, a shared refreshment, a couple of laughs, and a fellowship that is unsurpassed. Those who have been swept up in its spell know that no other game can match curling in its sportsmanship and camaraderie."

Only in Canada? Not!

Curling is most popular in Canada, Scotland, and the United States, but it's also enjoyed in a number of other countries.

The following countries belong to the World Curling Federation:

Andorra

Australia

Austria

Belgium

Bulgaria

Canada

Czech Republic

Denmark

England

Finland

France

Germany

Hungary

Iceland

Italy

Japan

Korea

Liechtenstein

Luxembourg

Tales from the Rink

The rule book of the Royal Caledonian Curling Club in Edinburgh, Scotland, specified that whiskey punch was to be the usual drink of the club to order to "encourage the barley crops." The early rules of the Montreal Curling Club—later renamed the Royal Montreal Curling Club—stated that the losing party was to pay for a bowl of whiskey toddy, which was to be placed in the middle of the table for the enjoyment of their opponents.

Tales from the Rink

"At the Brier, the parties are interrupted twice a day by curling games, but nobody complains, because curling is what they came to see."

—Jack Matheson, quoted in Doug Maxwell's *The First Fifty*.

Mexico

Netherlands

New Zealand

Norway

Romania

Russia

Scotland

Sweden

Switzerland

U.S. Virgin Islands

United States

Wales

Many of these countries are new to the game. The World Curling Federation estimates that approximately 15 other countries have established organized curling during the past decade alone.

In Canada, the sport is played in every province and territory, but is most popular in Saskatchewan where one in four people curl—a rate of participation that's five times as high as the national average.

Tales from the Rink

There are more than twice as many curlers registered in Saskatchewan as in the entire United States.

In the U.S., curling is most popular in Wisconsin, Minnesota, North Dakota, and in the New England, Great Lakes, and mid-Atlantic states. According to the United States Curling Association, there are also pockets of curling activity in other states, including Alaska, Washington, California, Texas, Colorado, Nebraska, Kansas, Missouri, and North Carolina.

In the Beginning...

Curling is a sport with a long and proud history, which you choose to ignore at your own peril. Failing to provide the appropriate rendition of the sport's history doesn't merely confirm that you're a novice. It also indicates that you haven't read *The Complete Idiot's Guide To Curling*—a major sin in our eyes at least.

As you've no doubt gathered, curling is a game that is steeped in tradition. Just whose traditions it relies upon, however, is a matter of great controversy. While most curling historians agree that curling has its roots in Scotland, some continue to argue that curling—or at least a game very much like it—actually got its start in continental Europe.

Both sides have dredged up some fairly convincing evidence. Those who argue that curling started in Scotland like to point to the famous Stirling Stone. The Stone—inscribed with the date 1511—turned up with a second stone dated 1551 when an old pond was drained in Dunblane, Scotland. If variations on curling were played in other countries prior to 1500, no evidence has been found—perhaps because these games were played with frozen clods of earth, thereby leaving no lasting evidence.

The pro-continental forces, in turn, cite as evidence two oil paintings by the renowned sixteenth-century Dutch painter Pieter Bruegel—paintings that depict scenes of ice shooting, a game similar to curling. Other art works from the time show players sliding large discs of wood along a frozen waterway or playing a game called *kuting* that can best be described as curling with frozen lumps of earth.

The argument has been going on for well over a century—perhaps considerably longer. In 1811, The Reverend John Ramsay of Gladsmuir, Scotland, wrote *An Account of the Game of Curling.* He argued that curling was of Dutch or German origin. He based his theory on the fact that words such as bonspiel, curl, and rink were clearly of non-Scottish origin.

In 1890, Rev. John Kerr challenged Ramsay's opinions in his own book, *A History of Curling.* He pointed out that many other curling terms were of Celtic or Teutonic origin: channel stone, crampit, draw, hack, hog, skip, tee, and so on.

Whether the game actually originated in Scotland or not, the Scots certainly deserve to receive full credit for taking up the game with such great enthusiasm. By birth or adoption, the game is clearly theirs—even though they've agreed to share it with the rest of the world, and Canadians in particular.

Rock Talk

According to curling historian W.H. Murray, curling got its name because of the low murmuring sound (or "curr" according to the Scots) that a palm-sized curling stone called a loofie made as it slid along the ice. Curling gets its nickname "the roaring game" for similar reasons: because of the roaring sound that a curling stone makes on its way across the ice.

Tales from the Rink

Ice-shooting—a game similar to curling, but that involves throwing a 25-pound disk with a stick-like handle along the ice—is still played in Bavaria and Austria.

Curling in Scotland

The Presbyterian church records show that one early Scottish curler—Bishop Graham of Orkney—managed to get himself in hot water with the church by forsaking his pastoral duties. His transgression? "He was a curler on the ice on the Sabbath."

Tales from the Rink

The Scots are also credited with giving the world the game of golf, which, by 1457, had become so popular that the Privy Council ordered its abolition in favor of the more useful sport of archery.

Tales from the Rink

"Brute force must have characterized channel stone play in its heyday. The irregularity of the stones, and the inequality of their weight, must have meant that luck played too great a part in the game. If a stone like the massive triangular Grannie from Meigle (115 lbs.) could be got safely to the tee it could be allowed to lie unguarded.... Anyone who has played a game involving stones of disparate weight will know that a hard strike with a puny stone against one twice its size will cause the small stone to rebound rather than propel the giant forward."

—David Smith, *An Illustrated History of Curling.*

You couldn't blame Graham or others like him for taking advantage of the great ice conditions. Between 1500 and 1700, Scotland experienced a period of uncharacteristically cold weather, which today's climatologists refer to as the Little Ice Age. Nasty weather for farming but great weather for curling.

Early Curling Stones

The earliest curling stones were known as "loofies"—a term derived from the Scottish word "loof" (meaning "the palm of the hand"). These five-pound river stones were flat-bottomed and shaped like a hand, and were thrown underhand using a baseball-like sweep. Those loofies that had been worn smooth by the passage of water were known as channel stones. Channel stones became popular once it was discovered that their symmetrical shape allowed them to be thrown more accurately than other stones.

Kuting stones (slightly larger versions of loofies) were used from 1500 to 1650. They weighed anywhere from five to twenty-five pounds. While they were admittedly crude, they did boast a few bells and whistles, like indents chiselled to allow the thumb and finger to get a better grip.

Around 1650, someone got the bright idea of attaching a handle to curling stones to make them easier to control. (Makes you wonder how many stones went wildly astray over the previous century or two, and how many fingers were crushed by curlers who were somewhat lacking in the co-ordination department!)

About the same time, curling stones acquired the same kind of status that muscle cars would acquire a couple of hundred years later, with the strongest men seeking to equip themselves with the largest rocks.

Curling irons—not stones—were used in Quebec in the aftermath of the fall of Quebec City (1759). Legend has it that the curling-hungry men of the 78th Highlanders were looking to have some fun while they were stuck in the backwaters of Canada. They melted down cannon balls and made kettle-like curling irons. By the time the Montreal Curling

Club was founded in 1807, curlers were routinely using 45- to 65-pound irons.

While curlers in Quebec continued to use curling irons until well into the twentieth century, curlers in Ontario used curling stones right from the very beginning. A select few, however, decided to make the most of their natural surroundings, curling with wooden blocks that were wrapped in iron to add weight and prevent splitting.

When curlers from the two provinces competed, each side wanted to use its own type of stones. They compromised by holding separate matches using each type of stone. Not surprisingly, the Ontario curlers tended to dominate in the rock game and the Quebec curlers took home the honors in the irons game.

From 1800 onward, rounded stones were more the norm, but it wasn't until the second half of the century that full-scale manufacturing of curling stones began. In 1879, J.S. Turner of Toronto developed a stone that was suited to all ice conditions. His specifications were used by Andrew Kay of Ayrshire, Scotland, who began to machine-tool curling stones. For the first time, it was possible to play a game of curling with stones of equal weight.

Other improvements to curling stones came over time. The concave cup on the bottom of the stone reduced friction. Manufacturing techniques improved to the point where it was possible to manufacture stones of the same weight, height, circumference, running edge, and size of handle. At this point, curling clubs began to purchase their own sets of stones and the rest, as they say, is history.

Tales from the Rink

Before round stones became popular, curlers were responsible for finding their own stones. Those with heavier stones had the advantage on days when the ice was keen and fast. Those with lighter stones had the edge if the ice was damp and slow.

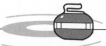

Tales from the Rink

"Today I saw a band of *Scotsmen* who were throwing big iron balls like bombs on the ice; after which they cried 'soop, soop,' and then laughed like mad; I truly think they are mad."

—A seventeenth–century French Canadian farmer's first impressions of curling, quoted in W.H. Murray's *The Curling Companion*.

Early Brushes and Brooms

When curling first began in Scotland, straw wisps and then standard household brooms were used to clear snow off the frozen lochs where games were held. Over time, these brooms began to play a role in the actual game.

Canadian curlers used straw brooms until around 1950, when corn brooms specifically

Tales from the Rink

Curling got a foothold in the U.S. in 1832, when a group of Scottish immigrants enroute to Chicago were shipwrecked on the shores of Lake St. Clair. Rather than moving on, the group decided to stay put. Almost immediately, they established the Orchard Lake Curling Club near present-day Detroit, Michigan, and played their first game using hickory blocks.

made for curling were developed. The curling brush—the dominant curling implement today—made its Canadian debut in the 1960s and 1970s. By the early 1990s, the brush had taken over 90 percent of the curling market.

Ice

The first curling games were played in the great outdoors. Because the climate in Scotland only allowed for a few weeks of good curling, when the weather was just right, curlers seized the moment, casting aside their family obligations in order to hit the ice. Apparently one wife was so annoyed by her husband's passion for curling that she exacted her revenge when he returned home after a curling frenzy in the winter of 1829–30. She set the table for dinner and then served him a curling stone.

Because they were so anxious to take advantage of the ice while it was available, early curlers played in appalling conditions. It wasn't uncommon to play in rain or snow, and for puddles to accumulate on the surface of the ice. In one memorable game in 1839, the Kilmarnock and the Fenwick curlers met for a game with 60 players per side. By the end of the game, there was so much water on the ice that some of the stones were completely submerged. Similarly, on February 25, 1853, one Scottish curler noted that "the water coming through the ice was rather troublesome."

Even if the ice was in relatively good condition, there was still the matter of clearing it. In 1801, a curling team from Ayrshire arrived for a day of curling only to discover to their horror that they had no tools to clean the ice. A gallant team member allowed his teammates to drag him up and down the length of the ice, thereby transforming himself into a six-foot-long human broom. The history books fail to tell us whether his efforts resulted in a win or a loss.

Tales from the Rink

Because there were so few days of good ice, Scottish curlers played well into the evening whenever the ice conditions were right. It wasn't unusual for a skip to dangle a white handkerchief from his broom to make the target easier to see.

In an effort to increase the number of possible curling days, in 1827, one enterprising Scot came up with an innovative solution on the grounds of his estate, aptly named "Curling Hall." John Cairnie—who went on to become the first president of the Royal Caledonian Curling Club, the mother of all curling clubs—built a clay-lined curling pond and flooded it with a quarter inch of water. He formed a club—"The Thistle" or "Cairnie's Own"—and flew a red flag to alert his fellow curlers when the ice was just right. "I do believe the generality of the people here think I am demented," Cairnie later admitted.

While the Scots struggled with a way to get the ice cold enough, Canadians struggled with a way to keep themselves warm. One Scot who spent three years living in Canada during the first half of the nineteenth century issued these words of caution to any curling enthusiasts who were thinking of emigrating just to get more ice time: "The weather is too cold even for the keenest curler to endure and the ice is covered very deep with snow…. Let no Scottish emigrants then, as heretofore, conceive that they will be gratified with plenty of this amusement. Thus it does not follow, that where there are plenty of men, water, and frost, there will be curling."

The solution for curlers in both countries was, of course, the covered rink. Curling rinks popped up in Montreal, Toronto, Hamilton, Ottawa, and Winnipeg during the mid-to-late nineteenth century. By 1900, most Canadian curling clubs had moved indoors. The indoor rinks forever changed the nature of the game by eliminating the effects of snow and natural imperfections in the ice.

It wasn't until after World War II, however, that covered curling rinks really came into their own in Scotland. The only way the curlers got their own rinks was by scooping up abandoned hockey arenas. Hockey briefly came into vogue in Scotland during the 1930s, but didn't ignite the same kind of passion as in Canada.

The Hack

Today, the term hack refers to a rubber starting block from which a curler begins delivery of the stone. As the name implies, early versions of the hack were nothing more than footholds hacked into the ice.

Over time, other products designed to give curlers a firm footing emerged. Early crampits were spike-like contraptions that were strapped to a curler's boot. They did the job well, but wrecked the ice.

In the late nineteenth century, hacks began to replace crampits. Early hacks were initially made of wood or steel but, by the late 1800s, they were being made of rubber.

How the Game Was Played

In the nineteenth century the numbers of players and the size of the house (the bull's-eye-like markings on the ice) varied considerably. Some versions of the game had anywhere from five to ten players, each delivering a single stone. According to Rev.

Tales from the Rink

Curling—or twisting—the stone didn't come into vogue until the beginning of the nineteenth century.

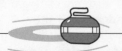

Tales from the Rink

Early games of curling involved 16 players—eight per side—with each player throwing a single rock.

Rock Talk

End   A portion of the game, similar to an inning in baseball. An end is complete when all sixteen rocks (eight per team) have been thrown. A standard curling-club game is usually eight ends, or about two hours long. Championship games, on the other hand, are 10 ends or about 2.5 hours long.

John Kerr's nineteenth-century book *History of Curling*, the house varied from two feet to ten feet in diameter.

In some places, curlers played a certain number of shots rather than a fixed number of ends. The first rink to obtain a score of 21 (or 31) was declared the winner. It wasn't unusual for a 21-shot game to last for longer than six hours. The historical record neglects to tell us how long it took to play a 31-point game. Perhaps everyone was too exhausted to keep track.

For the first few centuries, curling was a twenty-end game. Today, it stands at ten ends. The advantage of the shorter game is that it forces teams to keep the point-spread down. A comeback is simply that much more difficult in a shorter game.

The Grand Matches

The famous Grand Matches of Scotland got their start in the winter of 1846–47, when an uncharacteristically long cold spell kept the lochs frozen for nearly three months, enabling the ice on a loch at Penicuik House to achieve the necessary six-inch thickness. Three hundred curlers participated. When the last Grand Match was played at Lake of Menteith in 1979, 2400 curlers took part.

Between 1847 and 1979, the weather conditions were right for only 33 Grand Matches.

The Royal Caledonian Curling Club

Over time, groups of curlers organized themselves into clubs, the most famous being the Grand Caledonian Curling Club—later renamed the Royal Caledonian Curling Club—which was founded by John Cairnie in 1838.

When Queen Victoria and Prince Albert visited the Club some four years after its founding, they were presented with a set of curling stones—a gift given in the hope that Prince Albert would consent to be the club's first patron. When the stones were presented, Queen Victoria wanted to know how they were used. Lord Mansfield, president of the Grand Caledonian Curling Club, was happy to provide an impromptu demonstration on the oak-floored ballroom. Clearly Queen Victoria was amused: she and her husband both tried their hands at the game and Prince Albert agreed to become the club's patron.

The Old World Meets the New World

The Scottish curling team traveled to Canada and the United States in 1902. Team members were astounded—and more than a little envious—when they saw how the game had evolved in the New World.

They noted some crucial differences in the two games, and decided it was time to make some changes back home: "There's not the slightest doubt that the hack is superior to the crampit," one curler wrote. "We should abandon the crampit."

They were also quite taken by the indoor curling rinks. One of the tour's organizers had this to say: "It is not simply in the quantity of frost they have that our Canadian children are so happy. Their advantage as compared to ours is that they can attend to business all day, and adjourn to the rink in the evening....In the majority of cases they can have every kind of comfort in their retiring-rooms, and can either play or do the plate-glass skip business, i.e., criticise those who are playing."

The Scots were in for another culture shock when they met the Canadians again for the first-ever world championship, the 1959 Scotch Cup. By that point, the Canadians had mastered the takeout game—something the Scots had until then considered to be utterly unsportsmanlike. The Scots decided that since they couldn't beat the Canadians, they might as well join them. After mastering the takeout game and its evil twin the slide delivery (terms we'll be talking about later in this book), the Scots managed to win their first victory against the Canadians in the Scotch Cup of 1967.

Rock Talk

A takeout game focuses on removing your opponents' stones from play. A draw game, on the other hand, focuses on the placement and guarding of your own rocks.

The Olympics

Curling was first introduced as a demonstration sport during the first Winter Olympic Games, held in Chamonix, France, in 1924. It then made a second appearance at the 1932 Winter Games in Lake Placid, New York. The game disappeared for over fifty years, but was then reintroduced as an Olympic demonstration sport at the 1988 Calgary Olympics, with teams

Tales from the Rink

More than 80 countries carried television coverage of curling events during the Nagano games.

from Canada, Denmark, France, Germany, Norway, Sweden, Switzerland, and the United States competing for medals.

Between 1990 and 1992, the World Curling Federation increased its membership from 17 to 28 countries, thereby surpassing the Olympic requirement of 25 countries on at least three continents.

Curling was approved as a medal sport after the Albertville Olympics in 1992. It was actually introduced earlier than anticipated because the Japanese volunteered to introduce it at Nagano. Because Olympic rules say that host countries are entitled to six-years notice of the introduction of a new event, curling's medal debut could have been delayed until the Salt Lake City Games in 2002.

Clearly, being in the Olympic spotlight has already reaped rewards for curling. Curling clubs throughout the world reported additional business as a result of the sport's inclusion in the Winter Olympic Games.

The Least You Need to Know

➤ Curling is popular for a number of reasons: it's fun, it's affordable, and it can be enjoyed by people of all ages and from all walks of life.

➤ The sport is enjoyed in more than 30 countries, but is most popular in Canada, Scotland, and the United States.

➤ Curling was well established in Scotland by the early sixteenth century. It spread to Canada in the mid-eighteenth century and to the United States a short time after that.

➤ The sport made its debut as a medal sport at the 1998 Olympic Games in Nagano.

Chapter 2

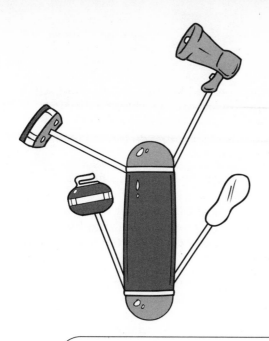

The Gear

In This Chapter

➤ Brushes and brooms

➤ Shoes and sliders

➤ The stopwatch

➤ Gloves

➤ Clothing

➤ The ice

➤ The rocks

➤ The scoreboard

➤ Measuring devices

Curling equipment can be divided into two basic categories: the stuff you supply and the stuff that's waiting for you at the rink.

The first category consists of brushes and brooms, shoes and sliders, clothing, and optional accessories like stopwatches.

The second consists of the scoreboard, measuring devices, ice maintenance equipment, and, of course, the ice and the rocks themselves.

Brushes and Brooms

While curling clubs usually have a few brushes and brooms kicking around, most self-respecting curlers quickly run out to purchase their own. After all, there's a certain cachet to owning your own broom or brush. Using one of the curling club's brooms, on the other hand, is like using someone else's toothbrush: you'll do it in a pinch, but it's certainly not something you want to make a habit of doing.

Curling brushes and brooms have come a long way since the early days when household whisks and straw brooms were used. While the key advantage to these early whisks and brooms was the fact that they were readily available, neither were particularly suited to withstanding the vigorous sweeping of the game. After all, most brooms designed for standard household use don't get this type of workout on the homefront—unless, of course, they're owned by Martha Stewart.

During the first half of this century, circular cross-section straw brooms came into vogue. (Don't know what we're talking about? Just picture the sturdy type of broom that witches carry on Hallowe'en.) One popular version of the broom incorporated a leather strap that stiffened the broom and increased the noise it made. The only problem with these brooms was that they still tended to shed, leaving a trail of debris on the ice that was anything but rock-friendly.

Then the folks in product development got smart, coming up with brooms that didn't shed. One such broom—the "Rink Rat"—was made up of three nylon thongs wrapped in resilient foam, covered in three cloth covers, and then bound with a plastic belt to hold everything together. It not only did a good job of polishing the ice and left little debris but also generated the most impressive thumping noise.

As the century progressed, the curling world switched to brushes. The Europeans were first to embrace this new sweeping implement, but the Canadians and Americans soon caught on—convinced, no doubt, by scientific studies that showed that brushes could be swept more effectively and with less effort. The first generation of brushes suffered from one major design flaw, however. They tended to shed bristles that, when they fell in front of a rock, caused the rock to make drastic changes in direction and speed—something that could bring a curler to tears.

In recent years, the brush has evolved. Brushes are now manufactured from plastic composites that generate little if any contamination. Many have curved handles that allow the sweeper to apply more pressure. They even have pivoting mounts to enable the head to align itself with the ice surface over a wide range of handle angles—making them a flexible and powerful tool.

From the Skip

You can expect to pay $30–$40 for a horsehair brush, $40–$50 for a hog's-hair brush, and $75 or so for a high-end synthetic brush. Pick up a power-grip handle ($15), a brush cover ($3), and a slider bar for the back of your broom ($10) and you're ready to hit the ice.

While synthetic brushes have proven to be very popular, it's still possible to purchase brushes that are made with hog's hair and horse hair.

Hog's-hair brushes come in two varieties: soft and stiff. Soft hog's-hair brushes are popular on keen ice while stiff hog's-hair brushes work best on frosty ice.

Horsehair brushes are known for their ability to remove frost from the ice without freezing or clogging.

If you decide to purchase a hog's-hair or horse-hair brush, you should plan to replace it every

From the Skip

You can access the Web sites of curling equipment suppliers galore from John Murphy's home page: www.geocities.com/Colosseum/ 9424

year because the bristles will dry out and become brittle. To ensure that you get a full season's enjoyment out of your brush, store it upright (bristles up) in a cool, dry place.

There's just one more issue to discuss while we're talking brooms. As you may have noticed, many of today's top players have two brooms: one for sweeping and one for stabilizing themselves during their delivery slide. Some of the brooms used for sliding bear little resemblance to a sweeping device: they are covered with sliding tape and feature modified handles and other gizmos designed to assist the curler during the delivery of the stone.

Should these modifications be allowed? Some think not, envisioning a day when some over-enthusiastic curlers will incorporate a set of ice skates in their sliding brooms. Besides, current designs of brushes already incorporate a sliding surface on the non-sweeping side—reason enough, according to many players and spectators, that curlers should be limited to one broom.

Shoes and Sliders

While you can get away with wearing your running shoes to the rink for a while, if you plan to take up the sport seriously, you'll probably want to purchase a pair of bona fide curling shoes.

As you might expect, there's a pair designed to fit every foot and budget. Bargain-basement models can be had for under $50, or you can pick up the Cadillac of curling shoes for $150 plus.

If you're left-handed, you're also left-footed. This means that you need to purchase a pair of "lefty" curling shoes that have been specially designed to incorporate sliders on the heel and toe of the right shoe and a good grip (a.k.a. a rubber sole) on the left shoe. Right-handed curlers, on the other hand, need sliders on the heel and toe of the left shoe and a good grip on the right shoe.

Before curling shoes became common, curlers bought a slip-on slider that covered the

Tales from the Rink

Ken Watson is generally credited with changing curling forever by introducing the Long Slide. By today's standards, his was a very short slide, as it involved releasing the stone at the tee line. He brought about this drastic change by taking his foot rubber off his lead foot, exposing the slippery leather sole. If you have ever forgotten to take the protection off your slider foot and have had that foot grip the ice, you will see how much more strength is required to throw a rock without a slide.

While the "Watson Slide" came to its end with the curler midway between the hog and tee lines, many of today's curlers slide out well beyond the hog line, and can, for fun, slide the whole length of the ice. What brought this about? Sliders made of new materials, better techniques, and better ice.

Rock Talk

Hog Line   A line located 21 feet from each tee. A rock must be released before the near hog line, and travel beyond the far hog line, or it will be removed from play.

Tee Line   A line passing through the tee at right angles to the center line. It marks the point at which an opposing stone may be swept.

sole portion of their "sliding" foot. These were at first made of various plastics like high-density polyethylene, but Teflon soon became the standard as it was the slipperiest of the plastics. Curling shoes soon appeared with a Teflon sole, followed by a complete Teflon surface from heel to toe.

Sliding has taken much of the physical strength out of the game, opening it up to a much wider range of sizes and shapes of curlers. There is no need to lift the stone and swing it in order to generate the speed required to propel the stone down the ice—a recent development that we'll be discussing in greater length in Chapter Six.

Some curlers prefer to use a removable slider made of Teflon. Half-sole and full-sole sliders can be purchased for about $20 to $30. Stainless steel sliders are also available.

The Stopwatch

One of the modern curler's most useful tools is the stopwatch.

Until a few years ago, one could only express the condition of the ice by using such words and phrases as "fast," "slow," "real fast," "faster than it was last Sunday," and so on.

Clearly this method of analyzing ice conditions was anything but scientific. The defini-

Tales from the Rink

Vincent Vernet of the St. Paul Curling Club in St. Paul, Minnesota, found out firsthand that a good pair of curling shoes can really take you places both on and off the ice.

"I had lined up a job interview one afternoon, so to save time I brought my black 'power suit' to work so I could change on my way to the interview.

"After putting on my suit at a gas station, I was about to reach for my dress shoes when it suddenly dawned on me that I had forgotten to bring them along. What was I going to do? Wear my dirty old tennis shoes with my three-piece suit? No way!

"A smile of relief came over my face when I remembered that my curling shoes—which I keep in the trunk of my car all winter long—were black. I put on my curling shoes, found the parking spot closest to the entrance of the prospective company, and gingerly walked on the sidewalk, lacking a cover to put over my red brick slider.

"I finished the interview and the interviewer was none the wiser about my predicament."

tion of "fast" versus "slow" varied considerably from curler to curler, and some curlers' memories proved less than reliable when it came to comparing the ice conditions from one occasion to the next.

A few years ago, someone decided that it would be helpful to be able to come up with a number to rate the quality of the ice and, after experimenting a little, discovered that the stopwatch was the tool they needed.

Here's how it works. By timing how long it takes for a draw shot (a shot that just has enough strength to reach the target end of the ice) to cover a certain distance, you obtain a number that describes the speed or slipperiness of the ice.

Now here's where it gets a little complicated: the higher the time in seconds, the faster (or slipperier) the ice. While that concept probably seems about as clear as the ice itself, it really does make sense if you think about it. Here's why: the slower a rock can be when released and still reach the tee line, the slipperier the ice is (since the speed is slower it takes more time to make the trip). In other words, the ice conditions have to be pretty slippery to allow a slow-moving rock to make its way down the length of the ice.

Gloves

While a thin pair of standard-issue gloves are suitable for curling, some curlers prefer to wear specially designed leather, deerskin, or lycra gloves instead. If you decide to go this route, expect to pay approximately $30 for a pair of decent curling gloves.

21

The secret to choosing a pair of gloves is a pair that's warm enough and yet not so bulky that it interferes with your ability to play the game.

Clothing

Curling doesn't have the same sort of dress code as golf and tennis. Curlers are a practical lot who are more concerned with comfort than fashion.

Some curlers purchase pants and jackets that have been specially designed for curling, but the majority get by wearing street clothing that is loose fitting and warm.

One quick tip before we move on: it's a good idea to dress in layers so that you can re-move an outer layer or two if you begin to heat up.

The Ice

Until now, we've focused on the equipment that you're expected to supply: a brush or broom, gloves, clothing, a stop watch, and so on.

Now let's consider the other equipment required to play the game, namely the stuff you'll find at the rink.

It goes without saying that you need ice to curl. Since this is an Idiot's Guide, however, we owe it to you—and our editors—to give you a crash course in Icemaking 101.

You'll note that all of the measurements given in this chapter are in feet and inches rather than meters. This is because curling developed in Anglo-Saxon countries, which have traditionally used imperial rather than metric measurements. Because the mea-surements are much neater when they're expressed in the imperial system, for the most part, we've decided to stick with imperial measurements in this book. If you're bound and determined to pay homage to the Gods of the metric system, you can do your own conversions by multiplying the number of feet by 0.3048 to obtain the num-ber of meters. (We told you it was a lot neater if you stuck with the imperial system!)

As you know, the game of curling is played on a slab of ice that must adhere to clearly defined specifications. The ice dimensions are defined in the rule books and standard-ized worldwide, with only minor variations allowed. (See Figure 4.1 on pp. 38 and 39 for a diagram of the ice.) A sheet of ice is generally 146 feet in length and 14 feet 2 inches in width (15 feet 7 inches in the United States). In order to conserve width, some rinks have no dividers between adjacent sheets of ice (no side boards) and the amount of clearance between the house and the edges of the ice varies from one and one half to two rock widths or more.

The lines defining the house are normally painted on the concrete base on which the ice is made. The target area—the house—consists of four concentric circles (circles that are inside one another). The circle diameters are one foot, four feet, eight feet, and twelve feet. A small hole—the tee—is made at the center of the house, a marking that becomes the official center from which all measurements to determine whether rocks are in the house and which are closest to the center are made. It is not unusual to find that this official center isn't actually centered in the painted circles, so calling for a measure when rocks are about the same distance from the tee makes good sense—unless, of course, the opposition is willing to concede that your rock is closest!

The hack refers to rubber cups set into the ice. They vary slightly in terms of design but are typically situated four feet from the end of the rink (six feet behind the back line).

The tee line is a line running parallel to the ends of the rink through the center of the rings. The tee line marks the point on the rink after which the skip is free to sweep an opponent's rock with the aim of having it slide as far back as possible or even out of play.

Rock Talk

Button   The area immediately surrounding the tee. The button is one foot in diameter.

Skip   The player who, alternating with the other team's player, normally plays the last two rocks in an end; and who is responsible for directing the strategy of the game.

Tee   The center of the house.

The hog line is situated 21 feet in front of the tee line and parallel to it. It marks the point at which players must release their rocks. At the target end of the ice, a rock must cross the other hog line in order to be in play. Should it fail to do so, it is said to have been "hogged" and is removed from play before the next stone is played. (There is one exception to this rule: if a rock hits a rock that is in play and thereby fails to cross the hog line, it is considered to be still in play.)

The ice surface is made as level as possible, but then the surface is "pebbled" by sprinkling it with droplets of warm water that freeze on contact. Although there are machine pebblers that print an almost uniform pebble on the ice, the more common method of pebbling is manual. The person responsible for the pebbling wears a water tank that leads through a flexible hose to a sprinkler head. The technician turns on the water and, walking backward down the sheet, swings the spray head from side to side. The water travels upward for a short distance and then falls to the ice in a fine spray that freezes in seconds. Sheets of ice are usually swept and pebbled between games.

It is generally believed that the act of pebbling adds more build-up to the center of the sheet than it does at the edges and that explains why rocks normally tend to curl more from the center outward than they do from the edges coming inward toward the button—an aspect of curling that the more skilled players are able to use to their advantage.

Humidity does tend to condense on the cold ice sheet. The outer edges of the sheet, which do not get polished with brooms, often have a build-up of frost. This frost can slow a rock very effectively should that area of the ice be brought into play. In order to minimize this effect, many rinks dehumidify the air in the arena.

Tales from the Rink

The ice conditions at some curling rinks are legendary—like the notorious sheet eight at the St. Paul Curling Club in St. Paul, Minnesota. Sheet eight was on an outside wall, so the ice would heave when the weather was really cold and water would leak in from outside when temperatures rose and the snow melted.

Curler Donn Satrom tells how he used the poor ice conditions to his advantage on one occasion.

"We were playing on that sheet during one St. Paul International Bonspiel when the ice shifted, creating a slope upward from the center line toward the outside wall.

"Going into the last end, we trailed by one point but had last-rock advantage. As I came to throw the hammer, there were several rocks in front of the house, but only two stones in the circles. Our opponent's rock was on the tee line, just biting the 4-foot circle on the side of the house nearest the wall. We had a rock on the other side of the center line, also just biting the 4-foot at the tee line. We appeared to have shot rock, and I threw a takeout with the last stone of the end, planning that the shooter would stay in the house to score two and win the game.

"I threw my rock 'up the hill' and as it moved down the ice, it floated back toward the center line. The shot just caught the inside of their stone, pushing it out to the 12-foot circle, and then rolled out of the house. While we did not score two, it seemed our rock was now clearly shot since theirs had been moved out of the 4-foot.

"But, on sheet eight that day, the end was not quite over. After sliding out to the 12-foot (and the top of the hill), their stone slid slowly back downhill until it came to rest fully in the 4-foot. Had I not hit the stone, we were likely shot and would have to play an extra end. But instead, having moved our opponent's rock out of the 4-foot to the edge of the house, I enabled their stone to slide back downhill to score one and win the game."

The Rocks

The majority of the world's curling stones (a.k.a. rocks) are made in Scotland using granite that comes from North Wales. Only the highest quality granite is used because any flaws will not withstand the hammer blows received during a typical game. That said, it is not unheard of for a rock to break. In fact, the rules even make specific mention of what should happen should such a calamity occur: the largest fragment will be counted on that end.

Because of their high cost, modern rocks are made so that when they are worn, the rock can be turned over, the handle reversed, and the other side of the stone used.

Tales from the Rink

Norm Williams—a long-time member of the Peterborough Curling Club—likes to tell the story of Vancouver curlers Frank Avery and Rolly David and their prized Andrew Kay curling rocks from Scotland.

"They were pretty proud of those rocks," Norm recalls. "The rocks even had sterling silver handles."

During one memorable game at the Vancouver Curling Club in about 1935, the duo were playing in a bonspiel against Joe Dundas, a curler from Saskatchewan who had learned to compensate for the poor ice conditions on outdoor rinks in his home province by putting a lot of power behind his shots.

On the occasion in question, Joe set out to do a double takeout of Frank and Rolly's rocks—a shot that clearly horrified the rocks' owners.

Before Joe's rock could reach the other end of the ice, Frank and Rolly ran out on the ice and dragged their rocks to safety.

The center portion of the bottom of the stone is scooped out, leaving a circular ring on which the stone slides. The stone's contours are made according to standard templates and all surfaces are polished. The handle is offset so that the hand can be centered over the middle of the rock when lifting it. A rock is roughly a foot in diameter, 4 1/2 inches high not counting the handle, and weighs approximately 42 to 44 pounds (19 to 20 kg) but 44 pounds is the maximum as set by the Canadian rule book.

Tales from the Rink

Younger players play with 24-pound "junior stones."

Sixteen rocks are required to play a game, and each team's rocks are given different colored handles and tops so that they can be easily distinguished across the length of the ice.

The Scoreboard

The traditional scoreboard for curling is a unique and clever device. That said, it's testament to the intelligence of the average curler that we're capable of mastering the logic required to use this contraption.

The scoreboard is a horizontal board with numbers from 1 to 12 or 15 running from

Rock Talk

Vice-Skip The player who, alternating with the opponent's third, delivers the third two rocks of each end, who holds the broom for the skip, and who assists the skip with game strategy. The vice-skip is sometimes called a third or mate.

left to right. Over and under each number is a hook. The top row of hooks is for one team, usually defined by the color of rock handles they are using, while the lower set is for their opponents.

Scoring uses a series of cards, each with a number on it. For an eight-end game, these numbers would be from one to eight with a nine and ten perhaps being available in case of a tie after eight ends, and a need for extra play. The advantage to a traditional scoreboard is that it requires a minimal number of cards and is easily scored by the competitors. (The vice-skip is usually expected to mark up the score after each end.)

Suppose the red team scores two rocks on the first end. The "1" card (signifying the end) is hung on the red team's row of hooks directly over the number "2" (signifying the number of points) on the scoreboard. Suppose on the second end the yellow team scores one point. Then the "2" card (signifying the end) is hung on the yellow hook under the number "1" (signifying the number of points). Suppose that in the third end the yellow team "steals" and scores two more points. Then the "3" card (signifying the end) is hung on the yellow hooks under the number "3" (signifying the number of points, now that two points have been added to the one previously scored).

The scoreboard would now look like this:

```
RED          1
          1 2 3 4 5 6 7 8 9 10 11 12 13 14 15   B
YELLOW   2   3
```

The end hook marked "B" is for ends blanked (ends in which neither team scores). The card for the end is hung opposite the color of the team that threw last rock.

People who regularly watch curling on TV may never have seen a traditional scoreboard. This is because a simplified scoreboard is used on the tube. In this scoreboard, the center row of numbers refers to the ends and the number of rocks scored by each team is shown in the rows above and below, with a total shown at the far end of the board. This is how the score shown on our traditional scoreboard would appear on a simplified scoreboard on TV:

```
                                           Total
RED        2 0 0 0 0 0 0 0 0  0  0      2
           1 2 3 4 5 6 7 8 9 10 11 12
YELLOW  0 1 2 0 0 0 0 0 0  0  0      3
```

Measuring Equipment

Something else you'll find at the rink are measuring devices designed to assist in determining which team's rock is closest to the tee. There are two types of measuring devices: one designed to determine whether a particular rock is in the house (on or touching the painted rings on the ice) and one to determine which rock is closest to the tee (the center of the rings).

From the Skip

The basic rule of scoring is that a team counts one point for each rock that is closer to the tee than any opponent's rock. The scoring occurs after all sixteen rocks have been played.

The first type of measuring tool consists of a six-foot-long radius bar, which is anchored to the tee. It can be rotated to trace the outline of the house, thereby determining whether a particular rock is in or out.

The second type of measuring tool works like the protractor you used in high school math class. One point of the device is fastened to the tee. The other part is pulled up against a particular rock to measure its distance from the tee. A similar measurement is then taken of a second stone. The two measurements are compared, thereby determining whose rock counts and whose doesn't.

Before we move on, let's take a moment to consider a few of the finer points of measuring:

➤ If two rocks are measured and found to be exactly the same distance from the tee, neither rock counts. This means that the only rocks counted on this end are those closer to the tee than the two rocks in question. In other words, if the team winning the end has two rocks close to the tee and their third rock is the same distance from the tee as one of the other team's rocks, only the first two rocks count.

➤ If the rocks in question are so close to the tee that the measuring device cannot be used, then the skips must judge by sight alone whose rock is closer. If the two skips are unable to agree, a referee is called in to make the decision.

The Least You Need to Know

➤ Most curlers today use brushes made of synthetic substances, hog's hair, or horse hair.

➤ You can either purchase special curling shoes or wear a suitable pair of street shoes. If you don't purchase curling shoes or purchase a pair without a slider, you'll need to purchase a separate full-sole or half-sole slider. If you're left-handed, make sure you purchase "lefty's" shoes.

➤ It's up to you whether you want to purchase special gloves, pants, and other curling clothing. If you don't go with specialty clothing, look for items that are warm and that allow for ease of movement.

➤ A growing number of curlers are purchasing stopwatches to assist them in gauging ice conditions.

➤ There's an art to making ice, and a skilled curler quickly learns how to use the ice conditions to best advantage.

➤ A standard curling stone weighs 42 to 44 pounds (19 to 20 kg).

➤ There are two types of scoreboards: traditional ones found at most curling rinks and simplified versions used in television broadcasts.

➤ Rinks have special measuring devices used by curlers to see which team's rock is closest to the tee.

The Team

There are four positions on any curling team: lead, second, third (or vice-skip), and skip. In most games, the lead throws the first two rocks for the team, alternating shots with the lead from the other team. Similarly, the second throws rocks three and four; the third throws rocks five and six; and the skip throws rocks seven and eight. (You can find out about exceptions elsewhere in this book.)

Players tend to make their way up the ranks, starting out by playing lead, progressing to second and then third, and finally finishing their curling career by assuming the highly coveted job of skip. (Highly coveted by some people that is. Many people would rather land a position as an air traffic controller or heart surgeon than take on the position of skip. After all, there's a whole lot less stress!)

Unfortunately, a logical progression doesn't always take place. In some clubs, players are promoted to the position of skip on the basis of seniority rather than skill—something that can be very demoralizing to players who are assigned a team whose skip is not up to the challenge of the position.

From the Skip

The best way to improve your skills and your understanding of the game is to take advantage of a curling clinic early in the season.

Rock Talk

Although brushes are used almost exclusively in curling games today, the instrument held by the skip as an aim point is still referred to as the broom.

Rock Talk

Lead   The player who, alternating with the opponents' lead, delivers the first two rocks of each end.

In more competitive leagues, however, the laws of supply and demand (to say nothing of natural selection!) come into play. Good skips are able to attract the best players to their teams, while less-skilled wannabe skips are left with the choice of either settling for a second-rate team or playing vice or second on a first-rate team.

Just a quick grammar lesson before we move on. Because both men and women enjoy the sport of curling, it doesn't seem fair to use male or female pronouns exclusively throughout this book. That's why we're going to alternate back and forth from chapter to chapter. In some chapters, we'll assume that the team comprises men only, in others we'll assume that the team is made of up women, and—just to see if you're on your toes—sometimes we'll even pretend we're playing a mixed game. Until the grammar police come up with a non-gender-specific singular pronoun that will allow us to avoid those dreadful he/she constructions, we're afraid that's the best we can do.

The Lead

When you first hit the ice, you're likely to be assigned the position of lead. It's not that the position of lead is an easy job (witness the job description below!); it's simply that it's less complex than the other jobs on the team—and it gives the other three players the chance to undo any damage done by a novice!

At least two out of every three rocks thrown by the lead are likely to be draw shots—especially if she is playing in a league that follows the Free Guard Zone rule, a rule that specifies that players are allowed to bump but not remove three (or four) rocks of a given end if they are played between the hog line and the house. (We'll discuss the free guard zone later in this book). Some of the lead's draw shots will be around guards, so she must be accurate on the broom (curling jargon that means that her shots must consistently go where the skip indicates). The lead will also be asked to peel rocks (clear out rocks from in front of the house) on occasion—especially when her team has last rock. She must also be a strong sweeper who has the strength and stamina required to sweep six rocks each end.

Rock Talk

On the broom means that a particular shot started out on a line toward the skip's broom. If the skip misjudged the amount of curl or if the weight (speed) of the rock is not correct, it can be on the broom but still be a miss.

Draw shot A rock that is delivered so that it comes to rest in the spot indicated by the skip.

Guard A rock between the hog line and the house that is used to try to prevent the opposition from hitting a rock in the house.

Peel A takeout shot that removes a stone from play and rolls out of play itself.

Here's how a job description for the position of lead might sound:

The lead must:

➤ consistently hit the broom.

➤ be skilled at controlling weight between the tee line and hog line so that she can lay in short or long guards at will, or go into the house.

➤ be a strong sweeper (skilled at sweeping, physically fit, and able to judge the speed of rocks).

➤ be able to still hit the broom at takeout or peel weight.

➤ be a team player.

Rock Talk

Long Guard A guard near the hog line.

Short Guard A guard near the house.

Takeout weight A rock with sufficient speed to drive an opponent's rock out of play, beyond the back line is said to have takeout weight.

Peel weight Sufficient weight to force both the rock being hit and the shooter to clear the ice.

The Second

The second throws a wider variety of shots than the lead. She throws the full spectrum of weights, from long guards to takeouts in the back rings to delicate weights such as tap-backs, raises, and splits. Like the lead, she must sweep six rocks per end.

Therefore, the job description for the second might look something like this.

The second must:

➤ consistently hit the broom.

Rock Talk

Back Rings   The portion of the 8-foot and 12-foot rings behind the tee line.

Raise   The action of bumping a stone from one position to another position.

Split   Hitting a rock in front of the house so that both it and the shooter end up in the house (an angle hit on a rock).

Tap-back   A very gentle hit.

Weight   The amount of force or speed on a rock as it makes its way down the ice.

Rock Talk

Wick-in A wick where a rock near the edge of the ice is used to direct the shooter nearer to the button.

➤ throw all weights and be able to switch between different weight shots.

➤ be a strong sweeper, physically fit, and able to judge rock speeds quickly and accurately since she is usually the person responsible for judging weight on the lead's rocks.

➤ be a team player.

The Third or Vice-skip

In some leagues, they're called thirds. In others, they're called vices. Whatever you call them, they have an important role to play. The vice is called upon to make every possible curling shot, including the more complex shots that tend to spook less-experienced players: raises, wick-ins, and so on.

As the name implies, the vice-skip gets to fill in as skip when the skip is throwing her rocks. Consequently, she needs to be able to fulfill the job description for a skip. Because she is called upon to sweep four rocks in each end, she must be a capable sweeper. To put it simply, the vice needs to be the most versatile player on the team.

A job description for the position of vice would look something like this.

The vice must:

➤ consistently hit the broom.

➤ know how to execute the full spectrum of curling shots—the easy ones, the difficult ones, and everything in between.

➤ be a strong sweeper.

Rock Talk

Vice and third mean the same thing. They refer to the player who throws rocks five and six for her team, and who holds the broom and acts as skip when the skip is throwing her own rocks.

➤ fill in as skip, judge the course of rocks, and guide the sweepers as they attempt to bring the rocks in on line (on the desired path).

➤ get along well with the skip and be confident enough to contribute helpful suggestions on shots and strategy.

➤ be a team player.

The Skip

In addition to being able to make all of the curling shots, the skip must have a good understanding of strategy. She must also be a leader—someone who is able to motivate and encourage her players to work together as a team.

A job description for a skip might look something like this.

The successful candidate for the position of skip must be able to:

➤ judge ice, be able to mentally note how shots behave on various parts of the ice, and commit this information to memory (in other words, no Idiots need apply!).

➤ be a skilled strategist and have a knack for performing a risk-benefit analysis on any given shot.

➤ be able to anticipate what is required to keep a particular rock on course from the moment that the rock is released (anticipate and estimate curl before it occurs).

➤ handle the pressure of the job, and not let it affect either her shot-making abilities or decorum.

➤ quickly assess the opponents' individual and collective strengths and weaknesses.

➤ function as a leader, motivating, coaching and involving her team, and listening to their suggestions.

➤ be an alert opportunist—someone who is able to respond quickly when the unexpected, or even unthinkable!—happens.

➤ hit the broom and ideally have "button" weight in her back pocket (curling jargon that means that the skip can, at any time in the game, throw a rock to the button).

Tales from the Rink

The Honourable John D. Arnup, a member of the Toronto Cricket Skating and Curling Club, likes to tell the tale of a skip at his club who was obsessed with winning. "It was said of him that if he could beat you 24–2, he would never ease up until the last rock was played.

"One of the legends that was linked to him—which may be a myth—concerned a game that was close and tense. His lead was sweeping the second player's rock when he fell—in front of the rock.

"Instantly the skip bellowed, 'Sweep him!'"

The Recipe for a Good Team

You will note that hitting the broom and being a team player are prerequisites for all team positions.

Hitting the broom is an obvious need. The best sweeping in the world can only compensate for minor errors in line and, to execute a strategy, a team needs to make as many of its shots as possible.

A less obvious but equally important requirement is the ability to work together as members of a team. If the primary goal of the game is to have fun—an almost sacred tenet in the world of curling—then there's no room for temper tantrums or inflated egos on the ice. Players who give the game their all, who are compatible on and off the ice, and who put the team's needs ahead of their own are likely to enjoy playing together. If you belong to such a team and you all share a love of competition, you've got a real winner on your hands.

The true test of a team is the ability to stick together in good times and in bad, for better and for worse. (Kind of has a nice ring to it, now doesn't it?) There are unfairnesses that can and do rear their ugly heads in games. A brush hair or other contamination spoils a key shot; an opponent misses the broom, but makes a lucky wick-in or raise and ends up putting a rock behind cover; or stones are poorly matched (behave differently on the ice) and the team loses several ends before it figures out the problem, wasting additional ends as it struggles to sort stones.

If team members can take these situations in stride, laughing at them over a few drinks at the end of the game rather than losing their composure on or off the ice, the game will continue to be fun. And that, in our minds at least, is the only reason to play.

Body Language

Before we wrap up this chapter on teams, it makes sense to take a few moments to talk about the ways that teams communicate on the ice.

Since most rinks are relatively noisy places—the sound of rocks cascading down a large number of sheets of ice tends to have that effect!—and since the rules outlaw the use of walkie-talkies or other communication devices, teams need to be able to rely on as many non-verbal signals as possible.

While each team tends to develop a non-verbal language of its own, there are signals that are fairly widely used. Next time you tune into the World's or some other type of high-profile competition, see how many of these signals you can spot.

The universal signal used by skips is the one you see before every shot. The skip taps the ice where she wants a particular shot to end up, and then holds the broom at the point of aim. If the shot is a hit, the skip indicates how hard she wants the shot to be by indicating the strength of the shot with her broom. (She taps the rock to be hit, and then uses her broom to indicate how far back the shooter would go if it didn't hit the rock.) Back-line weight, hack weight, and backboard weight are the three common weights indicated by a skip.

If the shot is a gentle raise (a shot in which one of the rocks in play is moved only a few feet, sometimes called a tap-back), she will hold up her broom and slide one hand down the handle to indicate how far she wants the rock moved. Some teams indicate the weight required by having the skip draw her hand across her body after indicating that it is a hit. If her hand is at her waist, she is calling for medium-weight takeout; if her hand is at her shoulder, she is calling for heavy weight; and if it is at her knees, she is calling for light weight.

Once the rock is released, some skips move their brooms to where they judge the rock to have been aimed so that the sweepers know if the rock is slightly narrow or wide of the broom—something that allows them to adjust accordingly. This signal is also useful to the curler delivering the rock because it lets her know immediately if there was a fault in her delivery.

In most situations, the sweeper next to the rock concentrates on watching the rock, judging its speed, and ensuring that her brush does not touch it. The front sweeper alternates between looking down and looking up to see if the skip wants to alter the sweeping pattern because of line (how close the shot is following the path she wanted it to follow). Some skips use their brooms to indicate a need for maximum sweeping, or hold up a hand to tell the sweepers to stop sweeping and consequently let the rock curl more.

Calling the Shots

While hand signals are obviously useful, in the heat of battle, most skips will rely on verbal signals, too. Everyone has heard the call "Sweep! Sweep!" and knows what that means. Other on-ice messages aren't quite so easy to decipher, so here are a few translations:

➤ CLEAN   Sweep gently to clean the ice in front of the rock, but don't sweep hard enough to polish the ice.

➤ NEVER   The rock needs to curl, so hold off on sweeping and give it a chance to do so. (Good sweepers will stay with the rock just in case they're called upon to work their magic after all.)

➤ HURRY HARD   Put maximum effort into sweeping. "Hurry" means use fast strokes; "hard" means put lots of pressure on the brush.

In general, teams should have a complete set of non-verbal signals.

Occasionally, the skip will have to change the shot while the rock is partway down the ice, and he needs an agreed-upon signal to do this, but, for the most part, the sweepers should control sweeping for weight, the skip for line.

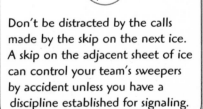

Don't be distracted by the calls made by the skip on the next ice. A skip on the adjacent sheet of ice can control your team's sweepers by accident unless you have a discipline established for signaling.

The Least You Need to Know

➤ A good lead needs to be able to consistently hit the broom; be skilled at controlling weight between the tee line and hog line so that she can lay in short or long guards at will, or go into the house; be a strong sweeper; be able to hit the broom at takeout or peel weight; and be a team player.

➤ A good second needs to be able to consistently hit the broom; throw all weights and be able to switch back and forth between different weight shots; be a strong sweeper; and be a team player.

➤ A good third (or vice) needs to be able to consistently hit the broom; know how to execute the full spectrum of curling shots; be a strong sweeper; fill in as skip; get along well with the skip and be confident enough to contribute helpful suggestions on shots and strategy; and be a team player.

➤ A good skip needs to be able to judge ice; be a skilled strategist; be able to anticipate what is required to keep a particular rock on course from the moment that rock is released; handle the pressure of the job, and not let it affect either her shot-making abilities or decorum; quickly assess the opponents' individual and collective strengths and weaknesses; function as a leader; seize opportunities as they arise; and be a highly skilled player.

➤ Most teams use a combination of non-verbal and verbal signals on the ice.

Chapter 4

The Rules

In This Chapter

➤ How the game works

➤ How the game is scored

➤ How the rules have changed

➤ International variations on the rules

➤ House rules

While curling is a challenging sport to learn, the rules of the game are surprisingly simple. Two teams made up of four players each take turns throwing rocks down a sheet of ice with the team that lost the coin toss going first. Teams alternate throwing rocks with each player on the four-player team throwing two rocks. After all 16 rocks have been thrown, the score for the end is calculated by determining which team's rock or rocks are closest to the tee. A point is scored for each rock that is closer to the tee than any of the opponent's rocks.

The skip directs the game and holds his broom

Rock Talk

An end is kind of like an inning in baseball. Most competitive curling games have ten ends while club games are eight ends.

Championship games will go into subsequent ends to break a tie.

as the target or aim point for each of the players when it is their turn to throw. He also indicates which direction or turn he wants on the handle and the distance he wants the rock to travel (a.k.a. the weight). He lets the team know the purpose of the shot so that the sweepers can use their own judgment in determining how much they should sweep a rock since sweeping makes the rock travel further and curl (curve) less.

That's our *Reader's Digest* condensed version of how curling works. But since we've been contracted to write an entire chapter on this topic, we're going to take this opportunity to give you a crash course on the rules of curling. We won't tell you enough to allow you to hang out your shingle as a referee, but we will provide you with enough information to hit the ice without making a total Idiot of yourself. Then, as you master the finer points of the game, you can flesh out your knowledge of the game by consulting the complete Canadian and American curling rules that we've included in Appendix B.

The Markings on the Ice

You can't understand how curling is played unless you understand what all the lines and circles on the ice actually mean.

Curling is played on a sheet of ice that conforms to the standards set out by the Canadian Curling Association, the United States Curling Association, or some other curling authority. While there are minor variations between countries, a typical Canadian curling rink is shown below.

The first marking that you're likely to notice as you look down the ice is the aptly

Figure 4.1 The ice

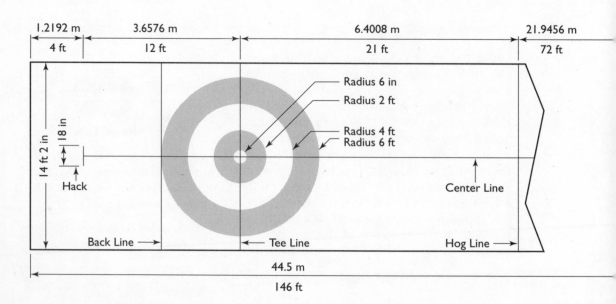

named center line—the line that extends lengthwise down the ice. Its purpose is to make it easier for sweepers to know where they are on the ice sheet as they look down at their brooms, and some feel it helps when aiming rocks—especially on shots near the center line.

In some rinks, you'll find two additional lines on either side of the center line. These extra lines are typically painted four feet from each side of the center line. Their purpose is to further aid the sweepers in determining their exact position on the ice.

The side lines are the vertical markings on the ice that indicate where the area of play ends. Any rock that touches or overhangs the side line is immediately deemed to be out of play and must be removed to avoid colliding with other rocks.

Because curling is played in two directions (ends 1, 3, 5, 7, and 9 are played in one direction and ends 2, 4, 6, 8, and 10 are played in the opposite direction), the entire rink is symmetrical. When you're delivering a stone, you aren't concerned with the markings directly in front of you; you're aiming for the markings at the other end of the ice.

At both ends of the ice, you'll find a set of concentric circles (circles inside one another). They are identified by their width and are consequently known as the 4-foot circle, the 8-foot circle, and the 12-foot circle. The smallest circle is known as the button. These sets of circles make up the area known as the house. The small hole in the center of the button is known as the tee.

Between the end of the rink and the house is the hack—two footholds that are set into the ice to give a curler's foot something to grip on to while he pushes off to deliver the

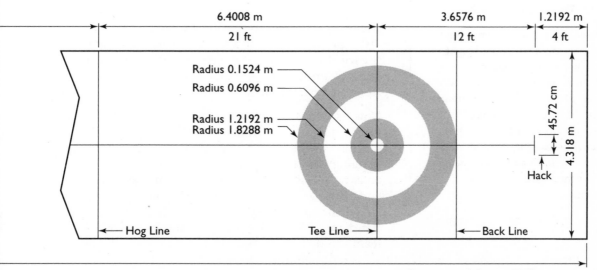

Conversion: 1 foot = .3048 metres

stone. The hack is located four feet from the end of the rink at a point that is sometimes referred to as the foot line. Each foothold is situated a maximum of 3 inches
from the center line. A right-handed curler must use the left hack, while a left-handed
one must use the right.

The next marking on the ice as you gaze up the rink is the back line. You can ignore
the one closest to you when you're shooting because it doesn't really mean anything.
The one that determines whether your rock is deemed to be out of play is located 10
feet from the other end of the ice, at the outer edge of the house.

The tee line at your end of the ice is important, however. It marks the point of no return when it comes to delivery. Once your stone passes this line, it cannot be called
back and replayed.

The next line on the ice is the hog line. It's situated 21 feet from the tee line. It marks
the point by which you must release your stone when you're executing your delivery.
The hog line at the target end of the ice is also important. A rock is considered to be in
play if on delivery it crosses that hog line completely—the exception being if it hits a
rock in play, in which case it need not completely cross the hog line.

The next line on the ice (beyond the hog line at the target end of the ice) is the tee line
in the middle of the house. Your team has full sweeping rights over your rock until it
passes this line. Then the skip from the other team (or his designate) can sweep your
rock in an effort to take it out of play (past the back line at the other end of the ice).

Tales from the Rink

Stones have a maximum weight of
44 pounds, a minimum height of
4.5 inches and a maximum
circumference of 36 inches. The
rules of curling neglect to define
the shape of the "running"
surfaces on the bottom of the
rocks, presumably because rock
manufacturers and repair facilities
have these critical factors
standardized.

The Rocks

Now that you've mastered the markings on the ice,
let's talk about how the rocks fit into the game.

To play a game of curling, you need two sets of eight
stones, color-coded so that they can easily be
distinguished from one another across the length of
the ice. Traditionally, the team that does not have
last rock on the first end chooses which color of
stones it wishes to use.

Now let's consider what happens if you
momentarily forget what color your stone is and
play one of the other team's stones. Aside from
hanging your head in shame and promising to buy
an extra round of drinks for your teammates at the
end of the game, there's not much you can do.
Under the rules of curling, the shot is allowed to
stand. Once the rock comes to rest, one of your
team's undelivered stones is used to replace it, and
the rock that you—ahem—borrowed is returned to the hack end.

There are some other strange situations that don't often occur—but that you'll want to know about nonetheless: having a rock break in the midst of play or having the handle come off during delivery. If a rock breaks in a rock-to-rock collision, the largest fragment is used to score that end and then the rock is replaced with a (theoretically) more robust stone. If the handle comes off during delivery, the team delivering the stone has the choice of letting the shot stand, or putting the rocks back in their original positions and replaying the shot.

Teams and Skips

As we stated a little earlier on, teams normally consist of four players, each of whom delivers two rocks. Once the order of throwing rocks is established in the first end, it cannot be changed during the game.

The skip usually throws the last two rocks for a particular team—but not always. The critical factor is consistency. As we just stated, once the order of players has been established, it cannot be changed at any point during that game. Similarly, the player who is designated to hold the target broom for the skip must do so for the entire game.

Three-player teams are allowed if a player is missing or if illness or injury prevents a player from continuing and no alternate is available. In this case, the first two players throw three rocks each, while the third curler throws two.

The skip is the on-ice equivalent of a quarterback, and is consequently charged with

From the Skip

Getting to choose the color of your stones is small compensation for forfeiting last-rock advantage. Teams will go to great lengths to obtain last-rock advantage—and will intentionally blank an end to keep it. We'll be talking more about last-rock advantage in our chapter on strategy, but for now make a mental note that this is one situation in life where it's better to be last than first.

Rock Talk

The rocks are referred to by number, starting with the first rock thrown by a particular team ("rock one") and ending with the final rock thrown by that team ("rock eight"). In competition, each player uses the same two rocks in case there is a minor variation between stones.

Rock Talk

Curling teams are usually named after the skip. The team led by Jane Smith is therefore known as the Smith Team or the Smith Rink.

Tales from the Rink

To say that co-author Rod Bolton is a competitive curler is a gross understatement—something his teammates found out the hard way back in 1985.

When Rod suffered a heart attack in the middle of a game at the Humber Highlands Curling Club, his teammates had a hard time convincing him to head to the hospital rather than finishing the final few ends.

The worst part of the whole ordeal, according to Rod, was finding out that his team had conceded the match after he left for the hospital—something that adversely affected the team's standing in that draw.

directing the play. While many skips today are more democratic than the skips of yesteryear, it's a foolhardy player indeed who deliberately ignores the directions of the skip.

Who Goes Where

In order to avoid on-ice traffic jams, the rules of curling clearly establish who goes where. As you might expect, there are separate rules for the non-delivering team (the team that is not throwing a rock) and the delivering team (the team that is throwing a rock).

The Non-Delivering Team

The rules clearly state that the skip and vice-skip (a.k.a. "third") may stand behind the back line at the playing end, but they must be sure that they do not move or position their brooms in a way that distracts their opponents. The skip may stand in the house behind the player holding the broom. He must remain stationary during stone delivery and be sure that his broom does not interfere with or distract from the play.

At the delivery end, the curler whose turn it is to throw next rock must stand near the backboard and remain still and silent during his opponent's delivery. (Guess this explains why John McEnroe took up tennis, not curling.) The other player or players on the non-delivering team stand at the extreme edge of the sheet, between the two hog lines, being sure not to obstruct either the opponent's vision or the play.

The Delivering Team

The rules state that the skip or vice-skip (in this case, the person holding the broom) may be positioned anywhere behind the hog line at the target end of the ice. He is the only player from the team allowed in this area during stone delivery.

Special Delivery

A player delivering a stone is allowed to talk to his teammates and make preparatory swings or movements in the hack, but once the stone is either released from the player's hand or has reached the nearer tee line, it is considered to be in play and consequently cannot be stopped and rethrown.

The player must release the handle before the rock reaches the nearest hog line or he is subject to a penalty. That penalty is that the non-offending team is allowed to let the shot stand or remove the rock that has been illegally delivered and replace all other stones moved by it to their previous positions—whichever option works to their best advantage.

If a player misses his turn and throws only one rock, play continues and he throws the last rock for the team on that end. If, after the skip (or fourth player) has thrown two stones, it suddenly becomes obvious that one of the players on the team has thrown only one stone, unless it's obvious who made the error, it is assumed that the lead erred and he is given the responsibility for throwing the team's last rock.

If a team throws two rocks in succession, play continues and the non-offending team is either given the opportunity to throw the last rock or two consecutive last rocks, depending on who had last-rock advantage.

If the penalties for messing up seem to be a little harsh, it's certainly for good reason. They're intended to serve as a strong deterrent to making these kinds of errors, however accidentally they may be committed.

A Touched Stone

By "a touched stone" we don't mean a stone that has gone a little crazy after making one too many trips down the ice. What we're talking about is a stone that has been interfered with by one of the players—typically a sweeper.

Here's what the rules say: if the players on the delivering team touch the stone while it is in motion—either with their bodies, clothing, or brooms—it is considered to be a touched stone and is consequently subject to one of the following three penalties once it completes its travel:

Dire consequence #1: The play is allowed to stand.

or

Dire consequence #2. The touched rock is removed, and any rocks it touched are replaced in their original positions.

or

Dire consequence #3: The stones are placed in the position that would have resulted had the stone not been touched.

As you might expect, the skip of the non-offending team gets to mete out the punishment, choosing whatever works to his team's greatest advantage. While the third alternative is a little trickier to invoke in club play, where the players don't have access to an officiating referee, it should not be ruled out if it is the fairest alternative. (This is one of those situations where curling distinguishes itself as a classy game. Can you imagine NHL hockey players chatting civilly about what would have happened if one of the players hadn't inadvertently touched a puck with a high stick, and conceding that the fairest thing to all concerned would be to grant the wronged team an extra goal? Hardly.)

When a stationary stone is displaced and it is behind the play, it is replaced in its original position. (The skips simply agree on the position of the stone, with or without the assistance of an objective bystander such as an official.)

On the other hand, when a rock is touched ahead of the play, in a manner that alters the course of the rock being played, then the three alternatives outlined earlier in this section are presented to the skip who has been wronged, and he decides which alternative works to his team's greatest advantage.

Sweeping and Brushing

Between the tee lines, the members of the delivering team are permitted to sweep the rock being delivered (or any of their team's rocks that have been set into motion by the delivered stone).

Behind the tee line, only one player from each team is permitted to sweep his own team's rocks, and only the acting skip can sweep an opponent's rock. First choice as to who can sweep a rock beyond the tee line goes to the team owning the rock but, if the choice is not to sweep, the opponent must not be prevented from sweeping. One word of caution to novice curlers who might be tempted to disgrace themselves on the ice: it is not considered to be morally acceptable to sweep one of your own rocks without pressure or vigor in order to prevent the opposition the opportunity to sweep it. It's the on-ice equivalent of letting someone butt into line or sneaking a few extra items through the express line at the grocery store.

The rules of curling state that sweeping is to be done within six feet of the rock and the sweeping motion is to be from side to side, evenly across its entire path, finishing on either side of the delivered stone. This latter rule is virtually impossible to enforce and will likely be stricken from the rule books in the not-too-distant future. We predict that eventually players will be allowed to sweep different parts of the path in front of the rock to different degrees in order to increase or decrease the amount of curl.

Scoring

The scoring of curling is relatively simple—it's a matter of counting rocks. (The only tricky part to scoring is figuring out how to use the traditional scoreboard, but you mastered that particular skill in Chapter Two, right?)

When all 16 rocks have been delivered, a team counts one point for each rock that lies within the house that is closer to the tee than any of the rocks of its opponents.

The two skips (or vice-skips, if they are the ones in charge at the time) must agree on the score before any rocks are moved. In some situations, agreement on one or more rocks is easily reached, but a measure is required for a second, third, or some other rock. With both skips' agreement, the "agreed-to" rocks can be removed to facilitate measurement. An obvious situation that would necessitate moving a rock would be if one rock covered the tee, thereby preventing the use of measuring equipment.

If a rock is moved prematurely (before the skips agree on the scoring) and the rock in question was a potential counter, the benefit of the doubt is given to the non-offending team. The moral of the story? Don't touch the rocks until everyone agrees on the score for the end.

Measuring

The art of painting rings is somewhat inexact. To make matters worse, the rings are covered by several inches of ice. This explains why official measuring equipment is often used to determine the position of a particular rock, even when a visual judgment seems possible. Since the tee may not align with the painted rings, and since rocks may vary slightly in diameter, the official measure is deemed to be from the tee to the closest part of the stone.

Here's what the rule book has to say about the use of measuring devices. (You'll want to read this section carefully because there are a few surprises!)

First of all, until the 16th rock comes to rest, no physical device can be used to determine if rocks are in the rings or closer to the tee. No matter how badly you want to know whose rock is closest to the tee midway through an end, you're forced to rely on visual cues rather than measuring equipment to make this judgment. Remember what your Mama taught you: patience is a virtue.

At the edges of the sheet of ice, in situations in which only painted lines exist, visual judgments determine whether a rock is in play. Once a rock goes out of play, it's out of the game—even if it somehow manages to make itself back on to the playing area.

If rocks close to the tee cannot be measured with the measuring equipment supplied and you can't tell by looking whose rock is closer, then the two rocks may be declared to be tied. Unless there is also a rock clearly closer than the tied rock, the end will be declared a blank (an end with no score).

When opposing rocks are the same distance from the tee (at least so far as the measuring devices are concerned), they may also be declared tied. In this case—unless there are rocks closer to the tee—the end will be declared a draw (there will be no score). It doesn't matter how many other rocks are in the house, if they're farther away than the tied rocks, they don't count.

Tales from the Rink

In his book *The First Fifty*, Doug Maxwell describes Ken Watson's heartbreakingly close encounter with an eight-ender (a perfect end in which all eight of your rocks are in the house but none of the opponent's). "With seven rocks in the house, it looked good. The sweepers were working his rock and a couple of feet before the house, the lead—Charlie Kerr—dropped an ash from his cigar. The rock ground to a halt inches from perfection." Could this be the origin of the no-smoking regulation found in the Canadian Curling Association rule book?

Rock Talk

If you'd like to check out the international curling rules for yourself, you can find them at the World Curling Federation Web site: www.curling.org

Equipment

Dried-out brooms, shedding brushes and even defective or dirty sliders or slider protectors can put contamination on the ice, which can ruin a shot. As a result, in most tournaments, officials reserve the right to inspect any clothing or equipment that may come in contact with the ice.

Because there aren't too many officials kicking around your average curling rink, the onus is on the players themselves to use good judgment. Since one hair can spoil a shot, one shot can determine an end, and one end can be key to the outcome of the game, players should police themselves when it comes to preventing contamination from reaching the ice surface. Smoking on the ice is outlawed in the rules, and most rinks provide motorized-brush shoe cleaners to remove debris that might otherwise be tracked onto the ice. Unfortunately, one of the worst culprits when it comes to on-ice debris is an item sometimes supplied by the rinks themselves: rental brooms and brushes that have seen better days and that are no longer fit for use.

The Free Guard Zone Rule

Now we're going to switch focus momentarily and talk about an important rule for curlers who make it to the big leagues: the Brier, the Tournament of Hearts, the Olympics, and the World Curling Federation Championships. What we're talking about is, of course, the Free Guard Zone Rule.

By the 1990s, curling was becoming—dare we say it—a boring sport to watch on television. The skill of the players had progressed to the point where players were simply knocking out one another's rocks repeatedly. To add a bit more sizzle to the game, the World Curling Federation introduced the four-rock, Free Guard Zone Rule, which specifies that players are allowed to bump—but not remove—the first four rocks of a given end if they are delivered between the hog line and the house. The Canadian Curling Association followed with a variation on the rule—the three-rock rule—in 1994.

Chapter Seven provides a detailed explanation of the art of peeling (taking a rock out in front of the house without passing either your opponent's or your own rock through the house in a way where either rock might do damage). We won't repeat that discussion here, but we will briefly touch upon the rules concerning the free guard zone.

The free guard zone is that area of the ice between the hog line and the tee line, but excluding the house. Any rock touching the tee line (at the edge of the circle) or biting (touching) the 12-foot ring at the front of the house is not considered to be in the free guard zone. However, a rock that is in play because it hit another rock that is either biting or in front of the hog line is considered to be in the free guard zone. If there is any doubt as to whether a rock at the edge of the rings is in the free guard zone, the six-foot radius bar may be used. Note: this is the one exception to the "no measuring" rule during the course of an end.

By now you're probably wondering what the big deal is about the free guard zone—why it matters whether a rock is in the zone or not.

It matters a great deal, and here's why. Under the Canadian Free Guard Zone Rule, if the first two rocks thrown in an end come to rest in the free guard zone, they cannot be removed until after the third rock has been thrown. They can be hit and moved, even moved into the house, but they cannot be removed from play.

Rock Talk

Russ Howard is generally credited with inventing or developing the Free Guard Zone Rule, originally called the Moncton Rule as it was first tested in competition in Moncton, N.B.

Rock Talk

International competitions use a four-rock rule that is basically the same as the three-rock rule except that free guards cannot be removed until after the fourth—rather than the third—rock has been thrown.

Should a team knock an opponent's free-guard-zone rock or even one of their own free-guard-zone rocks out of play, then the other team is given two choices: they can either let the play stand as it is; or have the free-guard rock returned to its position before the offending shot and have the rock just delivered removed from play.

Don't miss this bit of fine print. Once a rock is declared a free-guard stone, it remains so until after the third rock on the end is thrown. This is why it so important for skips to be in agreement on the free-guard-rule status of each of the first two rocks before the next rock is thrown.

House Rules

Most official rules assume the presence of a referee. As you can imagine, there aren't many referees on hand at most curling clubs—or even at most local bonspiels.

Because they can't pull a referee out of a hat each time the need for one arises, many clubs have house rules or traditions that the new curler or new member should know

Rock Talk

In a "Draw to the Button" competition, a curler from each team sends a rock down the ice. The rock that is closest to the button is declared the winner. This is a popular way of breaking ties when there isn't time to play an extra end.

Rock Talk

In curling, a burned or touched stone rock has been illegally touched by a player on the delivering team while it is still moving. Touched can mean with broom, clothing, or body parts.

about before hitting the ice. Here are just a few of the house rules you might expect to encounter at your friendly neighborhood curling club:

1. Although the official game is 10 ends with extra ends to break ties, most clubs play an eight-end game because it fits better into a two-hour time slot. The two-hour time allocation allows rinks to schedule two games in each of the morning, afternoon, and evening periods. Ties are allowed to stand in many clubs. In others that don't allow ties, they're broken through various "Draw to the Button" competitions because of time limitations.

2. Most clubs have sweepers "declare" a touched rock as soon as it occurs and the rock is immediately taken out of play. This avoids the difficulties involved in "replacing rocks to their original positions" or worse still, putting rocks in the positions that they would have reached had the rock not been "burned."

3. Where curlers are rated in forming balanced teams, the rules specify which procedures the skip is to use in rearranging the order of his team when using spares (substitute players) or playing a three-person team because one of the players is absent.

4. Many rinks have not yet adopted the Free Guard Zone Rule, but it's likely that in years to come the rule will become universal.

5. Many rinks allow any player to hold the broom when one member is absent. This allows the members of the team to share the sweeping load more equally.

The Least You Need to Know

➤ The painted circles at either end of a curling rink are known as "the house."

➤ The hack refers to the set of rubber footings imbedded in the ice to give curlers better footing to push from when they deliver their shots.

➤ The hog line is the line partway down the ice that indicates the point by which curlers must release their rocks.

➤ The tee line is located in the middle of the house. Once an opponent's rock has passed the tee line, the opposing skip can sweep to encourage the rock to go out of play.

➤ The back line at the target end of the rink marks the point at which a rock is deemed to have gone out of play—once all of the rock comes to rest on the other side of the line.

➤ The rules of curling specify who gets first rock, who gets to choose the color of the rocks, and so on. The rules even address situations in which the rocks crack while in play or a player accidentally throws one of his or her opponent's stones!

➤ While curling is becoming an increasingly democratic game, for the most part, the skip still calls the shots (literally!)

➤ When all 16 rocks have been delivered in an end, a team counts one point for each rock that lies within the house that is closer to the tee than any of the rocks of its opponents.

➤ Under the Canadian Free Guard Rule, if the first two rocks thrown in an end come to rest in the free guard zone, they cannot be removed until after the third rock has been thrown. They can be hit and moved, even moved into the house, but they cannot be removed from play.

➤ Many clubs have house rules or traditions that the new curler or new member should know about before he hits the ice. They provide guidelines on handling a variety of situations, including a tie or the absence of one of the players.

Part II
Where Science Meets Strategy: The Total Game

Now that you've mastered the fundamentals of the game (well, on paper at least!) it's time to put some of that newfound knowledge to work.

Over the next few chapters, you'll learn about the science behind the sport (inquiring minds need to know!) and the secrets to on-ice success. We'll even take you inside the mind of a skip—an exercise that is guaranteed to have you thanking your lucky stars that you get to play lead for a while....

Chapter 5

Cool Science

In This Chapter

➤ What makes a rock curl?

➤ The science of sweeping

➤ What happens when two rocks collide

➤ Putting science to work for you

If you still have flashbacks about the horrors you endured in high school physics class, you might be tempted to skip this chapter entirely. While you are well within your rights to do so—after all, we don't give out detentions for missing class!—you do so at your peril. Curlers who lack an understanding of the scientific principles behind the game of curling are curling with one hand tied behind their backs—something that's unlikely to do much for their game.

What Makes a Rock Curl?

Let's start out by tackling the number-one physics question about the game of curling, namely what makes a rock curl?

If you think back, way back, to that boring lecture on friction that your physics teacher gave you back in high school, you can figure this one out for yourself. Just in case you've repressed the memory, let us remind you of a simple scientific principle: static friction is always greater than sliding friction. In other words, it takes more force to get something moving than to keep it moving. Here's an example that most of us can

53

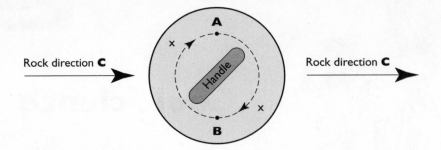

Figure 5.1 What makes a rock curl?

From the Skip

When you're planning your shot, keep in mind that a rock will travel on a relatively straight line until it slows down enough to start to curl.

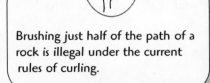

Brushing just half of the path of a rock is illegal under the current rules of curling.

relate to (unfortunately). If you've ever tried to push a car that has broken down, you've no doubt noticed that it's much more difficult to get the car moving than to keep it moving once the wheels have started to roll.

Now let's consider how this basic rule of science makes its presence felt on the ice. Figure 5.1 shows a stone moving in direction C and rotating clockwise as shown by arrow x. The dotted circle in the diagram represents the rubbing surface—a ring on the bottom of the rock. At point A, the speed of rubbing on the ice is the speed of the stone down the ice plus extra speed due to rotation. At point B, the rubbing speed is the speed of the stone minus the speed due to rotation. Since the speed of rubbing is slower at B than at A, the friction force is higher and the rock curls toward B. As the rock slows down, the percentage difference between the two speeds becomes increasingly greater, causing the rock to curl more in its last few feet of travel.

The Science of Sweeping

Now let's consider the science of sweeping. Although it is not currently legal under the rules, brushing half of the path of a rock can affect the curl. If you brush the path in the direction the rock is curling, you will reduce curl, but if you brush the path in front of the rock on the other side, you will increase curl. The reason for this is obvious: the rock curls because of a difference in the force of friction on the two sides of the rock. Sweeping the "slow" side of the rock decreases the difference in friction force, while sweeping the "fast" side increases it. If our prediction regarding changes to the sweeping rule come to pass, then the art of sweeping will become one step more complicated and more important. (We can practically hear skips yelling "straighten" or "more curl" in future bonspiels!)

Between a Rock and a Hard Place

Now let's talk about what happens when two rocks collide—that is, what happens to both the rock that has been hit and the rock that did the hitting (a.k.a. the shooter). The rock that has been hit moves in a line that extends through the centers of the two rocks and through the point of collision, and the shooter moves at right angles to that line.

There is some small variation from these theoretical angles as a result of rock-to-rock friction and ice static friction, but the variations are generally so small that they can be ignored. They are of greater interest to a physicist than a curler!

Now let's consider how these scientific principles help to explain what happens with some common hits: a half-rock hit, a quarter-rock hit, and a three-quarter rock hit.

In a three-quarter rock hit (see Figure 5.2), the shooter deviates 75.5 degrees from its original path and the hit rock goes 14.5 degrees in the opposite direction.

A half-rock hit occurs when the shooter goes off at 60 degrees in one direction, while the rock that has been hit goes off at 30 degrees in the other direction. (Here's a neat little fact to amaze your teammates: the rock that has been hit travels almost twice as fast after the collision as does the shooter!)

In a quarter-rock hit, the shooter deviates 41.5 degrees from its original path and the hit rock travels 48.5 degrees in the opposite direction. This time the hit rock travels at about the same speed as the ongoing shooter.

Becoming an On-ice Einstein

Since you're unlikely to don a lab coat and carry a protractor with you to the rink, you're probably wondering how you can put your newfound scientific knowledge to work on the ice. The good news is that your skip will do a lot of the thinking for you. The bad news is that you have to be able to follow his logic!

Here's an example of the type of shot that benefits from a little on-ice science.

Assume that rock A in Figure 5.3 is on the button and that you want to wick off rock B in order to hit it. If you sight along the back surface of rock A and draw an imaginary line through to the front of rock B, that is where your shooter must hit rock B on collision. To hit that point, the center of our shooter must be twice as far out from the center line of rock B than is the point we want to hit. As you can see, rock C is the rock that is being wicked in.

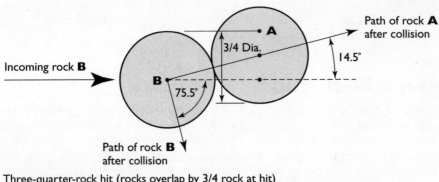

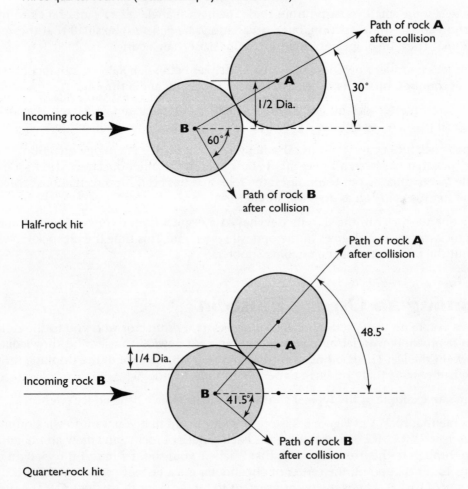

Three-quarter-rock hit (rocks overlap by 3/4 rock at hit)

Half-rock hit

Quarter-rock hit

Figure 5.2 Hits and angles

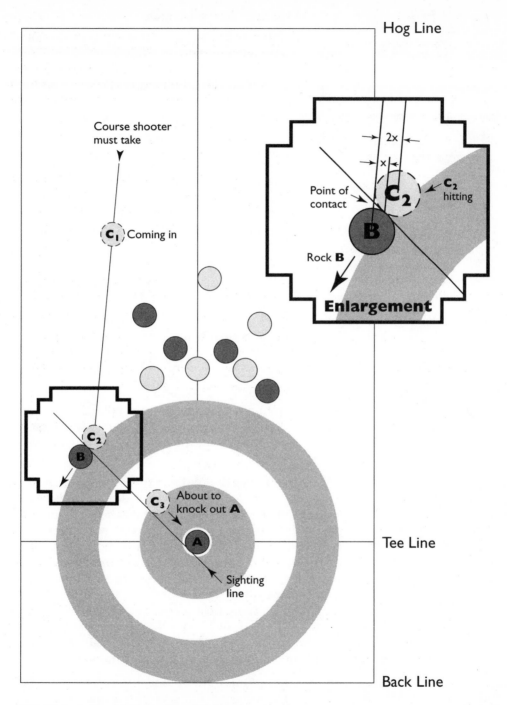

Figure 5.3 Calculating hit point for wick-in

Rock Talk

Wicking off a rock means to use it as a bumper and bounce your rock in off it.

Rock Talk

Turn   The rotation put on the rock during delivery.

Curl   The curling motion of the rock.

Tales from the Rink

Putting turn on the stone while delivering it didn't come into vogue until the late nineteenth century.

Another Angle

Another scientific fact that you can use to your advantage has to do with raises. When rocks hit dead on, the rock that has been hit moves at a speed that is almost equal to that of the rock that hit it (say 95 percent). On the other hand, a rock that is angled in on a raise starts to move at a speed that is less than that of the shooter: a three-quarter rock hit has the hit rock move on at about 90 percent of the shooter's speed; a half-rock has the hit rock move on at just over 80 percent of the shooter's speed; and a quarter-rock has the hit rock move on at just over 60 percent. The moral of the story? The greater the angle of a raise, the faster the shooter needs to be when it hits the other rock.

Avoiding an On-ice Knuckle Ball

Have you ever wondered what would happen if you tried to send a rock down the ice without applying any curl? To put it simply, you'd find yourself stuck with a 44-pound knuckle ball.

Don't understand what we're talking about? Allow us to pull out our chalk and chalkboard for a moment and run through another quick lesson in physics.

A rock that is sent down the ice without an in-turn or an out-turn is known as a dead-handle rock. Dead-handle rocks are unpredictable beasts. Sometimes they acquire a curl as they go down the ice. Sometimes they do tricks, making their way down the ice in an "S" curve. Other times they do what you would expect them to do, making their way straight down the ice. Most of the gyrations they perform can be explained away by variations to the sliding surface of the rock or by the fact that the rock picks up some frost on one side during its travel. Since consistency and predictability are the keys to success on the ice, dead-handle rocks are bad news. Skips lose hair over dead-handle rocks as well as their equally evil twins— rocks that were given insufficient rotation and lose their turn in transit.

Another equally unpopular animal at the rink is the spinner—a rock that has too much curl. Contrary to what you might expect, spinners curl less than rocks with slow rotations. This is because the rubbing speed on the bottom of the rock—caused by the spin—becomes large as compared to that due to travel down the ice. Consequently, there is less of a difference in friction between the two sides of the rock than there would normally be. This is why good teams try to have all their players put on the same amount of turn on their rocks.

The Least You Need to Know

> While it sounds like a good idea in theory, it's not a good idea to attempt to vary the amount of turn on your rock as a way of modifying the amount of curl. Consistency is the key to success on the ice, not trying to re-invent your delivery each time you step in the hack.

➤ Curling stones curl because the friction on one side of the stone—the side most affected by the rotation—is greater than on the other side of the stone. As the rock slows down, the percentage difference between the two speeds becomes increasingly greater, causing the rock to curl more in its last few feet of travel.

➤ Although it is not currently legal under the rules, brushing half of the path of a rock can affect the curl. If you brush the side in the direction the rock is curling, you will reduce curl, but if you brush the path in front of the rock on the other side, you will increase curl.

➤ The rock that has been hit moves in a line that extends through the center of the two rocks at the point of collision, and the shooter moves at right angles to that line.

➤ The greater the angle of a raise, the faster the shooter needs to be when it hits the other rock.

➤ A rock that is sent down the ice without an in-turn or an out-turn is known as a dead-handle rock.

➤ A rock with too much curl is known as a spinner.

Chapter 6

Basic Skills

In This Chapter

➤ The keys to a good delivery

➤ The traditional delivery

➤ The non-lift delivery

➤ The art of sweeping

We've chosen to devote this chapter to the two basic types of skills required to play the game: delivery and sweeping.

If you've had a chance to flip through any other curling books, you've no doubt noticed that the bulk of them zero in on the slide delivery. Because it is so popular, we have chosen to cover it first and then move on to discuss the non-lift delivery—a new type of delivery in which the stone is never lifted off the ice except to clean the running surfaces. As you will see later in this chapter, we predict that in the very near future, the non-lift delivery will replace the slide delivery as the delivery method of choice. (Remember, you read it here first!)

We also devote a portion of this chapter to a skill that every curler needs to master: sweeping. While you may assume that the time you spent sweeping the front porch or the back patio as a kid is training enough when it comes to sweeping, think again. There's more to wielding a broom than you might think. A whole lot more, actually.

Special Delivery

Before we discuss the two basic types of delivery, let's take a moment to focus on the keys to a good delivery. In our not-so-humble opinion, a good delivery involves:

1. aiming your body correctly in the hack.

2. swinging the rock on both back and forward swings along the aim line to the target broom.

3. grasping the rock correctly so that "putting on curl" will not push the rock sideways.

4. tucking the body in behind the rock with the sliding foot almost under the body's center of gravity.

5. being balanced and stable (both mentally and physically!) during the delivery and release.

6. using the broom correctly to assist balance.

7. using a repeatable and accurate method of weight control.

8. releasing the rock cleanly, before the hog line with a handshake-like follow-through motion.

Now, let's get down in the hack—mentally at least!—and consider the task at hand. The first time we run through the steps involved in a successful delivery, we'll give you a bird's-eye view of the entire process. Then we'll zero in on the specifics and tell you exactly how you should be positioning the various parts of your body to ensure the most effective delivery.

First Things First

The first thing you should do when you're preparing to deliver a stone, after taking your position in the hack, is to clean the bottom of the rock to be sure that it is free of frost or debris. Most curlers use their broom to do this, turning the rock over and polishing the bottom. They often go over the running surface with their hands or gloves to be sure that their cleaning job has been successful.

As you squat in the hack preparing to deliver, look at the skip's broom and in your mind draw a line—the aim line—from the skip's broom to

To avoid creating new problems for yourself, either turn sideways when cleaning the rock, or make a point of sweeping the area where the rock was cleaned before placing the rock on its running surface. Some curlers give the rock a spin after they put it down in order to be sure that it slides smoothly.

Tales from the Rink

Ken Watson is credited with pioneering the modern slide delivery at the St. John's Curling Club in Winnipeg in 1930. Legend has it that Watson and his team discovered the slide one night during a practice session when the lead forgot to slip a rubber on his shoe before delivering his stone. He skidded twenty feet down the rink—and into the history books. The slide helped to give curling a racier image—one that helped to popularize it with teenagers and twenty-somethings. It also reduced the amount of strength and physical effort required to throw a stone, opening up the game to others who might not traditionally have had the strength to play.

the center of the hack. Square your body so that you face the target broom and be sure that the rock is centered on the aim line.

If you are a right-handed curler, your right foot will be in the left hack. Your left foot, which will become your sliding foot, will be kept close to the hack, either perched on the outside edge of the hack, or on the ice just in front. You hold your broom—to help you balance—in your left hand.

What happens next involves several simultaneous actions, or ones that follow each other in rapid succession. You lift the stone, swing it backward along the aim line like a pendulum, and then reverse the motion and swing the rock forward toward the broom. As the rock passes over the hack and in the direction of the target broom, your right "pusher" leg is fully bent and, as you move forward with the rock, it is ready to propel you forward like a coiled spring. As you move the rock backward with your throwing arm straight, your shoulders will automatically be lifted to the point where the stone is directly under the shoulder. As you swing farther back, the stone will be lifted. The shoulder height should remain fixed at this point so that on the forward swing the stone returns smoothly to the ice.

While all this is going on, what is your left foot doing? As you swing the rock backward, this leg reaches behind and close to the hack, acting as a counterweight to prevent the weight of the rock from tipping you over sideways. As you come forward, you have to tuck your sliding foot under you and slide on it during the next stage of delivery. This prevents you from falling on your face! Because you have not allowed the sliding foot to swing out sideways during the delivery, you are able to bring it across and under you without too jerky a maneuver. The rock must be well ahead before the non-sliding leg is brought under the body and in line with it.

Now let's consider where the broom and the left hand fit into this whole maneuver. The left hand holds the brush or broom partway down the handle so that the sliding surface (the back of the brush head) is touching the ice to the front and slightly to the side with the handle behind your left shoulder. (Note: Some curlers lock it under their left armpit for added support).

As you begin the backswing, the brush lifts off the ice, providing more counterbalance to the weight of the rock but, as you swing forward and place the rock on the ice, the broom also touches the ice, somewhat like training wheels on a bike.

As you begin your slide with the rock, your back foot comes out of the hack and provides some front-to-back stability by sliding lightly on the ice. (Most curlers turn this foot sideways.) For a proper slide, the majority of the weight must be on your sliding foot, with the broom and rear leg playing minor rolls in maintaining balance. The body should be erect so that your wrist is over the stone.

Now what about the curl? When we first look at the skip, he indicates how fast a rock he wants and where he wants it to end up. He also indicates in which direction he wants the rock to turn, usually by extending one arm horizontally. A right arm calls for a clockwise turn—an in-turn—while a left arm means a counter-clockwise turn—an out-turn (assuming a right-handed curler).

In order to prepare for the turn you rotate the stone so that the handle is cocked about 60 degrees in the opposite direction to the rotation you want before you start your delivery. During the backswing, the handle does not rotate. During the forward swing, however, the handle may or may not rotate, depending on whose technique you decide to follow. (Some experts suggest you start the rotation during the forward swing; others suggest you put the curl on during the slide.)

Tales from the Rink

From the beginning, the slide delivery has been a source of controversy. The Royal Caledonian didn't know what to make of it when it first caught wind of this innovation. After consulting with member clubs in both Canada and the United States, the Scottish club ultimately ruled that the slide was admissible. But when Stan Austman of Saskatchewan slid all the way down the sheet of ice and placed his final stone on the button, it was obvious that some type of limitation was required. As a result, rules were put into place to limit how far the curler could slide. As it currently stands, the stone must clearly be released before the hog line, but the slide can continue unlimited after that.

Whichever method you adopt, putting on the curl should be a smooth and automatic action rather than an afterthought at the end of the slide when the arm is fully extended and the probability of inadvertently pushing the rock sideways is high. A high body position with the wrist over the stone allows the hand to impart a pure turning force that is free of any sideways thrust.

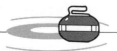

Tales from the Rink

Ken Watson—three-time Brier champion—advocated starting the rotation during the forward swing, but many current experts recommend that the curl be put on during the slide. The discrepancy in technique can probably be explained by the longer slides of modern curling.

If you watch high-level competitions on television, you will note that some players start to rotate the rock in the wrong direction, and then reverse it prior to release. It would seem that the reason they turn the rock in both directions is to have any sideways thrusts from putting on curl cancel each other.

Whichever method you adopt should become automatic. Once the handle has been twisted in the right direction, curl should be in the right direction and amount without further thought. Two to three complete turns in the travel down the ice is the recommended amount of curl.

The speed of the rock should be determined by the extent of backswing, by the force put into the forward swing before the rock is laid back on the ice, and by the back leg push off—not by an arm push during the slide. When the rock first touches the ice on the forward swing, the arm is not fully extended. At the point of release, the arm is fully extended and the rock has turned to the point where the handle aims straight down the ice and the final hand release is a motion not unlike extending the hand for a handshake.

From The Skip

A word to the wise: if you are going out to curl for the first time, before you try a slide delivery on the ice, do a dry run on the carpet first. It's hard enough for a beginner to assume the correct position without also having to worry about the effects of a slider (the slippery contraption that allows you to slide down the rink).

Four Not-so-easy Steps to a Slide Delivery

Since the delivery is so critical to the sport, it's worth considering the elements of a successful delivery once again and in greater detail.

Now that we've walked you through the process of delivering a stone, let's consider how your body should be positioned during each phase of the delivery.

A good slide delivery involves four basic steps: getting yourself into the correct position and then leaning slightly forward, drawing and swinging the rock backward, swinging the rock forward in a smooth motion, and then sliding out of the hack (the rubber foothold in the ice).

Let's consider each of these elements separately and see what you need to pay attention to during each stage of the delivery.

1. Get into the correct position in the hack and then lean slightly forward. Your first task is to assume the correct position—something that is much easier said than done! What you're trying to do is to get yourself into a squatting position with the ball of your non-sliding foot resting against the back of the hack and your sliding foot jutting slightly forward. Don't let your knees flare out; instead keep them close together, directly over your feet. Your upper body should be upright and relaxed, with your shoulders positioned square to the target, and your eyes

should be looking forward toward the skip's broom (not the rock she wants you to hit). Your throwing arm should be straight, and your balance arm (the arm that holds the broom) should be kept straight as well, but off to the side. Ideally, the broom should be resting on the back of your body, with the handle behind your left shoulder. Cock the handle of the rock so that it will produce the curl that the skip has requested.

Once you've assumed the correct position as described above, your next step is to move your sliding foot forward slightly so that your upper body, stone, and broom begin to move forward.

2. Swing backward. Next, you start to draw the rock back along the ice and your rear end raises out of the squatting position. Your head and shoulders should remain upright, and your throwing arm should continue to be straight. At this point, the bulk of your weight should be on your non-sliding foot. As you continue to draw the rock back, it will raise your shoulder until the stone is directly under the shoulder. Shoulder height should be frozen at this point, and the rock will swing backward in a pendulum-type motion and transfer your weight to the leg that is in the hack. At this point, your sliding foot also swings back to a point behind the hack—a maneuver that allows you to maintain your balance.

Make sure that the position is comfortable. No part of your body should be rigid or tight.

Just a few words of caution: don't push the rock down the ice or use any exaggerated hand motions as you release the rock or the rock will go off course. And, whatever you do, don't hold onto the rock past the hog line or the rock will be deemed to have gone out of play.

The rock speed should be determined by the speed at which you come out of the hack, not by a shove or a push during delivery.

3. Swing forward. Once the rock reaches the maximum backswing, gravity will make it want to swing forward like a pendulum, and you can add speed with your arm in order to get the correct weight. Since the shoulder has remained fixed, the rock should be exactly at ice level at the bottom of the swing, providing a smooth transition to a sliding motion.

4. Slide out of the hack. As the rock now starts to slide along the ice, you push with your hack leg and slide forward, being careful not to lean on the rock for balance or to allow it to drag behind the rest of your body. Your shoulders should be parallel to the ice, your sliding foot tucked under your center of gravity, and your

brush (which continues to be held out to the side) should be at least as far forward as your sliding foot. Depending on the length of slide you use, you either started the rock turning on the downswing or during the slide so that the rock handle has reached the straight position when it is released.

The Non-lift Delivery

The lift delivery that we just described in great detail may look good on paper, but it's actually wrought with weaknesses and difficulties. Don't believe us? Consider the evidence:

1. There is a severe weight shift when the rock is lifted and again when it is placed back on the ice during the forward swing. Shifting forty-plus pounds of rock weight can upset the curler's balance—and do quite a number on his back.

2. The aiming eye and the stone aim line are not over one another but on near parallel paths. This makes aiming more difficult—similar to what you experience if you purchase a camera that doesn't allow you to look through the lens directly.

3. The stone can bump the ice, throwing the shot out of line. (Just envision the type of rough landing you get to experience when you put your life in the hands of a frighteningly inexperienced airline pilot!)

4. The sliding foot must do a difficult and very athletic maneuver. First, it must swing back as a counterbalance to the rock weight during the backward swing; then it must let the rock get ahead of it and move sideways in order to tuck itself under the curler's body and behind the shot rock. (And you thought that Twister™ was tricky!)

5. The thrusting leg is offset a small amount from the swing of the rock rather than being in line with it.

The non-lift delivery either eliminates or improves upon all of these weak points.

In the non-lift delivery the starting position of the curler is quite similar to that used in the lift delivery—although there are subtle differences. Because there is no need to counterbalance the weight of the stone, the back leg and sliding broom can be more compact, and they are not forced sideways.

The delivery is accomplished along a line bisecting the push-off foot, and the aiming eye can be over the same line. The rock is first drawn back along the aim line, and then pushed forward with a combination of leg thrust and arm push. The sliding foot is tucked under the body as in the lift delivery, but because it does not go through a backward swing, and because it is tightly beside the push-off foot, the distance it must travel is smaller and the maneuver is simpler.

Since the stone never leaves the ice, there are fewer opportunities for shifts in body weight to throw the curler off balance—good news for those of us who are co-ordination challenged.

Rock Talk

Weight refers to the amount of force or momentum on a rock as it makes its way down the ice. Draw weight means using enough force to cause the rock to end up on the playing surface—usually in the house. Guard weight means using enough force to cause the rock to stop short of the house. It then either protects a rock already in the house from being easily hit or provides a protected area in which a rock can be easily hidden. Takeout weight means using enough force to push an opponent's rock through the house and out of play. Hack weight means using enough force to take out a rock and send it as far as the hack. Bumper weight means using enough force to send the rock to the back end of the rink. Peel weight means using sufficient weight to force the rock being hit and the shooter to clear the ice. Rocks thrown with guard or draw weight curl the most, while rocks thrown with takeout weight curl the least.

Because most of the other aspects of delivery—positioning the body, putting on curl, and stone release—are similar to the lift delivery, to save paper, we have not repeated them.

As you've probably gathered by now, we've got a bit of a bias when it comes to delivery. We believe that the non-lift delivery is intrinsically superior to the lift delivery, and are not surprised that there appears to be a trend toward the non-lift delivery, particularly amongst younger players and countries that are new to the game.

The Art of Sweeping

The next skill that you need to master is sweeping.

Sweeping clears the ice of any frost or debris that might cause the rock to slow down or go off course and polishes the pebble in the ice, thereby reducing friction and allowing the rock to go farther and straighter. (Here's a neat bit of trivia that will amaze your family and friends: the sweeping motion actually causes a portion of the pebble to melt away temporarily, creating a thin film of moisture that acts as a lubricant between the ice and the stone.)

From the Skip

It is possible to sweep gently to clean the ice without having much effect on the curl or distance traveled. The loss of one rock to contamination on the ice is too many, and this simple low-energy sweep, although not foolproof, provides worthwhile insurance.

From the Skip

Effective sweeping can cause a rock to travel ten to fifteen feet farther than it otherwise would have traveled.

The two players responsible for sweeping the stone are those who aren't directly involved in the play at the time (i.e., they aren't taking their turn to deliver a stone or holding the broom to indicate where a particular shot is to go—a role of the skip or acting skip).

The two sweepers stay alongside and slightly in front of the rock as it makes its way down the ice. Since the sweepers are closest to the rock and traveling with it, they are in the best position to judge its speed and the need for sweeping. The skip, on the other hand, is a better position to see the line the rock is taking.

When you're sweeping, you should stand with your hips at a 45 degree angle to the path of the stone. Ideally, your feet should be slightly more than a shoulder's width apart, and your knees should be slightly bent. Leaning forward at the waist will ensure that most of your body weight is over your sliding foot. Use your gripper foot (your non-slider foot) to propel yourself down the ice without lifting the slider foot. Make sure that you're sweeping directly in front of the stone at all times since the rules require that the brushing stroke go completely across the stone's width.

The rules allow for unlimited sweeping from the point the rock has been released until the rock makes it across the tee line at the target end of the rink.

The Least You Need to Know

➤ A good delivery involves four basic steps: getting yourself into the correct position and leaning slightly forward, swinging the rock backward, swinging it forward in a smooth motion along the aim line, and then sliding out of the hack.

➤ There are numerous advantages to the non-lift delivery—something that helps to explain the growing popularity of this type of delivery, particularly with curlers who are new to the sport.

➤ Weight refers to the amount of speed or momentum on a rock as it makes its way down the ice.

➤ The purpose of sweeping is to clear the ice of any frost or debris that might cause the rock to slow down or go off course, and to polish the pebble in the ice, thereby reducing friction and allowing the rock to go farther and straighter.

➤ The rules of curling allow you to start sweeping as soon as the rock has been released, and to continue doing so until the rock makes it across the tee line at the target end of the ice.

Hot Shots

Now that you know how to deliver and sweep the rock (well, on paper at least!), let's talk about the various shots that the skip may call upon you to make.

There's a lot to master in this chapter, so don't expect yourself to absorb everything the first time through. You'll want to read this chapter a couple of times before you play your first game. You might even want to tote your handy Idiot's Guide with you to the

From the Skip

Don't be surprised if some of these shots are called something slightly different at your club. You only have to attend one out-of-town bonspiel to discover that there are regional variations in curling terminology.

Rock Talk

An eight-ender means that your team has scored eight points in an end—something that is a rarity to say the least. In an eight-ender, all eight of your team's rocks end up closer to the tee than any of the other team's rocks. Bottom line? An eight-ender makes a hole in one look like child's play. See Chapter 9 for more details on eight-enders.

rink, and refer to it briefly between ends—unless, of course, you're too embarrassed to have your teammates discover that you're an Idiot! (Don't feel this way; they've probably got their own copy stashed away at home!)

If the jargon begins to make your head spin, take a deep breath and flip to the glossary in Appendix A. It's a quick and painless way to begin to decode the mysterious language of curling.

Now that we've issued all the necessary disclaimers and reminded you why you were so smart to pick up this particular curling book, let's move on to our discussion of the basic curling shots.

The Draw

The draw is the most fundamental and widely used shot in curling. It simply means sending a rock down the ice so it ends up where the skip wants it to end up.

Here's how it works.

The skip decides whether he wants an in-turn or an out-turn (in other words, whether he wants the rock to curve or curl in a left-to-right or right-to-left motion), estimates how much the rock will draw, taps the ice where he wants the rock to end up, and then sets his broom as a target for the thrower.

When executing his delivery, the curler must keep two important facts in mind: the weight required to reach the target area and the distance his sweepers can carry (i.e., make it go farther than it normally would) a rock. He tries to deliver the rock at the broom with a weight that would fall about 50% of that carry distance short of the target if it were not swept. Underthrowing allows for a margin of error that isn't possible with overthrowing.

Once the curler releases the rock, the sweepers take control. They watch the ice ahead of the stone to ensure that it is kept clear of debris. They quickly judge how much sweeping the rock requires to reach the target area and vary the intensity of their sweeping accordingly. As the rock nears the target area, they continue to estimate the need for sweeping. In some cases, they are aided by instructions from the skip, but when line or direction is not a factor, most skips leave the sweeping judgments to the sweepers.

The Freeze

The freeze is a draw shot in which the target spot on the ice is a location where, if played properly, the rock thrown will come to rest against another rock.

A freeze makes the front rock very hard to remove. The backing of the rock behind it means that the power of a hit is transmitted through the front rock to the back one, removing the back rock but leaving the front rock unscathed. Only a precise hit near one edge will move the front rock any distance, and significant power is required.

A corner freeze means that the contact point is off center. (Yes, we know: it's difficult to find a real corner on a round rock!) Corner freezes are easier to remove than ordinary freezes. Most hits will move or remove both rocks. A hit at 2 (see Figure 7.1) removes both rocks but saves the shooter. A hit at 3 removes rock C and the shooter, but leaves rock D. A hit at 1 can remove rock D and the shooter, leaving rock C.

When a rock is almost totally hidden, a corner freeze to it acts like a handle of extension to the rock. Hitting the "handle" at the next opportunity can move or remove the original rock. If you look at Figure 7.1, you will notice that rock E is hidden behind rock G, but made vulnerable by the extension handle provided by freezing rock F to it.

The Takeout

When we talk takeout, we're not talking fast food—we're talking a hard, fast shot. As the name implies, this shot involves taking a rock out of play by hitting it hard enough to drive it beyond the house. If the rock that is being hit is hit nearly dead on, the shooter can be kept in play. A hit can be intentionally just off-center so that the shooter can be used as a guard or a counter. This strategy is referred to as hit and roll.

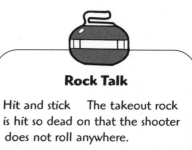

Rock Talk

Hit and stick The takeout rock is hit so dead on that the shooter does not roll anywhere.

Normal weight for a takeout is usually hack weight or slightly greater. If a curler throws heavier, the sweepers can do little, if anything, to affect the shot.

Guards

Guards are just what the name implies—rocks that are placed between the house and the hog line with the express purpose of hiding other rocks behind them, or protecting rocks that are already in favorable locations.

A guard near the house is called a short guard, while one near the hog line is called a long guard. A long guard is easier to draw around, but harder to raise onto the rock hidden behind it. A short guard, on the other hand, is more difficult to draw around, but easier to raise onto the rock hidden behind it.

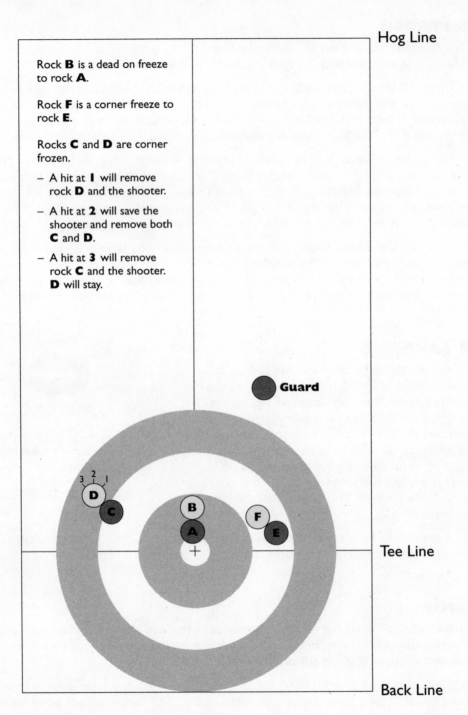

Rock **B** is a dead on freeze to rock **A**.

Rock **F** is a corner freeze to rock **E**.

Rocks **C** and **D** are corner frozen.

— A hit at **1** will remove rock **D** and the shooter.

— A hit at **2** will save the shooter and remove both **C** and **D**.

— A hit at **3** will remove rock **C** and the shooter. **D** will stay.

Hog Line

Guard

Tee Line

Back Line

Figure 7.1 The freeze

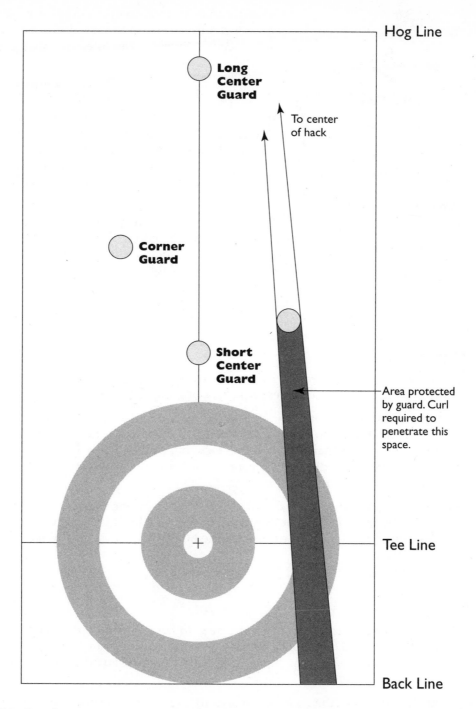

Figure 7.2 Guards

From the Skip

You can think of the space protected by a guard as being the area that would be in its shadow if a bright light were shone at it from the middle of the hack. Only by curling can rocks penetrate into that area.

Guards can be located on or near the center line (center guards) or placed about four feet on either side of center, in which case they are called corner guards.

In order to be most effective, in most situations a guard should be placed on an imaginary line that joins the center of the rock to be guarded with the middle of the hack. Once the rock that is to become the guard crosses the hog line, the sweepers and the skip should keep that imaginary line in mind, and getting the rock on line should take precedence over anything else.

A case can be made that when the ice does not curl equally in both directions, the line on which the guard is placed should be biased to make the guard as effective as possible. For example, if the ice curls "in to out" more than it curls "out to in"—a common situation on club ice—the ideal guard situation is closer to the center line.

Tap-backs

There are two ways to protect a rock from being knocked out by your opponents—use a guard or place it in front of an existing rock or group of rocks.

We have already talked about using the freeze as a method of providing backing to a shot. Another method is to bump an opponent's rocks to the area of the house behind the tee line and, rather than putting these rocks out of play, leave them where they are in order to make it more difficult for your opponent to knock out stones you place in the house in front of them.

This strategy of building a fence or wall across the back of the house is sometimes re-ferred to as playing "chap and lie" weight. The danger with this strategy is that, should your opponent clear all of your rocks from the house, you are leaving him with addi-tional potential counters.

Ports

A common situation facing a curler is the need to have his stone pass between two or more guards or obstructing stones. These gaps between stones are called ports and there is a science to negotiating them—especially when the guard stones are different distances from the target.

Fortunately, the curl of the rock can be used to increase the clearance the rock has and the probability of making the shot. What's more, the amount of curl—and hence the

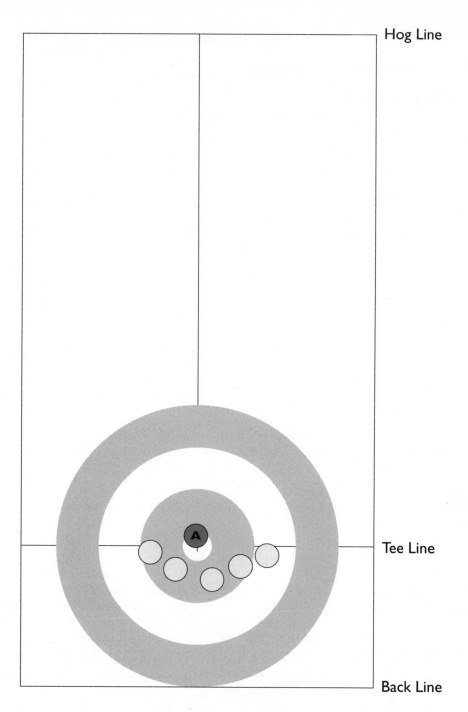

Figure 7.3 Tap-backs

Hog Line

Tee Line

Back Line

Tales from the Rink

While skill is important, sometimes it's sheer luck that carries you through a particular end—something seventeen–year–old competitive curler Ryan Chapman discovered during a game at the Bridgewater Curling Club in Bridgewater, Nova Scotia.

The boys' competitive team that Ryan belonged to was playing against a group of older men in an effort to improve the teenagers' level of play. Because one of the teenagers was unable to make it out for the game, coach Dave Carr took to the ice with his team.

During the first part of the game, Dave stumbled, fell on his back, and, in doing so, knocked the rock down the ice. His rock went through an extremely small hole between two guards, took out the other team's shot rock (the rock closest to the tee), and settled in close to the tee. A dream shot.

They're still talking about it a good year and a half later.

weight of the shot used—may increase the clearance. Consider the following two examples:

In Figure 7.4, a slow rock just over tee-line weight with an out-turn (counter-clockwise turn) is required to get through the port between the first and second guard.

In Figure 7.5, a clockwise-turning rock at heavy weight (backboard or greater) will have more clearance negotiating the port than a slower rock with either curl or the opposite turn on a fast rock.

Because port shots require such precision, anything a skip can do to increase the tolerances (margins for error) helps to improve the probability that his team will make the shot.

The Raise

As we discussed earlier on, the introduction of the Free Guard Zone Rule (a.k.a. the three-rock free guard rule in Canada and the four-rock free guard rule internationally) has led to a greater accumulation of rocks between the house and the hog line than was previously the case in curling. This, in turn, has increased the frequency with which two difficult types of curling shots—the raise and the raise takeout—are used.

Let's talk about the raise first (see Figure 7.6). This is a shot where a team promotes a rock from in front of the house to a position nearer the button or tee line. On a straight raise, the rock doing the raising can become a guard for the rock it promotes. An angle raise can put a rock behind cover, sometimes in a position where it is extremely difficult to remove. One form of the angle raise is called the split. Here, a rock close to but outside of the rings is raised into the house on an angle so that the lightly thrown rock that raises it wicks off and ends up being in the house, too.

The Raise Takeout

Now let's consider the raise takeout—a shot where a stone in front of the house is hit and propelled in such a manner as to hit and remove an opponent's rock (see Figure 7.7). This is especially useful when one of your rocks is guarding one of your opponent's. A perfect raise takeout replaces your opponent's rock with one of your own and then guards it with the rock that did the raising.

Obviously, if the rock being hit for the raise takeout is also your opponent's rock, then you want it to "corner" the target rock, not hit it dead on, so that both rocks are knocked out of the rings.

Why are shots like the raise and the raise takeout not played more often? The answer lies in the accuracy required. To raise a rock onto one ten feet behind it, you must hit the first rock within about one inch of the aim point to even touch the second rock. To remove it, you must be even more accurate. To remove it and have it stick requires still higher accuracy. When one considers that from point of release to the hit on the rock being raised is a distance of about 80 feet, the accuracy seems almost unbelievable—and yet the top players make a significant percentage of such shots.

The Wick

To get to a part of the ice that is behind guards or to hit out a rock that is well protected, you can bounce off a rock at the side of the rings and ricochet to the target or target area. This is probably one of the most exciting shots in curling, partly because the end result is often an unexpected surprise.

Let's go back to fundamentals for a moment and consider what happens when two rocks collide.

As Figure 7.8 shows, the hitting rock goes at right angles to the hit rock. The hit rock travels on a line through the centers of the two rocks at point of contact. Note that the point of contact is halfway between the aim line and a parallel line through the center of the target rock. (As you may recall, we discussed this subject in greater detail back in Chapter Five when we explored the physics of the game of curling.)

When two rocks hit at a 45 degree angle, both rocks continue at about equal speed. The nearer we get to a dead-on hit, the greater the velocity of the hit rock after collision and the lesser the velocity of the shooter. Conversely, the finer the hit, the more the shooter will maintain its velocity and the slower the hit rock will move.

If you are trying to wick in to remove an opponent's stone and the angle is severe, the shot must be made with considerable force in order for the shooter to continue to its target with sufficient momentum to remove the target stone. When you are trying to

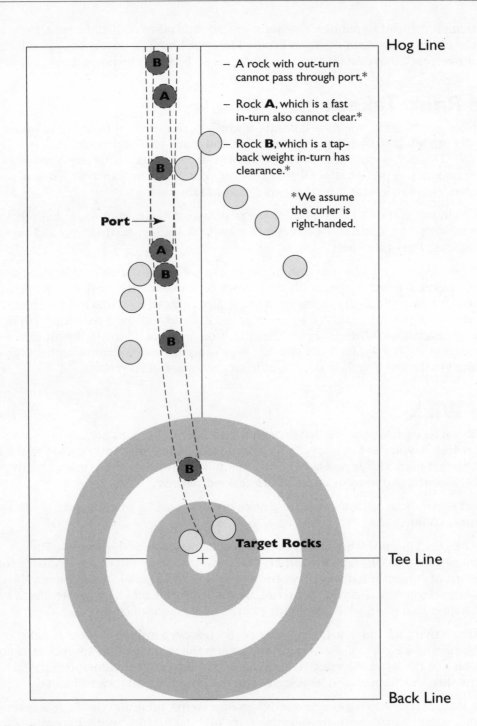

Hog Line

— A rock with out-turn
cannot pass through port.*

— Rock **A**, which is a fast
in-turn also cannot clear.*

— Rock **B**, which is a tap-
back weight in-turn has
clearance.*

*We assume
the curler is
right-handed.

Port →

Target Rocks

Tee Line

Back Line

Figure 7.4 Ports

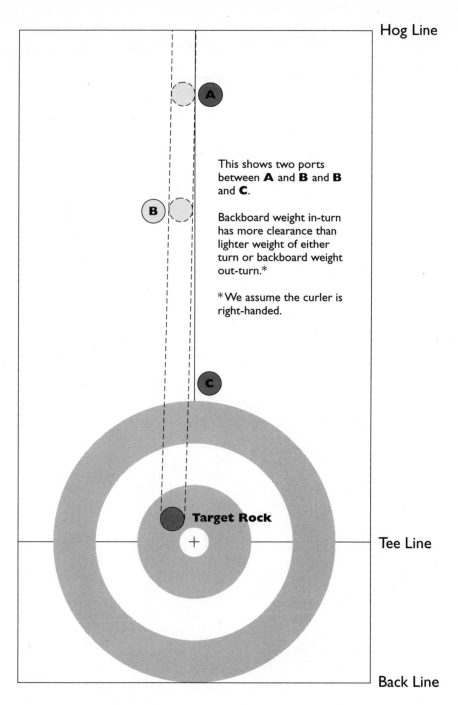

Hog Line

This shows two ports between **A** and **B** and **B** and **C**.

Backboard weight in-turn has more clearance than lighter weight of either turn or backboard weight out-turn.*

*We assume the curler is right-handed.

Target Rock

Tee Line

Back Line

Figure 7.5 Ports

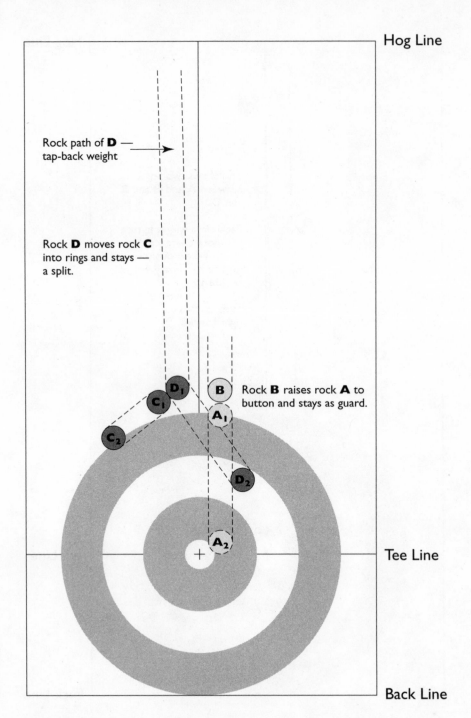

Hog Line

Rock path of **D** —
tap-back weight

Rock **D** moves rock **C**
into rings and stays —
a split.

Rock **B** raises rock **A** to
button and stays as guard.

Tee Line

Back Line

Figure 7.6 Raises and splits

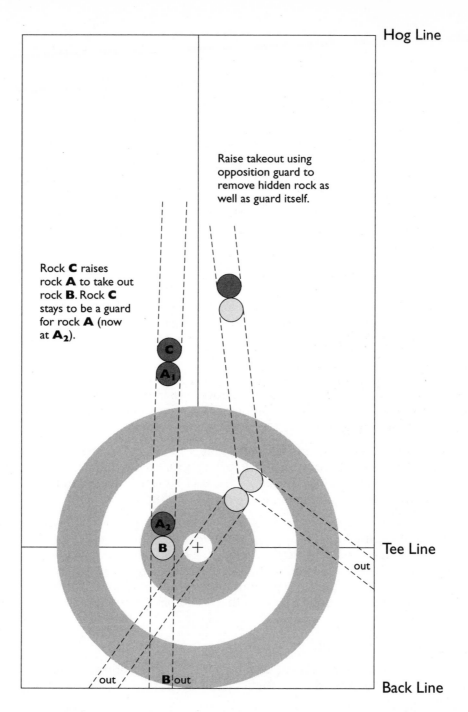

Hog Line

Raise takeout using opposition guard to remove hidden rock as well as guard itself.

Rock **C** raises rock **A** to take out rock **B**. Rock **C** stays to be a guard for rock **A** (now at **A₂**).

C

A₁

A₂

B

out

B out

Tee Line

out

Back Line

Figure 7.7 Raise takeouts

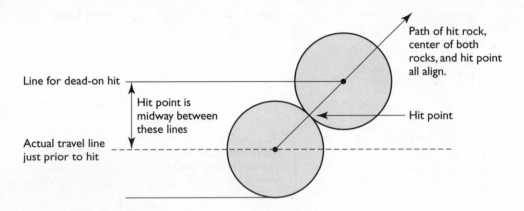

Figure 7.8 Geometry of a hit

wick in behind guards and come to rest at or near the button, there are often several alternatives: a fast rock can be sent with a small angle on the target stone, a lighter weight can be used at a wider angle on the hit, or you can use one of the various combinations in between. Just keep in mind that the lighter shots will end up deeper in the house. (See Figure 7.9.)

Note that the point of contact is halfway between the aim line and a parallel line through the center of the object rock (the rock being hit). This is a point that many skips—and TV commentators for that matter—do not seem to fully understand. As a result, the broom positions set are sometimes questionable.

What's more, some skips overlook the possibility of a double takeout when the two rocks are on the same horizontal line. Remember that the wicking rock leaves the front face of the first target rock and it can hit the back surface of the second target rock and still remove it. This often provides enough angle for the shot to work.

A half-rock shot—one that is aimed at the edge of the target rock after taking any curl into account—will wick off at approximately 60 degrees to the aim line (the line that the rock was on immediately before it made the collision) and drive the target rock at a 30 degree angle to that line in the opposite direction. Obviously, you can't expect to execute shots of this complexity without understanding the geometrical principles that make them work. (Now don't you wish that you'd paid attention in math class?)

Freebies

In pool and snooker they refer to them as puts and sets—shots that are so easy that any Idiot should be able to make them.

Freebies (a.k.a. gifts) take two forms. In both cases, they involve rocks that are either very close or touching. In one case, the line joining the centers of the rocks is aimed at

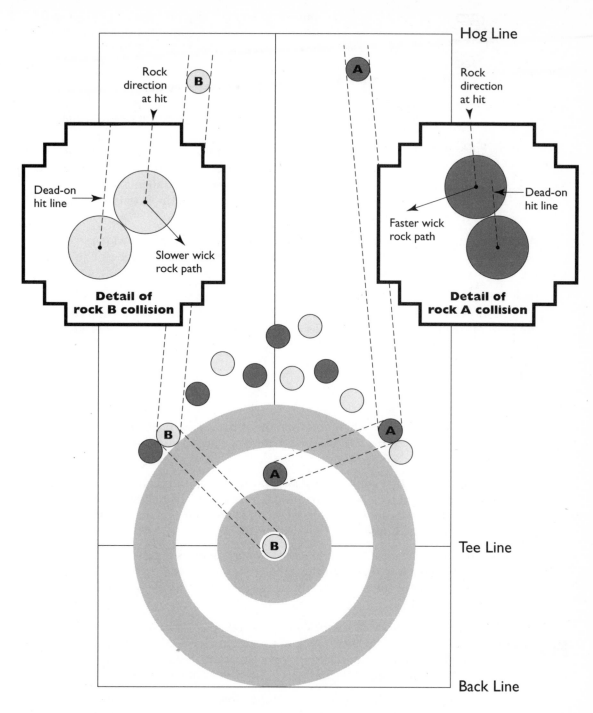

Hog Line

Rock
direction
at hit

Rock
direction
at hit

Dead-on
hit line

Slower wick
rock path

**Detail of
rock B collision**

Dead-on
hit line

Faster wick
rock path

**Detail of
rock A collision**

Tee Line

Back Line

Figure 7.9 Wick-ins

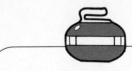

Rock Talk

Frozen   Rocks that are touching one another.

Near-frozen   Rocks that are almost touching one another.

the button or a target area. In the other case, the tangent line to the point of contact aims toward the button or target area. (See Figure 7.10.)

Remember how we said that raise shots are easier when the rocks are close together? Frozen or near-frozen rocks are like an aimed gun: with a wide tolerance on the hit, the back rock will be propelled along the line joining the centers of the frozen rocks. When this happens to be a shot that is advantageous, you have a freebie. On the other hand, if you detect that such a freebie is available to your opponent, a gentle tap to spread the frozen rocks may be in order!

When rocks are situated side by side, and are frozen or near frozen, a wide range of hits on one of the rocks will propel it along a line at right angles to the line joining the center of the two rocks.

Each type of shot is shown in Figure 7.10. Although such shots do not occur very often, always be on the lookout for them, particularly when there are a lot of rocks at the front of the house. Remember: both shots can be used to either promote a rock (light-weight hit) or to use the second rock to take out an opponent's rock (heavy-weight hit).

The Peel

When your team is ahead or when your opponent has a rock in the house that is well guarded, you will likely want to remove a guard or potential guard from in front of the house.

While raising might at first seem like a good option, there's one significant problem: trying to raise the guard rock back onto a hidden rock runs the risk that a slight miss will leave your shooter as a replacement guard and give your opponent a free shot to put another rock in the house or put up still another guard.

This situation calls for a shot known as a peel. A peel involves removing a rock in front of the house in such a way that both the shooter and the offending rock are taken out of play without either of them passing through a part of the house where they might do damage.

This calls for a hit finer than a half-rock, since the objective is to see that the shooter goes to one side of the ice, the guard rock to the other. The direction of the peel will be dictated by the location of other rocks. In some situations, we may want to avoid a possible second hit. In others, a second hit could work to our advantage.

If there are two guards in play and they are either close together or staggered in their distance from the house, we may wish to do a double peel using either the shooter or

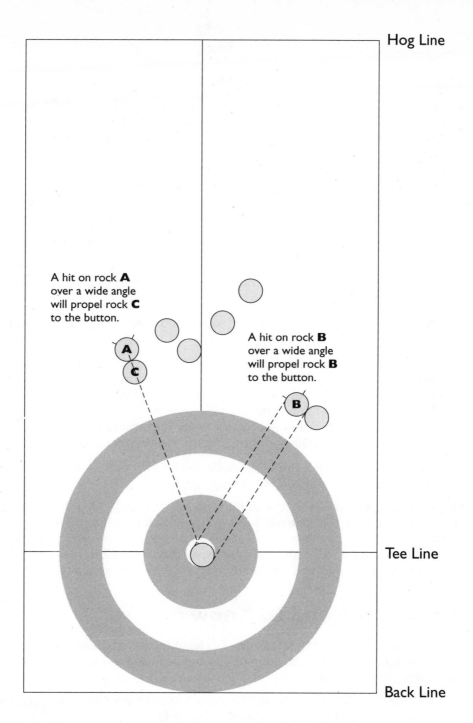

A hit on rock **A** over a wide angle will propel rock **C** to the button.

A hit on rock **B** over a wide angle will propel rock **B** to the button.

Hog Line

Tee Line

Back Line

Figure 7.10 Freebies

Tales from the Rink

If at first you don't succeed—you could be the next Ernie Richardson. Legend has it that the four-time Brier winner failed to get a single rock in the house when he first tried the game at age 13. "I had tears in my eyes after the game," he later told journalist Doug Maxwell. "I was never so discouraged in my life." Concluding that curling was "a lousy game," he focused instead on hockey, football, baseball, and tennis for the next eight years. It was only at that point—after having become accomplished at billiards, a game that in its collision angles is not unlike curling—that he decided to try his luck on the ice again. He eventually became skip of the famous Richardson family rink. The rest, as they say, is history.

the farthest guard to make a second collision with the closest guard and hopefully have all three rocks taken out of play.

While peeling is an important skill for any curler, too much of a good thing can be, well, boring. Here's why.

By the early 1990s, high-level curling teams had became so effective at peeling rocks that two basic strategies developed. If the score was tied and the team had last rock, they would peel all rocks put up by the opposition, blanking ends (scoring zero) until the last end, gambling that they would be able to score since they would still have last-rock advantage. Similarly, if they got two rocks up, they would peel all rocks until the tenth end last rock, leaving the opposing skip the ability to score only one point.

Such tactics led to scores of 2 to 1 and similar small rock counts, and the game became so predictable that it was out and out boring.

Not surprisingly, the powers that be in the world of curling decided that a change was in order, and the Moncton Rule was followed in quick succession by the three- and four-rock Free Guard Zone Rules. While these rules aren't often used at local rinks, if you manage to make it to a cash spiel (a bonspiel played for money) or a national or international tournament, you'll certainly need to know how to play "the Zone."

The Least You Need to Know

➤ There are a number of different shots to learn in curling, including the draw, the freeze, the takeout, guards, bumpers, ports, the raise, the raise takeout, the wick, freebies, and the peel.

➤ With the Free Guard Zone Rule, the use of high-risk shots like raises and raise takeouts has become much more common and necessary.

Chapter 8

More of a Good Thing

> **In This Chapter**
>
> ➤ Why strategy is important
>
> ➤ What a skip needs to think about
>
> ➤ How strategy changes over the course of a game

Because of the amount of strategy involved, curling is often compared to such games as chess and snooker. The analogy is a good one: rather than merely focusing on the shot you're about to make, you need to be thinking two or more shots ahead—anticipating what your opponents will do and figuring out what your next move will be.

While the skip is generally responsible for setting the strategy throughout the course of the game, most skips welcome input from the members of their team. (It's just a few die-hard traditionalists who insist that they're in charge of the ship, and don't want to hear anyone else's ideas.) Even if your skip decides to pull rank on you, it's important to understand what's going on in his head so that you will know what he's expecting from you. That's why we've decided to start out this chapter by giving you a crash course in strategy.

Strategy 101

Here are some basic principles that hold true in the majority of curling games. (You will note that we say the majority of games. As you will soon discover for yourself, there are no absolutes when it comes to curling!)

From the Skip

Force your opponent to surrender last-rock advantage by making him take a point rather than blanking the end.

l. 'Tis better to blank an end than to walk away with only one point.

What we mean by this is that it's better to sacrifice the point you might take in this end in order to have last-rock advantage in the next end.

Just one bit of fine print to note before we move on: you don't want to use this particular strategy if it's last end and the score is tied. In this case, you want to take your point, pick up your marbles, and go home.

2. Good ice is nice. Bad ice can be nice too.

There's no question about it: ice conditions affect strategy. The trick is to find ways to make the ice conditions work for—not against—you. Here are a few tips on strategies that work well on various types of ice:

Straight ice—ice that does not curl much, even at draw weight—makes guards more effective, but the guard must be put on after the rock that you wish to protect is in place because you won't be able to draw around it either. Raising rocks into the house rather than drawing around guards can be more effective, and raising is easier at tee-line weight.

Swingy ice—ice that curls a lot—makes long guards relatively ineffective and makes raise shots more difficult.

Unbalanced ice—ice that tends to favor either inward curls or outward curls—demands that guards be placed in a slightly staggered pattern in order to obtain the best protection.

Non-uniform ice—a sheet of ice with conditions that vary from one spot to another—can even provide opportunities. In some rinks, for example, frosty ice builds up near the edges of the sheet. If you force your opponent to play into these areas, you can tremendously increase the difficulty of his shots.

3. The scoreboard ruleth.

As is the case in many sports, the score often dictates what type of approach to use. An early lead of more than a few points will call for a conservative hitting game, while being down several rocks early on in the game may call for a more aggressive approach—for example, a draw game with many rocks in play. (Although this type of draw game is riskier, it may be the only way to score two or more rocks in an end. Many of the better skips start out the end with an aggressive draw game, but if halfway through the end they see little chance of building up an end, they bail out and go for a blank.)

4. Practice makes perfect.

Unless you are very familiar with both the ice and your opponents, the first few ends of a game are a bit of a feeling-out process. Try to learn as much as you can about the ice at the start of the game by making a variety of shots over as much of the ice surface as possible. If you pay close attention to how each rock responds, you can find out how much draw there is (how much a rock will curl in various parts of the ice) and how takeout-weight rocks behave. This is also a great opportunity to size up your opponents' strengths and weaknesses.

From the Skip

Sweepers should judge the ice early on so that they'll know how much broom work will be required in subsequent shots.

The homework you do at the start of the game will pay off in later ends. Having a better feel for the ice will ensure that difficult shots such as coming around short guards, freezing, and shooting through ports have a much better chance of succeeding.

5. Look before you leap.

Before you get into the hack, consider as many outcomes as possible to a particular shot—the best and worst possible scenarios and everything in between. Not all shots end up where they are supposed to, so it's important for the entire team to consider in advance the good or bad outcomes that might result if a particular rock went off course.

From the Skip

Even after a shot has been missed, you may want to sweep the rock to prevent it from doing further damage.

Here's an example of what we're talking about. It's not unusual to see a rock that was supposed to be taken out hit a stone at the back of the house or at the edge of the circles instead and stay in play. Prior knowledge of such a possibility could in many cases lead to the skip altering the sweeping pattern to avoid this particular outcome.

Similarly, it's sometimes possible to turn a takeout into a double if things go well. Once again, the skip can control the sweeping in order to get the best result.

Note: Some shots may be scrapped entirely after the team considers what could go wrong and decides that the potential benefits don't merit the risk. Rather than being greedy and trying to get four points out of an end rather than three, a team might choose to avoid a risky shot that could potentially end up raising an opponent's rock to the button.

Don't cut the rest of the team out of the decision-making process if you have the opportunity to skip. Instead, involve them in the brainstorming process as much as possible. As a rule of thumb, eight eyes are better than two.

6. Think twice. Then think again.

Before you choose your shot, make sure that you have evaluated all possible alternatives.

Obviously, this is often much easier said than done—particularly if the ice is cluttered with rocks. Rather than settling for the first shot that comes to mind, look for freebies and other wide-tolerance shots that are likely to yield rich rewards.

7. Keep your house in order.

Keep the center of the ice clear when you have last rock, or try to capture this area—clutter it with your own rocks—if your opponent has last rock. While this strategy may sound obvious, it's surprising how often it gets missed.

A skip should be coach and cheerleader to his team. While players sometimes make mistakes or forget key points to their deliveries, there's a right way and a wrong way to pass along advice. When your turn comes to play skip, don't criticize another player harshly or embarrass him in front of the rest of the team. Remember: nobody tries to make a bad shot.

8. Let your opponent be the guinea pig.

Learn from your opponent's mistakes by watching his every rock. Be sure to note the actual line taken by each rock—not just the intended line. The reason is obvious: you may have to duplicate his shot or base a shot on his, and you want to know both where he actually aimed and what happened.

9. Focus, focus, focus— especially if you're the skip!

Although a good skip always tries to anticipate what is going to happen on shots made by both his own team and the opposition, there is always the chance that an unexpected wick or an unusual set of collisions in a cluster of rocks may produce a need to sweep a rock to the button or even to get it to bite the rings—or to sweep an opponent's rock out of (or to the back of) the house.

It is not only embarrassing to a skip, but also demoralizing to his team when he is caught "asleep at the switch."

10. *Gamble a little.*

As the old expression goes, "Nothing ventured, nothing gained." High risk shots—e.g., long raises, medium or long raise takeouts, freezes, and long doubles or long wick-ins—can really pay off for your team, and should be used in the following situations:

➤ When a near miss is still useful. A long raise or raise takeouts, if not successful, may still help to remove a problem guard. Likewise, the freeze may still be useful if it becomes a gentle tap-back, near freeze, or chap and lie.

➤ When the reward justifies the risk. A shot that, if successful, could be a game winner certainly warrants consideration.

➤ When there is no other alternative. If you don't gamble, you're going to lose, period.

The Final Exam

There are literally millions of situations that can arise in a curling game, and since it is impossible for us to cover more than a few of these scenarios in this book, we're going to do the next best thing to meeting you down at the rink for a couple of games: walk you through parts of an imaginary game as seen through the eyes of one skip and give you the chance to put your newfound knowledge of strategy to work. (Think of it as the final exam—except that we give you the answers along the way.)

Here goes.

Our team is playing in a regional bonspiel at a rink we have never played before and against a skip whose team we know very little about. After the usual introductions and handshakes, our vice tosses a coin to decide who goes first. We lose the toss, so we have to throw first rock. Our lead chooses the red rocks as he always does: it's his lucky color. The skip from the other team reminds everyone that we are playing the free guard zone and after exchanging "Good Curling" salutations, we're set to begin.

As I make my way to the far end of the rink with the skip from the other team, I think about how I'll play that first end. Although our team usually plays an aggressive come-around style, I feel there are too many unknowns—the ice, the rocks, and the opposition, to name a few. I decide that I'll be ultra-conservative and place the first rock in the house, preferably at the front of the 4-foot ring. I assume that the rock will draw about two feet and, after tapping my broom on the ice to show where I want the rock, I set my broom on the tee line at the edge of the 4-foot circle calling for our lead to deliver an in-turn.

The ice turns out to be a little heavy and, despite the vigorous sweeping by our second and vice, the rock comes to rest on the center line, just short of the rings, in the free guard zone. It turns out that this is the other skip's home rink and he decides to be aggressive from the start, ignoring our rock and putting up a corner guard. I watch his rock and it draws about two feet from his broom on the center line and ends up midway between the house and hog line on the skip's left-hand side of the sheet. Rocks are shown numbered in the order in which they were played in Figure 8.1.

Deciding to become a little more aggressive, I decide to try to draw into the house behind my first rock, although, to be honest, I have two other possibilities in mind. I will set the broom to have the shot just skim by the guard at minimum clearance on the draw shot, knowing that if I misjudge, we have the chance of making either a split or even a raise of our first stone. Tapping the same spot as I had on the first shot—top of the 4-foot—I take another rock-width of ice (one rock wider in broom placement) and call for our lead to deliver the same turn, same weight. The path on the ice is now partly polished and our lead places the rock in behind the first rock at the top of the 4-foot, although it is not completely buried.

Given the placement of our lead's stone, the other skip is now faced with a variety of dilemmas or possibilities:

1. He could hit my front rock and try for a double takeout—the risk being that he might miss the second rock and leave another guard in the center of the ice or that he could be too exact and have my first rock hit the second and stick (not roll away).

2. He could leave my stones to deal with later on and try to go behind his first guard—the risk being that I would put up a long guard on my rock staggered slightly to the right of my short-guard, but further protecting my short-guard rock and clogging up the center of the house still further, something he didn't want with last rock.

3. He could try to draw around the other side of my short guard, but try to get nearer to the button than my rock. This would be a difficult shot as no one had tried that curl on that side of the ice, and he would be guessing at how much the rock would draw on that side of the house. If it hung out (didn't curl enough), I would have an easy takeout with a chance to roll behind either my guard or his corner guard.

4. He could try to take out my shot rock with a medium-weight takeout, playing the ice closely and knowing that if he missed the shot rock, he would at least take out my short guard.

He decides to go with the fourth alternative, and he succeeds in removing my rock. Unfortunately for him, his shooter rolls out of the rings.

I now know that part of the ice reasonably well, and decide to try a split on my short guard. There is the possibility that one rock may roll behind his corner guard, but even if we don't get that bonus, we could end up with two rocks in the house well separated. (We like having rocks that are well separated because it's harder for our opponents to double them out. It's kind of like using a divide-and-conquer strategy on ice.)

Earlier on in the game, our vice used his stopwatch to time our lead's last draw. He now gives this number to the second, who is able to use this number to gauge the

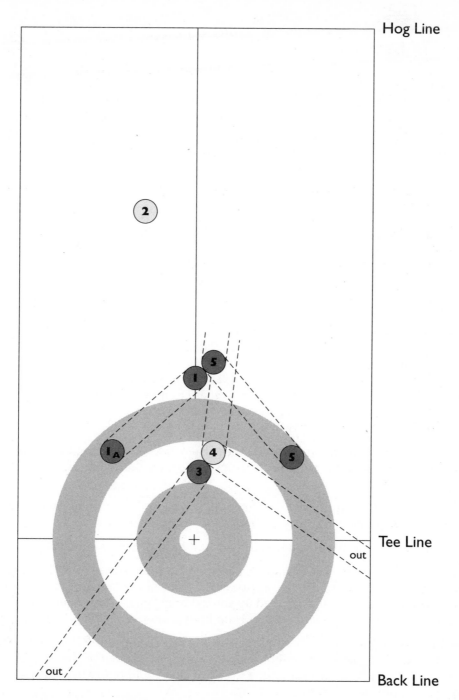

Hog Line

Tee Line

out

out

Back Line

Figure 8.1 Strategy Game, First End, First Five Rocks

Rock Talk

Shot rock   The rock closest to the tee.

Rock Talk

Biting the front of the rings
Barely touching the front of the rings. A rock that bites the house is counted as being in the house.

conditions of the ice and then deliver a stone with perfect tee-line weight. We end up with a perfect split—in other words, both of the rocks are the same distance into the house and in front of the tee line. We don't manage to get the left rock completely behind the corner guard, but we are still pleased with the shot. (Ecstatic, no. Pleased, yes.)

The other skip then switches to a hitting game. The first thing his team tries to do is to get a roll behind our guard. Then they try to roll over near our other rock, hoping that we will hit and stick and set up an easy double.

Our second and vice respond well, in each case hitting out the opponent's rock and then rolling enough to keep the two rocks separated in the house. The exchange of rocks continues until the other skip's first rock rolls out of the house after taking out one of our rocks.

Now I'm faced with a dilemma: what to do with my last rock. I could try to put it on the button and force the opposition to hit and stick or give up a steal of one (allow the other team to take one point on the end). Or I could become a little more aggressive and try to put the rock in the house, but up-front enough to guard as much of the button as possible. Such a rock would have to be far enough forward so that if it hit the rock dead on, it would leave our second rock as shot.

I come out a little light, but our lead and our second save the shot by sweeping it so that it bites (touches) the front of the rings, almost on the center line. (Thank heaven this is a team sport.)

The other skip is up to the task and, taking the side of the ice I had shown him during the early ends, draws almost to the button—counting one.

Our team is pleased. We now have last rock and have given up only one point.

The second end, on the other hand, is a near disaster (see Figure 8.2). The other team's lead puts the first rock in the house, just at the front of the button. Our lead—not fully realizing how much the ice has sped up since the first end—comes out too strong when I call for a corner guard, and ends up in the house.

The other team then lays its second rock on the center line at the front of the house, where it acts as a guard on the shot rock. It's also close enough to the rings that it could potentially be used for a split, a situation that could put two of our rocks in the house if we were to remove his shot rock.

The hitting game is on. The free-guard possibilities have been wasted. To make a long

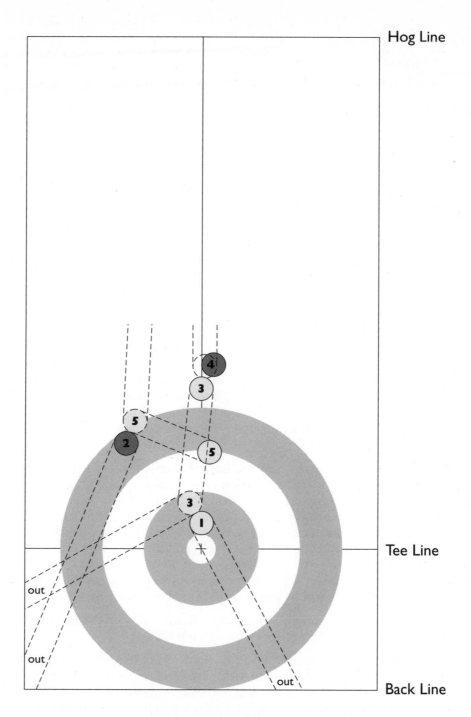

Hog Line

Tee Line

Back Line

Figure 8.2 Strategy Game, Second End, First Five Rocks

Rock Talk

A steal occurs when the team that does not have last rock scores one or more points.

story short, we make a raise takeout double, but leave our shooter (rock 4) out front as a potential guard. The skip from the other team throws a stone that hits and rolls off our first stone and gets behind rock 4. Another raise takeout clears the opposition from the house. Unfortunately, rock 4 doesn't stick, and we still have a rock out front. Successive attempts to hide rocks are followed by takeouts, and, in the end, we are able to blank the end and retain last rock.

Let's skip ahead (no pun intended!) to the tenth end. The game is all tied up, but the other team has last rock. We need a steal to win.

I call a short team meeting before we hit the ice. Everyone agrees that our best option is to try to plug up the front of the house and keep the other team hitting. We agree not to worry about getting a rock in the house until later in the end; to overlook most of the opposition's counters (rocks that are in the house); and to concentrate on trying to capture the front of the house.

Our lead is able to lay his first rock as a guard, placing it about two feet in front of the rings and just a few inches from being square on the center line (see Figure 8.3). The skip from the other team calls for his lead to throw his rock through the house, but holds his broom one rock's width from our guard, signaling that he wants to try to move our rock off center without taking it out of play. The lead almost makes the shot, but catches too much of our rock and rolls it to the sideboard. We replace our rock in its original resting place (since it was in the Free Guard Zone), and I call for a long center guard in an effort to keep our rocks as far apart as possible, while still clogging up the middle.

Having already wasted one rock, the skip from the other team feels compelled to try to double out our two rocks by raising the long guard onto the short. He comes close, perhaps too close, as he ends up driving our front rock through the house while leaving his shooter almost in its place, rock 4 knocking out rock 3. I call for another guard from our second. I tap the ice halfway between the two rocks in play, then set my broom one width farther from the center line than I did in placing the long guard. I don't want to hit his front rock, and realize that a bit of stagger between the guards would make them a tougher target for doubles. Our second comes through and our sweepers deliver the rock within inches of the target area (rock 5).

The skip from the other team decides to play a straight peel on the front rock, a shot that his team executes perfectly (rock 6 knocks out rock 4).

I need to widen the blockade in front of the house, so I call for a "near biter" (a rock that almost touches the house) just to the right of the center line. I expect it to be hit, but hope that the shot will either stick or roll nearby. Again, our second places the rock as requested. The skip from the other team calls for a hit with a roll behind our short guard. The shot is almost perfect, but rolls too far and "shows" on the other side of the center line, just in the rings (rock 8 hits on rock 7).

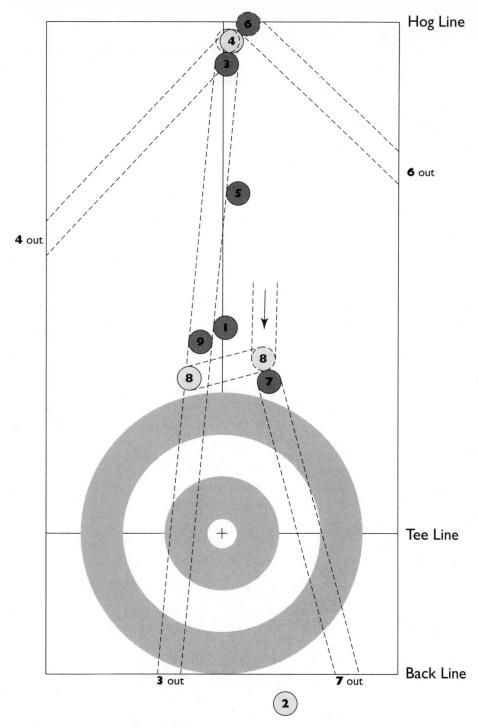

Figure 8.3 Strategy Game, Last End, First Nine Rocks

Now I need to decide which side of the house we should try to plug up next. I choose to call for a freeze to the other skip's last rock as it would be hard to remove and, if we get a good angle on his rock, it would prevent him from raising it into the button area. Our vice's rock doesn't curl as much as I would have liked, but it covers the opposition's stone in a way that makes both a raise and a double takeover difficult (rock 9).

I can almost hear the other skip thinking out loud. "Left side of center is hopelessly plugged up. We'd better get a rock in on the right before it is too late."

I think our staggered guard (rock 5) spooks him a little as he takes too much ice and his vice's rock ends up being hung out. The sweepers stop sweeping in order to let the rock curl, and the rock ends up in front of the house, biting the front circle almost at the first position of our rock (rock 8). (See rock 10 in Figure 8.4.)

Knowing that I have a means of getting a rock in the house with an angle raise on rock 9, I choose to hit out his rock 10 and stick so that he cannot raise it in behind cover (rock 11). The other skip feels that he now knows the exact ice to draw in behind my rock (rock 11) and calls tight ice, hoping to draw into—or at least very close to—the button. He almost makes his shot, but the rock touches our guard, leaving his rock about three feet to the right of, and just short of, the button (rock 12).

I couldn't leave rock 12 sitting out there as an easy wick-in target for the other skip, and so I decide to hit it out, hoping to get a roll behind cover. I hit it dead on (rock 13). The skip from the other team decides to try the same thing off my rock, but he too hits dead on and moves his stone only a few inches toward center (rock 14).

I have no doubt as to what I want to do with my last rock. I want to raise our vice's last rock (rock 11)—the one that the other skip had nudged on his draw attempt—to the front of the button. I know that if I get the angle right, my shooter will partially cover the other skip's rock on the rings, leaving him some difficult choices. I have noted by this time the ice taken by my opponent on his draw attempt (and how his shot worked out), and this gives me guidance as to where I will have to put the broom. I call the team together to be sure that everyone knows what the shot will be. I make sure that the vice knows that line on the tap-back is more critical than the weight, and then I head down to the hack.

From the Skip

Most curlers become more confident as the game progresses and they begin to get a feel for the ice.

I feel pretty certain that the ice is right, but having just thrown heavy weight on my first rock, I am a bit concerned about getting my draw weight right. I review my fundamentals as I prepare to shoot: rock clean, shoulders square to the shot, weight very clearly in mind, rock handle cocked for the proper turn.

As I release the rock, I suddenly remember that I haven't told the sweepers to be sure that the rock path is clear of debris, so I yell, "Clean, clean!"

Our vice watches the line of the rock and our sweep-

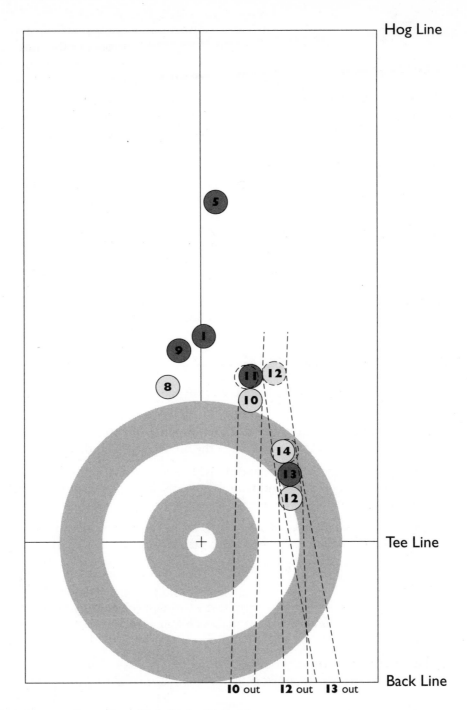

Hog Line

Tee Line

Back Line

10 out   12 out   13 out

Figure 8.4 Strategy Game, Last End, Rocks 10 to 14

From the Skip

One final word on strategy: you can lose games because of poor strategy, but the best strategy in the world won't do you any good unless all players on the team are able to make their shots.

ers watch the speed. Our tap-back comes off like clockwork, raising our guard behind cover to where it bites the front of the button and the shot rock moves over a few inches to partially cover the other skip's last rock (rock 14).

The other skip calls a team meeting. The team discusses every alternative, eventually zeroing in on their best option: angle-raising the skip's first rock (rock 14) to the button. A difficult shot at any time, this shot is made all the more difficult by the fact that it will probably decide the game. The team members debate which ice to take, and speculate about whether there will be frost build-up and slower ice to contend with since they will be using a part of the ice that hasn't been used so far in this end.

By the time the skip gets down in the hack, he is both excited and apprehensive. The shot comes out a little too strong, and the sweepers sweep too hard for too long. The skip just touches the edge of the target rock and it moves only a few inches. End of game; end of story. (We hope you like happy endings!)

The Least You Need to Know

➤ Last-rock advantage is worth more than one point. Don't relinquish it for less than two points, if you can help it.

➤ Study the ice on both your own and your opponents' shots. Make sure that you note actual line of shot, not just where the broom was placed.

➤ Modify your strategy to fit ice conditions. The score, ice conditions, who has last rock, the end being played, and your opponents' and your teammates' strengths and weaknesses are all key factors in strategy.

➤ When faced with a number of alternative shots, carefully weigh the chances of success (width or tolerance) versus the potential benefits.

➤ Involve your team in key decisions.

➤ While it's a good idea to have a strategy in mind for a particular end, you need to be willing to change your strategy midway through the end if you unexpectedly miss some shots or your opponent makes an abundance of particularly brilliant shots.

➤ A skip must be alert throughout the entire game and continually plan ahead. (What can we say? The hard work goes along with the glory.)

Chapter 9

Variations on a Theme

In This Chapter

➤ The Skins Game

➤ Singles

➤ Pairs

➤ The Points Game

➤ How ties are broken in competitions

➤ The Eight-ender

There are probably hundreds of games played with curling equipment, although the four-person team standard version is by far the most popular.

Although we don't intend to cover all variations of the game, in this chapter we will discuss a few of the more common variations in order to give you an idea of how versatile—and fun—the game can be.

Tales from the Rink

In floor curling, circular disks weighing two pounds each are sent down a 36-foot-long and 8-foot-wide rink made of hardwood, linoleum, well-laid tile, or smooth cement. The rules state that the floor should be prepared with "a light sprinkling of shuffleboard wax or cornmeal or a mixture of both." You can find a copy of the rules online at www.bcgames.org/senfloor.html

The Skins Game

The "skins game" is a game played for money. Like its golf counterpart, it has been popularized by T.V. The game follows the same rules as normal curling with minor exceptions relating to scoring and last-rock advantage. There is a prize for each end, normally cash, and the value per end is tapered so that ends go up in value as you approach the tenth and final end. The rules specify that you either win an end, tie an end, or lose an end. If you have last rock, you must score more than one point to win. If you score one point, you tie, but lose last-rock advantage. If the end is blanked or your opponent scores, you lose the end, but keep last-rock advantage. There is no carryover of points from end to end. Each end is a win-lose-or-draw situation and, if a draw, the prize money carries over to the next end. The overall winner is the team that wins the most money.

Singles

A popular way of evaluating the strengths of players is to hold a one-on-one competition. A common version of the singles game has each player throwing four rocks each end. The two players take turns throwing their rocks, and no sweeping is allowed. Players judge their own ice as there is no skip to hold the broom. Scoring is similar to normal curling and the number of ends typically varies from six to twelve. Because there are no sweepers to help "carry" the rocks, heavier weight is required and weight judgment is more difficult.

Pairs

The pairs game is similar to the singles game, but involves a second player who holds the broom and/or sweeps. The number of rocks thrown by each player varies from two to four, and the number of ends is set to suit the participants. This game makes a good training exercise for players who want to improve their overall skill level.

The Points Game

Scotland has a "points game," which very much resembles the skills competitions held in conjunction with the Brier and other major competitions.

In this game, rocks are set on the ice at predetermined points and the competitor tries to make a series of skill-testing shots. In the first version of the game, players were given four tries at striking, wicking in, drawing, and guarding. Subsequent versions of the game have involved a wider variety of shots, including chap and lie, raising, chipping out a guarded rock, and drawing through a port.

Started in the 1800's in Scotland, various forms of the game persist to this day as a means of determining who is the more skilled curler.

The Tie-breaker

In competitions, it sometimes becomes necessary to break a tie. Some curling clubs put the curlers in question through the following skill-testing exercise in order to break the tie.

First, each of the leads tries to draw a rock to the button. (No sweeping or hitting are allowed, and each lead throws only one rock.) The player whose rock ends up closest to the tee and in the rings wins. If the exercise fails to produce a winner, then the seconds compete. If the same thing happens again, the vices compete, and so on. It is surprising how the combination of nerves plus the fact that sweeping is not allowed make this competition much more difficult than it sounds. What's more, it gives the lowly lead the chance to be a hero.

Tales from the Rink

Legend has it that there are games of curling played that closely resemble darts. In this variation of the game, each circle is assigned a point value, with the rocks closest to the button being assigned more points than those that are farther out. In dart-like fashion, the player throws her rocks, tallies up her score, and then clears the playing field for her rival.

An Eight-ender

No one goes into a tournament planning to score an eight-ender, but sometimes—usually after your team has thrown five or six of its rocks—the possibility presents itself, and you decide to go for it.

There's nothing more exciting to a curler than scoring an eight-ender. (It's the curling world's equivalent of bowling a perfect game.) If you register your accomplishment with the Ford Motor Company of Canada, you and your teammates will walk away with a collection of prizes that are guaranteed to turn a few heads at the rink: a fleece top, a personalized certificate, and an eight-ender pin. What's more, each team member's name goes into a draw for a snazzy new car.

103

Here's the scoop on scoring an eight-ender.

In most eight-enders, the winning rocks are lined up in two columns of four rocks each. Some have a few biters near the outer edges and fewer rocks lined up neatly in columns. The idea is to present as small a target as possible and to leave as much room as you can for the opponents' rocks to pass straight through the house without hitting anything.

Sometimes, when the ice is uneven, draw-weight shots will climb up on ridges in the ice whereas takeout weight shots stay in the valleys. A smart skip knows how to make the ice conditions work in her favor and, if she's lucky, her team may manage to score an eight-ender.

If you do manage to score an eight-ender, here's what you have to do:

➤ Leave the rocks where they are until you've lined up some witnesses—ideally, a curling club employee or member of the curling club executive.

➤ Record the names and addresses of the members of the scoring team, the opposition, and your witnesses.

➤ Run for a camera, or draw a clear sketch showing how you managed to pull off this miracle on ice. (You'll want it both to substantiate your claim and for bragging purposes down the road.)

➤ Record the details about how play progressed in the end while they're still clear in your mind.

➤ Obtain the appropriate eight-ender registration form from either your curling club or contact Ford Eight-Ender Program Headquarters, 3817 Bloor Street West, Etobicoke, Ontario, M9B 1K7.

Phone: 1-800-561-5067, fax: 1-800-561-7287.

The Least You Need to Know

➤ There are a number of variations on the game of curling, including the skins game, cash spiels, the singles game, the pairs game, and the points game.

➤ Sometimes a skill-testing exercise is used to break a tie in a competition.

Part III
Body and Soul

Now that you've figured out what's involved in playing the game, it's time to talk about ways to get on top of your game both physically and mentally.

In the next two chapters, we talk about ways to improve your overall fitness level and techniques for mastering the specific types of skills required for curling. We also give you a crash course in sports psychology and let you in on the secrets of successful curlers.

By the time you're finished reading this section, you should be well on your way to becoming the next Sandra Schmirler or Russ Howard—or at least a reasonable facsimile!

Chapter 10

Training Camp

> ### In This Chapter
>
> ➤ Fitness program components
>
> ➤ Individual practices
>
> ➤ Team practices

Now that we're getting close to the end of the book, it's time to let you in on one of curling's best-kept secrets. Regardless of what comedian David Letterman and other similarly unenlightened folks would have you believe, you can't play this sport with a beer in one hand.

Whether the rest of the world wants to believe it or not, curling is a sport that requires a certain amount of physical fitness. You will find the odd Drew Carey clone lounging around the rink—but you're just as likely to find his type at a typical game of pick-up hockey. Does hockey get slammed as a sport because a few of the folks who play it recreationally have an affinity for beer or are more than a bit out of shape? Hardly. Why, then, does curling take such a beating for the very same reason?

The problem seems to be that the jocks of the world don't consider curling to be fast-paced or aggressive enough to be considered a "real sport." The distinction of being a "real sport" seems to be reserved for sports like hockey, football, and soccer—basically any sport in which foul language is thrown around, players whine about the referees' calls, and/or bones are crunched. (Perhaps this explains why most curlers have long since stopped caring about whether some testosterone-charged Eric Lindros-wannabe considers curling to be a "real sport" or not!)

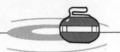

Tales from the Rink

"Those who knock it haven't tried it. Anyone who's curled appreciates the physical and emotional stamina required."

—Bill Tschirhart, a high-performance coach with the Canadian Curling Association.

If you haven't been active for some time, see your doctor before you start a new fitness program. Once you get approval to proceed, start slowly, only gradually building up the length and intensity of your workout.

But we digress.

The fact that we've included a chapter on training and conditioning tells you where we stand on the whole "real sport" or "couch-potato sport" issue. In fact, we believe that overall fitness training is every bit as important as the other topics we address in this chapter, namely improving your skills during individual practices and team practices.

Give It the Old One-two-three

A physical fitness program should incorporate three types of activities: cardiovascular training, flexibility training, and endurance training.

Cardiovascular Training

Cardiovascular training is the type of exercise that makes you huff and puff. (Actually, it shouldn't, because if you're huffing and puffing, you're working too hard. But you get the general idea.)

Strictly speaking, cardiovascular training refers to a continuous, rhythmical, and sustained type of movement that involves the large muscle groups of your body. The types of activities that fall into this category include walking, swimming, running, cycling, aerobic dance, rollerblading, ice skating, rowing, cross-country skiing, stair-climbing, and skipping. (Note: Steve Brown, coach of the U.S. Women's Olympic Team, cautions against choosing activities that are hard on the knees. "Curlers' knees take enough of a pounding as it is," he explains.)

The experts say that the cardiovascular component of your fitness program should last for 20 minutes or longer. They stress the importance of including both a warm-up and a cool-down as part of your workout in order to minimize injuries and soreness. (A warm-up allows your muscles to warm up gradually, thereby reducing the likelihood of injury, while a cool-down reduces problems with muscle spasms or cramping and prevents blood pooling, which can result in a drop in blood pressure and lightheadedness or fainting.)

Flexibility Training

Flexibility training is designed to prevent injuries. Competitive curlers incorporate flexibility training into both their regular fitness regime and their pre-game stretching rituals. (You've probably noticed curlers on TV stretching in and out of the lunge position before attempting their delivery.)

To be effective, each stretch should be held for fifteen to thirty seconds and should be repeated three to five times.

Here are some stretches recommended for curlers:

From the Skip

To improve your overall level of fitness, you should plan to exercise for thirty minutes or longer three to five times per week. (Anything less than three times a week doesn't do a lot to improve your level of fitness; anything more than that is overkill.)

➤ Shoulder stretches: Place the palm of your right hand on your left shoulder and pull your right elbow in. Then wrap your right arm over your head and pull downward on that hand. Repeat for the left hand.

Yes, Virginia, it is possible to have too much of a good thing. You should suspect you're overdoing it with your training program if you begin to experience a number of the following symptoms:

➤ insomnia
➤ irritability
➤ fatigue
➤ loss of appetite
➤ little or no desire to exercise or an obsession with exercising
➤ an increased number of colds and flus and
➤ an increased number of injuries.

Here's some more food for thought: too little exercise can also cause many of these symptoms. The moral of the story? Moderation is the key.

➤ Thigh stretches: Slowly swing your right leg from side to side, allowing your thigh to do the work. Then lie down on your side and do some leg lifts. Repeat for the left leg.

➤ Quadricep stretches: Lean against a wall for support and reach back with the right hand and grasp your right ankle. Hold for 10 seconds. Keep your hips forward and knees beside one another. Repeat using your left hand and ankle.

➤ Groin stretches: Move in and out of the lunge position. Make sure your right knee is directly over your right foot and ankle. Put your hands on either side of your right leg so that they can help to support your weight. Press your hips toward the floor. Repeat for the left leg.

➤ Pectoral muscle stretches: Do a push-up against a wall—ideally a corner.

➤ Back stretches: Stand up with your hands on your lower back and gently curve your spine backward.

From the Skip

If you have access to exercise equipment through a local gym, you might also want to incorporate the following types of exercises into your fitness routine: front leg raises (for your quadriceps), arm curls (to improve bicep strength), bench presses (for your arm and chest muscles), back raises (for your back muscles), and pull-downs (for your arms and shoulders).

Endurance Training

Endurance training involves exercising with progressively heavier resistance in order to increase the endurance of the musculoskeletal system.

An ideal endurance training program consists of exercises designed to improve leg strength and endurance, abdominal strength and tone, arm strength and endurance, and upper and lower back muscle and tone.

Sit-ups (for your abdominal muscles) and skipping (for your calf muscles) are two types of exercises that can be done anywhere, anytime, and that can do wonders for your on-ice endurance.

Individual Practices

If you're lucky enough to be able to book some ice time for yourself, put it to good use by practising some basic shots—like draws and takeouts.

Whatever you do, don't spend your time mindlessly shooting rocks down the rink, cautions Bill Tschirhart, the high-performance coach for the Canadian Curling Association. Throwing rocks without a specific goal in mind is a total waste of time. What's more, it can actually damage your game by encouraging you to develop sloppy habits.

You should also spend some time practising your delivery since it tends to be the most troublesome part of the game for beginners. See if you can bring an experienced curler with you to your practice and ask her to critique your delivery, paying particular attention to following faults:

➤ Poor balance caused by either an incorrectly positioned sliding foot and/or brush, poor timing and/or direction in the movement of the sliding foot, and/or excess leg drive (you push off too hard!)

➤ Poor accuracy caused by either poor balance, poor positioning, or poor aim.

➤ Poor release caused by incorrect grip, handle adjustment, release motion, and/or follow-through motion.

Poor balance can be corrected by practising the following types of drills:

➤ sliding forward without the stone and focusing on the movement of your sliding foot.

➤ checking your position to ensure that the sliding foot is properly positioned under your sternum.

➤ reviewing the correct positioning of the brush.

➤ improving the timing/direction of the sliding foot.

➤ accelerating gradually rather than in a sudden or jerky motion.

Poor accuracy can be corrected by practising the following types of drills:

➤ practising the delivery without the stone.

➤ focusing on keeping the stone on the line of delivery (directing the stone and sliding foot at the skip's broom) during the forward swing and slide.

➤ positioning the feet parallel to the line of delivery when you're standing in the hack and

➤ practising directing the sliding foot at a target inside the hog line without using an actual stone.

Poor release can be corrected by practising the following types of drills:

➤ practising the proper grip (grasping the stone with your fingers only as opposed to the entire palm of your hand).

➤ practising the proper amount of curl (between two to three complete rotations over the length of the ice).

➤ practising the correct follow-through motion (the handshake follow-through).

From the Skip

The camera never lies. Ask someone to videotape your delivery so you can study it yourself later. While you're watching the tape, be sure to pay particular attention to your downswing. How smoothly does the rock meet the ice?

From the Skip

Practise shooting rocks through ports. Place the rocks increasingly further away to increase the degree of difficulty.

Team Practices

Team practices provide an excellent opportunity to practise your skills and to learn how to communicate effectively both on and off the ice.

Some teams like to practice by playing a game of one-on-one or two-on-two so that everyone can practise the basic shots, gain further sweeping experience, and become more effective at responding to one another's signals and calls.

Be sure to devote at least part of the practice to working on your team's weight system. It's important for each player to be able to describe the ice in a manner that her team members will understand.

As we discussed in earlier chapters, some teams use stopwatches to rate the ice quality. It doesn't matter what type of system you use; just make sure that everyone uses similar terms to describe fast and slow ice. (After all, there's no point in coming up with some elaborate ice-rating system if no one can figure out what the heck it means!)

The Least You Need to Know

➤ A good fitness program for curlers should include cardiovascular, flexibility, and strength training.

➤ Use individual practice times to perfect your draw shots and your delivery.

➤ Use team practices to work on your skills and to ensure that you are able to communicate effectively with one another.

Chapter 11

Head Games

In This Chapter

➤ The importance of concentration

➤ Why focus matters

➤ Why some teams win and others don't

Curling is a complex game—one that is as much about strategy as the ability to make a particular shot.

What makes it a fascinating sport from a psychological standpoint is the fact that curlers are expected to conduct themselves in an appropriate fashion no matter how heated the game becomes.

Because you can't take out your frustration on your opponent by slashing him with a broom or body-checking her into the bumpers (unless, of course, your curling club is in a really bad part of town!), you need to be able to use your emotions to your advantage. That's where concentration and focus come into play.

From the Skip

A good level of physical fitness will help you to stay alert and mentally focused over the course of the game. Bottom line? When you tire physically, you tire mentally.

Attitude is Everything

It's true what Mom and Dad tried to teach you: attitude is everything. The secret to doing well in the game of curling (as well as the game of life) is to have a positive attitude. Rather than focusing on the possibility of failure, convince yourself that you're likely to make the shot. (So what if you end up being wrong. What have you got to lose—other than the end?)

But don't take just our word for it. Consider what Ernie Richardson, skip of the famous Richardson Rink from Saskatchewan, once had to say about the power of positive thinking: "Our rink always had a good mental attitude going into a competition. Hey, you can't even think the word 'lose' before you start. Think 'lose'—and you will. We thought 'win'—and we usually did."

Many curlers find it helpful to go through some pre-game rituals before they step into the hack, focusing on a few key words (e.g., "accuracy" or "weight") and then visualizing themselves making the shot. It's a technique that even the most highly trained athletes use to improve their game, so why not put it to work for you?

It's important to maintain this positive focus, even if the game isn't going exactly according to plan. Learn from your mistakes, but don't dwell on them. Instead, think ahead to the next shot. Above all, resist the temptation to let a rush of adrenaline encourage you to make a poorly thought-out shot.

From the Skip

Studies have shown that pre-game rituals play an important role in helping an athlete to achieve focus. That's why sports psychologists suggest that you go through a pre-set mental routine before stepping into the hack.

The Seven Secrets of Highly Effective Teams

There are good curling teams—and then there are great curling teams. Here's what sets the great ones apart:

Great Teamwork

Team members work well together, complementing one another's strengths and providing ongoing support and encouragement. Everyone understands her role on the team (reading the ice or calling the shots) and is able to deliver. "Most preparation takes place off the ice," notes Bill Tschirhart, a high-performance coach with the Canadian Curling Association. "This off-ice work includes team-building, goal-setting, and mental preparation."

Effective teams also share the same goals—whether it's to finish at the top of the curling club league or to make it all the way to the Worlds. Strong team dynamics was a major factor in the Schmirler Rink's win at the Winter Olympics in Nagano.

Great Communication—Both on and off the Ice

During the game, team members share valuable information on the condition of the ice and the opposing team's strengths and weaknesses and, after the game, they analyze the shots—the good, the bad, and the ugly. Believe it or not, the post-game debriefing is every bit as important to top curling teams as anything that happens on the ice.

"Teams that talk, win," says Tschirhart. "Remember, it takes four people to make a shot."

From the Skip

It's virtually impossible to stay focused for the two to three hours required to play a game. That's why top curlers (and beginner curlers who want to be top curlers when they grow up!) quickly master the art of taking mental time-outs between ends.

Great Time-management Skills

Team members know how to manage the time between shots. Rather than worrying about a problem at work or thinking ahead to the post-game party, they stay focused on the game, observing the other team's shots so that they can learn more about the ice and plan subsequent shots. (Remember: there's no law saying that you can't learn from the other team's mistakes!)

Great Relaxation Skills

Team members are able to relax on the ice, no matter how big the stakes. The best curlers are the ones who look cool as cucumbers as they step into the hack. Whether they use relaxation breathing (taking deep, slow breaths) or use positive self-talk (repeatedly telling themselves that they're going to make the shot), they are the picture of composure as they prepare to deliver the stone.

Great Minds

Team members have the ability to think on their feet and to plot their strategy a few shots in advance. Everyone can think of a great shot the morning after. The secret to great curling is to be able to come up with that shot when you need it—in the heat of the moment.

Great Composure

Team members are able to control their emotions. Like it or not, frustration is part of the game—even though it can be sheer torture to see the other team pick up a freebie

115

From the Skip

You can find a terrific article, "Mental Preparation: It's Not Just in Your Head," at **http://icing.org/coaches/advice/tschir2/tschir2.htm** The article, written by Canadian Curling Association high-performance coach Bill Tschirhart, discusses the use of visualization, imagery, and mental rehearsal.

when you're already down a few points. Rather than being upset by their opponent's good luck, team members focus on finding an even better opportunity to use to their advantage.

Great Discipline

Team members are able to enjoy a brief time-out between ends—and then get right back into the game. They talk to one another, laugh, and—for a few seconds at least—focus on something other than making the shot.

The Least You Need to Know

➤ Curling is a sport that demands tremendous concentration and focus.

➤ The most effective curling teams are those that work well as a team, communicate well both on and off the ice, manage their time well, know how to relax, are able to think on their feet, are able to maintain their composure, and are well disciplined.

Part IV
Have Rock, Will Travel

Now that you've learned how to hone your skills and improve your concentration and focus, it's time to put all that theory into practice in the curling world's equivalent of the final exam—the bonspiel.

In this final section of the book, we give you a taste of competition at the local, regional, national, and international level, covering everything from local bonspiels to international curling events.

Good curling!

Chapter 12

The Joy of Competition

In This Chapter

➤ How to find bonspiels in your area

➤ Ten easy steps to organizing a bonspiel

➤ When to set the VCR

The formal definition of bonspiel is "a curling tournament" but curlers around the world know that there's a whole lot more to a bonspiel: there's the chance to socialize with others who share your passion for the sport.

Some bonspiels are targeted at players who are out to enjoy some high-level competitive play. Others are aimed at curlers who are more interested in socializing than winning.

Where the Bonspiels Are...

If you're eager to experience a bonspiel, there are plenty out there to choose from. Here are some tips on finding bonspiels in your area:

➤ Talk to other curlers. As with anything else in life, the best way to find a bonspiel is through word of mouth. Ask other

Don't wait until the last minute to sign up for a bonspiel. The more popular events tend to fill up quickly. Some of the most popular events even have waiting lists that carry over from year to year.

curlers to give you the scoop on bonspiels in your immediate area as well as those out-of-town events that are worth attending.

➤ Check out the bulletin board at the curling rink. You're likely to find leads on more bonspiels than you could possibly hope to attend (unless, of course, you're young and foolish with more money and time than the rest of us old fogeys).

➤ Read curling newsletters and other publications. Your club and curling association newsletters are excellent sources for leads on bonspiels, as are publications such as *Sweep! Curling's Magazine* or *Canadian Curling News*. (You can find the contact information for these publications in Appendix D.)

➤ Hit the Web. Yes, you read that right. You can find out about bonspiels happening in your own backyard by searching the Internet. In addition to using any of the major search engines to find Web sites promoting upcoming events, you might also want to check out the Shot Rock Bonspiel Finder at www.bonspiel. com—a nifty tool that allows you to search for bonspiel information by date, location, and so on.

Tales from the Rink

According to Danny Lamoreux, manager of the Ottawa Curling Club in Ottawa, Ontario, there are three keys to a successful bonspiel: "Good ice, good rocks, and good beer!"

Ten Easy Steps to Organizing a Bonspiel

Chances are your club will host at least one bonspiel during the curling season. If you have the chance to help organize the event, go for it. It's a great way to meet people, have some fun, and help your club raise a bit of money at the same time. While organizing a bonspiel may sound like a big deal, it's no different from planning a wedding or family reunion—it's just a matter of scale.

That said, here are our ten top tips on organizing bonspiels.

1. Choose a date and a theme.

To ensure that you're able to attract as many curlers as possible, try to avoid choosing a date that conflicts with other bonspiels in your area. Because there's plenty to be done before the crowds arrive, allow yourself at least three months to plan and organize the event.

Try to give your bonspiel a theme. This is definitely one of those situations where creativity counts. Here are just a few ideas to get those creative juices flowing:

➤ The West Kildonan Curling Club in Winnipeg, Manitoba, is famous for its annual Crazy Spiel—an appropriately named event that celebrates all that's wacky about curling. Legend has it that manager and icemaker Joe Isfjord has been known to freeze Christmas trees and old tires into the ice as obstacles, paint a second set of rings in front of the house, and paint a set of rings at center ice so that curlers can throw from both ends!

➤ The Kingston Curling Club in Kingston, Ontario, hosts an annual Fisherman's Bonspiel during which curlers are treated to an unending buffet of top-quality lobster, crab, and other delectables. According to drawmaster Wayne Gilmour, some men have been making the Fisherman's Bonspiel a part of their curling season for the past forty years.

➤ The Riverdale Invitational Bonspiel (a.k.a. Do It On The Ice) is the largest gay and lesbian curling event in Canada, attracting approximately 30 teams each year. It's part of the circuit of gay and lesbian bonspiels, which include the Pacific Rim Cup (Vancouver in February), the Rotators (Toronto in November), and Apollo (Calgary in April).

➤ The Keene Curling Club in Keene, Ontario, hosts an annual Cordwood Bonspiel in which children are given the opportunity to curl with chunks of wood.

2. Decide upon the number of teams you would like to attract.

While you might not be able to attract 24 teams in the first year of your bonspiel, it's a number that seems to work well, both for cash-flow and scheduling reasons. If you

Tales from the Rink

While some curlers thrive on competition, others—like David Lindensmith—have found that a good game of pickup curling can reap some unexpected rewards.

At the Kingston Curling Club in Kingston, where Lindensmith curls, a "jitney" (a night of pickup curling) is held on Saturday nights when the ice is free.

"The basic idea is that whoever wants to show up plays in a pickup game, followed by dinner and cards and such in the bar. Everyone is welcome, club member or not. First-timers are interspersed with regular curlers. No one knows whom they will be playing with or against, and everyone realizes that they will likely be curling with people they haven't met before. The cost to participate is nominal, just enough to cover the cost of making dinner."

Two years ago, Lindensmith attended a jitney at his club. He had a great time getting to know Marguerite Daubney, one of the women he met that night, and the couple soon started dating. These days, the proud first-time parents are counting the days until their infant son, Michael, takes up the game himself.

have too few teams, you won't have the money for top-quality food and entertainment, and there won't be enough games going on to keep everyone pumped. If you have too many teams, on the other hand, it's difficult to have three draws and your event will have all the warmth and intimacy of a family reunion at a stadium.

3. Think in dollar signs.

An entry fee of $200 per team is about the norm for a cash spiel or bonspiel with all the frills (good food, good prizes, and good entertainment). Fun events like the Crazy Spiel cost less—more like $80 per team.

Your goal should be to break even on the entry fee. Every dollar you receive should be pumped into the food and entertainment budget, the prizes, and other costs of running the bonspiel. The only money your club should make during the weekend should come from the profits on sales in the bar.

4. Sell, sell, sell.

To attract as many out-of-town curlers as possible, advertise widely and as early on as possible. Make up fliers that can be pinned to bulletin boards in other curling clubs or included in newsletter mailings.

5. Delegate.

Running a bonspiel takes a lot of hands. Don't burn out a core group of volunteers or they'll scatter to the four winds when it's time to repeat the event next year. Instead of expecting everyone to help with every single event during the spiel, ask them to help out with one specific event (e.g., cooking breakfast on Sunday morning, working the bar on Saturday night, and so on). That way, everyone will have the opportunity to enjoy some of the fun.

From the Skip

Bribe the early-morning teams with a free breakfast. It's a great way to minimize griping and get everyone pumped for the game.

6. Bring on the food—and make it good.

Curlers love good food. It's a fact of life. It doesn't matter how great the prizes are or how well the entertainment is received, if you scrimp on the food, you'll have a lot of unhappy folks at the end of the day. So do everyone a favor and pass on the fried chicken, soggy french fries, and Ozzie-and-Harriet-style gelatin salads.

7. Remember the Golden Rule.

Don't expect anyone to follow a schedule that you wouldn't want to follow yourself, says Danny Lamoreux of the Ottawa Curling Club. If you schedule a team for a late-evening game Saturday night, don't expect them to be back on the ice at the crack of dawn Sunday morning. Curlers don't look favorably upon these types of schedules—particularly those curlers who are every bit as interested in the post-game commentary as what happens on the ice.

If you're pulling in curlers from farther away than your immediate area, take their travel time into account when you're setting up the schedule. You might want to finish the bonspiel on Saturday night or first thing Sunday morning to give people enough time to make it back home before they have to get up for work Monday morning.

To keep things fair, have the teams play on different sheets of ice during each round. That way, no one can blame the ice for their team's less-than-stellar performance. The ice for the final round can be allocated by drawing names from a hat.

Anticipate all possible outcomes and decide ahead of time how ties will be broken and what will happen if some of the games are running behind schedule. While you might not actually want to give this information to each team ahead of time, post it somewhere prominent so that people will know you had a game plan in place from the very beginning and that you didn't just wing it as special circumstances arose!

From the Skip

Decide what you'll do about games that drag on and on. Some clubs limit games to two hours; others simply accept the fact that some games will finish sooner than others.

From the Skip

When time constraints limit the number of games that can be played, a point system can be used to rank the various teams. A typical point system gives a team four points for a win plus one point per end won and one quarter point for each rock counted. The losing team also accumulates points for ends won and rocks counted.

One other important point before we leave the topic of scheduling. The surest way to kill a bonspiel (other than running out of beer, of course!) is to follow a schedule that allows one or more teams to fall out of contention too early on. If losing their first game makes what happens in subsequent games meaningless, that team is likely to lose interest. That's why round-robins and double knock-outs tend to make play more meaningful and enjoyable.

From the Skip

In a "fun" bonspiel (as opposed to a competitive bonspiel), plan to hand out prizes to the team with the worst overall performance, the one that loses the coin toss the most times, and so on.

8. Keep things moving.

Ensure that there's something to keep the curlers entertained at all times. Wayne Gilmour, drawmaster at the Kingston Curling Club in Kingston, Ontario, suggests that you have snacks and activities such as pop quizzes on curling available for curlers to enjoy between games. (And if you're looking for a booby prize for the losing teams, might we humbly suggest a copy of this book?)

9. Get the local business community behind you.

A bonspiel is good news for the entire business community. See if a local hotel would be willing to give out-of-town curlers a special rate on accommodations or whether the local Chamber of Commerce would be willing to provide free shuttle service between the rink and the hotel.

10. Get your house in order (literally!)

Spend a little time making sure that your house is in order before all your guests arrive.

Bring in an experienced icemaker to make "championship ice." (There's an art to making ice that can stand game after game of curling.) Ensure that the rocks are well matched. (An experienced curler from your club should be able to help you with this important task.) Make sure that there are plenty of rule books on hand, and that the officials that you've hired are familiar with the most up-to-date rules—particularly important if the Free Guard Zone Rule will be used in your bonspiel.

When to Set the VCR

Once you've been hooked on curling and have had the chance to participate in a few bonspiels of your own, you'll find that the TV set has almost magnetic appeal throughout the championship season.

Here are the events you won't want to miss.

Canadian Events

Labatt Brier

The Labatt Brier—which takes place each March—is the Canadian championship for men. It's the stuff of which legends are made. (If you want to get a sense of what this event is really like, try reading either Jean Sonmor's *Burned by the Rock: Inside the World of Men's Championship Curling* or Bob Weeks' *The Brier: The History of Canada's Most Celebrated Curling Championship*. You'll find both books listed in Appendix E.)

You can find out about next year's event by visiting http://cweb1.canadiana.com/brier

Scott Tournament of Hearts

The Scott Tournament of Hearts—which takes place each February—is the Canadian women's equivalent to the Brier. You can find out about next year's Tournament at www.itas.net/scott99

Cash Spiels and Skins Games Galore

Each year, corporate sponsors underwrite the costs of a number of high-profile cash spiels and skins games. You can find out about events such as the McCain SuperSpiel West, the McCain SuperSpiel, the McCain TSN Skins Game, and the JVC/TSN Women's Skins Game at the TSN curling page: www.tsn.ca/curling/curlingmain.html

American Events

United States National Curling Championships

You can find out about the Junior Nationals, Men's and Women's Nationals, and Mixed Nationals at the United States Curling Association Web site: www.usacurl.org/prog.htm

Tales from the Rink

U.S. Men's Olympic team member Mike Peplinski spelled out his proposal to wife Michelle in curling stones.

International Events

World Curling Championship

The World Curling Championship takes place each April, with the best men's and women's rinks from around the world competing for gold medals. You can find out about the upcoming season's events at www.curling.org/federation/calendar.html

World Juniors

Another popular event with TV viewing audiences is the World Juniors, which is held each March. You can find information about the event at the Canadian Curling Association home page: www.curling.ca

Winter Olympics

The 2002 Winter Games in Salt Lake City, Utah, will mark the second time that curling has been included as a medal sport. You can get the scoop on the event by visiting the official Web site at www.slc2002.org/home.html

Tales from the Rink

The Olympic spirit was alive and kicking at Nagano. Just ask Paul Martin. The fifty-year-old reserve on the men's curling team had the Olympic rings tattooed on his buttocks. "I've probably violated the copyright," he quipped.

The Least You Need to Know

➤ Participating in a bonspiel is a great way to meet other curlers. Don't feel intimidated just because you're a beginner. Just sign on the dotted line and mail in your entry fee.

➤ A good bonspiel requires a lot of upfront planning and organization.

➤ Some of the key events to tune into during curling season include the Brier, the Scott Tournament of Hearts, the Worlds, the World Juniors, the U.S. National Championships, and various cash spiels and skins games.

Chapter 13

100 Things Every Idiot Needs to Know About Curling

> ## In This Chapter
>
> ➤ Facts
>
> ➤ Stats and
>
> ➤ Trivia galore!

You've practised your slide delivery, mastered the lingo of the game, and have enough knowledge to bluff your way through the strategy part of the sport. Now it's time to teach you what you really need to know in order to win friends and influence people at the rink: curling trivia!

If you've dutifully read your book from cover to cover, you'll know the answer to many—but not all—of these questions. We've thrown in a few brain-twisters to really get you thinking—and a couple of questions where there is more than one correct answer. (Hey, this isn't supposed to be a final exam, so lighten up!) If you're really stumped on a particular question, simply flip to the back of the chapter and you'll find the answer in black and white.

Good Luck!

Curling Trivia

1. Curling got its name because
   (a) curling stones curl
   (b) of the low murmuring sound a curling stone makes as it moves down the ice

(c) the game was invented by the Earl of Curl, a Scottish nobleman who loved the great outdoors.

2. The famous Stirling Stone was found in the bottom of an old pond in what country?
   (a) Scotland
   (b) Ireland
   (c) England.

3. Early curlers in which two Canadian provinces curled with metal irons rather than stones?
   (a) New Brunswick and Quebec
   (b) Ontario and Quebec
   (c) Quebec and Manitoba.

4. What was Andrew Kay's contribution to the game of curling?
   (a) He was one of the sponsors of the Scotch Cup, the first world championship for curling.
   (b) His company, based in Aryshire, Scotland, was the first to machine-tool curling stones—something that made it possible to play a game of curling with stones of equal weight.
   (c) He was the fellow who came up with the so-called Free Guard Zone Rule.

5. In what year was the first Grand Match held in Scotland?
   (a) 1735–36
   (b) 1846–1847
   (c) 1920–1921.

6. What percentage of Saskatchewan adults curl?
   (a) 60 percent
   (b) 25 percent
   (c) 20 percent.

7. The Scotch Cup was sponsored by
   (a) the Scottish government

From the Skip

Is your knowledge of the history of the sport beginning to fade? Take a quick refresher course by flipping back to Chapter One.

(b) the Scotch Whisky Association

(c) the manufacturers of Scotch Tape®.

8. Which countries played in the first Scotch Cup?
   (a) Canada and Scotland
   (b) Canada, Scotland, and the United States
   (c) Canada, Scotland, the United States, and Great Britain.

9. How many curling clubs are there in Canada?
   (a) 1200
   (b) 1500
   (c) 3100.

10. How many Canadians watched curling on TV during 1997?
    (a) 5,000,000
    (b) 6,000,000
    (c) 12,000,000.

11. What were the audience viewing figures for the 1997 Brier and the 1997 NHL playoffs?
    (a) 1.44 million for the NHL playoffs and 1.36 million for the Brier
    (b) 1.44 million for the Brier and 1.36 million for the NHL playoffs
    (c) 1.5 million for each.

12. How many countries carried curling coverage during the Winter Games in Nagano?
    (a) 200
    (b) 80
    (c) 60.

13. What Canadian Curling Club is notorious for having a crooked run in its ice?
    (a) The Deep River Curling Club
    (b) The Lakefield Curling Club
    (c) The Galloway Curling Club.

14. The biggest change to the world of curling during the 1960s was
    (a) the switch to high-tech scoreboards
    (b) the switch from corn brooms to push brooms (i.e., brushes)
    (c) the introduction of time clocks.

15. The 1989 Brier attracted a record 151,530 spectators. In what city was it held?
    (a) Vancouver, British Columbia
    (b) Halifax, Nova Scotia
    (c) Saskatoon, Saskatchewan.

16. What famous Canadian curler had his hopes of an eight-ender dashed by a stray ash from another player's cigar?
    (a) Ed Werenich
    (b) Ken Watson
    (c) Ed Lukowich.

17. What Canadian curler commandeered a bus so that he could drive himself back to the hotel at the Perth, Scotland, world championships in 1967?
    (a) Ron Manning
    (b) Alfie Phillips, Jr.
    (c) Keith Reilly.

18. How much does it cost for a team to enter the playdowns for the Brier?
    (a) $500
    (b) $350
    (c) $200.

19. How much does it cost a team to enter the playdowns for the Scott Tournament of Hearts?
    (a) $250
    (b) $200
    (c) $150.

20. How many Canadian curlers enter the seniors' competition for curlers 50 and older each year?
    (a) 20,000
    (b) 35,000
    (c) 45,000.

21. What famous female curler and famous male curler faced off in the Battle of the Sexes in 1986?
    (a) Colleen Jones and Al Hackner
    (b) Marilyn Darte and Ed Werenich
    (c) Linda Moore and Ed Lukowich.

22. What Canadian curler was delighted to receive 25 cases of Labatt's Blue beer— shipped at a cost of $1000—at the 1990 world championships in Sweden?
    (a) Ed Werenich
    (b) Paul Savage
    (c) Russ Howard.

23. When a Scottish skip wants his teammates to sweep he yells
    (a) "Sweep! Sweep!"
    (b) "Soop! Soop!"
    (c) Words that must be censored in a family curling book.

24. Who is credited with creating the curling world's first artificial rink?
    (a) The Earl of Rink
    (b) John Cairnie
    (c) The Reverend John Ramsay.

25. In what month have most Scottish Grand Matches traditionally been held?
    (a) November
    (b) December
    (c) January.

26. Curling teams are traditionally identified by
    (a) the name of the rink they represent
    (b) the last name of the skip
    (c) the name of the organization sponsoring the team.

27. The oldest continuously operating curling club in the United States is located in
    (a) Milwaukee, Wisconsin
    (b) Detroit, Michigan
    (c) Hibbing, Minnesota.

28. Curling was first held as an Olympic demonstration sport in
    (a) 1924
    (b) 1928
    (c) 1988.

29. Which U.S. state has the largest concentration of curlers?
    (a) Wisconsin
    (b) Michigan
    (c) North Dakota.

30. Which of the following countries does not belong to the World Curling Federation?
    (a) New Zealand
    (b) The U.S. Virgin Islands
    (c) Ireland.

From the Skip

If it still sounds like Greek to you, turn to the glossary in Appendix A.

From the Skip

You can get the latest news on U.S. curlers at the United States Curling Association Web site: **www.usacurl.org**

31. U.S. Women's Olympic curlers Lisa Schoeneberg and Erika Brown knew each other long before they headed off to the 1998 Nagano Olympics. How did they know one another?
    (a) They are sisters.
    (b) Lisa used to babysit Erika.
    (c) The two worked together in a local restaurant.

32. Which member of the 1998 U.S. Women's Olympic curling team practised curling with tissue boxes and ash trays when she was a child?
    (a) Erika Brown
    (b) Lisa Schoeneberg
    (c) Lori Mountford.

33. A "burned" rock is one that
    (a) was damaged during the "burning-in" of the ice
    (b) is chipped
    (c) was touched by a sweeper while it was traveling down the ice.

131

34. The Silver Broom was sponsored by
    (a) a prominent janitorial supply company
    (b) a silver mine in Canada
    (c) an airline.

35. The winner of the skills competition held in conjunction with the Labatt Brier wins
    (a) an automobile
    (b) a snowmobile
    (c) a set of curling stones.

36. The skip of the first Olympic women's curling champions was
    (a) Sandra Schmirler of Canada
    (b) Elisabeth Hogstrom of Sweden
    (c) Andrea Schopp of Germany.

37. The curler known as "Fast Eddy" is Ed
    (a) Werenich
    (b) Lukowich
    (c) Ryan.

38. The curler nicknamed "the wrench" has the following last name
    (a) Werenich
    (b) Spanner
    (c) Piper.

39. Of the following prominent Canadian curlers—Wayne Middaugh, Mike Harris, and Russ Howard—which are also golf professionals?
    (a) Middaugh and Howard
    (b) Harris and Howard
    (c) all three.

40. The three families that have been prominent in world curling are the Somervilles; the Hays—and the Richardsons. Which of these families is from the United States?
    (a) The Somervilles
    (b) The Hays
    (c) The Richardsons.

From the Skip

Anxious to meet the First Families of curling? You can find out about their legacy in our Winners' Circle (see Appendix G).

41. There has been a Women's Curling Championship since 1979. What percentage of the time have Canadian women won the title?
    (a) 20 percent
    (b) 30 percent
    (c) over 50 percent.

42. The country that has the second most women's champions is:
    (a) Scotland
    (b) Sweden
    (c) The United States.

43. There has been a World's Men Curling Championship since 1959. In the forty years of competition, which country has won the competition the most often?
    (a) Canada
    (b) Scotland
    (c) Switzerland.

44. "Negative Ice" means
    (a) the ice is hard to read.
    (b) the ice is rough or chipped.
    (c) there is a slope to the ice and rocks curl in the opposite direction to that expected.

45. Your lead misses his second shot where you called for an in-turn takeout. You hold the broom in the same location for your second's first rock, but this time you call for an out-turn takeout. What is the most logical explanation?
    (a) The ice has changed.
    (b) Your lead is right-handed, and your second is left-handed.
    (c) You have negative ice.

46. A curler inadvertently uses a rock of the wrong color. What happens?
    (a) His rock is taken out of play and doesn't count.
    (b) Once the rock comes to rest it is replaced with a rock of the correct color and the rock thrown in error is returned to the delivery end of the ice.
    (c) There is a one-rock penalty.

47. A curler falls coming out of the hack but holds onto his rock so that it barely crosses the tee line. What happens?
    (a) He is allowed to go back to the hack and throw the rock again.
    (b) He must throw the rock from where it came to rest.
    (c) He forfeits his shot and is not allowed to rethrow.

48. When a team is forced to play with three players due to the absence or injury of their fourth team member, what is the greatest number of rocks the skip is allowed to throw on each end?
    (a) 4
    (b) 3
    (c) 2.

49. The tee is covered by a rock, making it impossible to measure to see which rock is second. What happens?
    (a) Only the rock covering the tee counts.
    (b) The end is declared a draw.
    (c) With both skips' agreement, the rock over the tee is removed and then rocks are measured in the normal way.

50. When rocks are nearly the same distance from the tee, the rock will be considered closest if it
    (a) has its center closest to the tee.
    (b) has any part of the rock closest to the tee.
    (c) is shown to be closest to the tee based on the painted circles in the ice.

51. A sweeper loses his slider and it hits the stone being swept, but does not disturb its path. Once the stone comes to rest, the opposing skip can
    (a) have it taken out of play and move any rocks it disturbed back to their original positions.
    (b) let the shot stand.
    (c) either (a) or (b).

52. Which of the following factors reduce the amount a rock curls during a given amount of travel: (1) excessive spin; (2) higher speed; or (3) more sweeping.
    (a) 1 and 2
    (b) 2 and 3
    (c) all of the above.

53. Some world-class tournaments do not allow a team to concede the game before a specified number of ends have been played, no matter how far behind they are in points. The reason for this is:
    (a) there are prizes based on total points.
    (b) the sponsors have prebooked a certain amount of TV time and would be left with nothing to fill the time slot.
    (c) it would look cowardly to give up.

54. There are often numbers on rocks in addition to the color markings. The reason for this is:
    (a) some players have lucky numbers they like to play.
    (b) so the rocks are always thrown in the same order.
    (c) so that each player always throws the same rocks, in case they behave slightly differently.

55. A red stone breaks into two pieces on the last shot of an end and, after all stones have been played, the smallest piece is closest to the tee but the largest piece is farther from the tee than one yellow opposition stone. How is this scored?
    (a) Reds count one.
    (b) Yellows count one.
    (c) No score is counted.

134

56. You are playing on a sheet of ice that has no side boards, only lines in the ice. A rock is delivered such that part of the rock crosses the sideline, but it curls back clearing the line before reaching the house. What is the fate of this rock?
    (a) It is allowed to remain in play.
    (b) It must be taken out of play as soon as it crosses the line.
    (c) It must be taken out of play when it stops moving.

From the Skip

You can brush up on the rules of the game by turning to Chapter Four.

57. A matched set of rocks means
    (a) they are all the same color.
    (b) they behave nearly identically in the amount they curl and the distance they travel.
    (c) they have identical weights.

58. In a ten-end game, the score is tied after nine ends. Reds have last rock in the tenth end, but nobody scores—the end is blanked. Who gets last rock in the extra end?
    (a) Last rock is determined by the toss of a coin
    (b) The yellow team
    (c) The red team.

59. In a mixed team, if the skip is a woman, which gender is the lead?
    (a) A man
    (b) A woman
    (c) Either a man or a woman.

60. A rock crosses the tee line and both skips want to sweep it. Which skip has first choice?
    (a) The skip of the team to which the rock belongs
    (b) The opposing skip
    (c) Whoever gets there first.

61. Joe brings his lucky broom to the curling match. It is a family heirloom and he has used it for years. The official asks to see his broom and tells him he cannot use it. What would be a valid reason for this ruling?
    (a) Everyone else is using brushes.
    (b) The broom has too long a handle.
    (c) The broom may put debris on the ice.

62. A rock can be sitting outside the hog line and still be in play if it
    (a) hit contamination and stopped there
    (b) hit a rock that had hit a long guard
    (c) is a burned rock.

135

63. Which two companies have sponsored the Brier (the Canadian Men's Championship) at some time?
    (a) Air Canada and MacDonald Tobacco
    (b) The Ford Motor Company of Canada and Scott Paper
    (c) MacDonald Tobacco and Molson's.

64. Which two companies have sponsored the World Championships at some time?
    (a) Air Canada and the Ford Motor Company of Canada
    (b) The Ford Motor Company of Canada and Scott Paper
    (c) MacDonald Tobacco and Molson's.

65. The Frances Brodie Trophy is given to recognize the women's World Curling Championships player who best demonstrates the spirit of curling. Brodie was
    (a) a designer of women's curling clothing
    (b) the first woman to score an eight-ender in world competition
    (c) a Scottish curling pioneer who helped to establish the first women's world championship in Perth, Scotland.

66. At what location was curling first played as a demonstration sport?
    (a) Nagano, Japan
    (b) Chamonix, France
    (c) Albertville, France.

67. After your vice delivers his two rocks, your team discovers to its horror that there are three rocks left. Either the lead or the second forgot to throw one of her rocks! Who delivers the last three rocks?
    (a) The vice throws one of the stones, and the skip throws the remaining two.
    (b) The lead delivers the next rock and then the skip throws the last two.
    (c) The skip delivers the next two rocks and then the lead throws the last rock.

68. A team notices that the other team's sweeping appears to be far more effective than their own. They decide to change the heads on the ends of their brushes when that end is completed. Under the Canadian rules, this is
    (a) not permitted
    (b) permitted.

69. Men are eligible to play as juniors for a limited number of years. This makes it difficult for a skip to win more than once—especially at the world level. Only one player has accomplished this feat to date. He is
    (a) Bob Ursel
    (b) Paul Gowsell
    (c) Peter Lindholm.

70. What is the greatest allowable circumference for a curling stone?
    (a) 31.4159 inches
    (b) 35 inches
    (c) 36 inches.

71. When curling is played under officiated conditions and a time clock is used, which team uses up time when a measurement is being taken?
    (a) The team that threw the last rock of that end.
    (b) The team that requested the measurement.
    (c) Neither team. Both their time clocks are stopped.

From The Skip

There's more to sweeping than just a good broom. Brush up (groan!) on your sweeping techniques by re-reading Chapter Seven.

72. A player may rethrow a rock in all but one of the following circumstances. In which case is he not permitted to rethrow the rock?
    (a) When the handle comes off the stone during delivery.
    (b) When the official in charge rules that there was a significant distraction during the delivery.
    (c) When the player forgets to remove the protective cover from his slider and the rock just reaches the first hogline.

73. A rock intended as a long guard just crosses the far hog line, but its final spinning action causes it to reverse direction and bite the hog line. Is the rock in play?
    (a) Yes. It should be left where it stops.
    (b) No. It must be removed.

74. Which U.S. state had more than one team at the first Olympic Trials in both the men's and women's events?
    (a) North Dakota
    (b) Wisconsin
    (c) Minnesota.

75. A Canadian Team is playing in the U.S. The Canadian skip says, "There's something different about your ice than the ice at our rink back home." He is right because
    (a) the circles in the house are different.
    (b) the ice width is different.
    (c) the distance from the tee line to the hack is different.

76. A curler who is delivering a stone fails to put turn on his rock because the handle has come loose on his rock. Is he allowed to replay the shot?
    (a) No, because the handle didn't completely separate from the stone.
    (b) Yes, because the loose handle ruined his shot.

77. In a ten-end tournament game, the red team is behind by a score of 9–6 at the end of nine ends. After six of the red team's rocks have been thrown, the red skip finds himself facing four of the yellow team's rocks in the rings, with no red stones, and so he concedes the game. The official score for the game is
    (a) 9–6 for the yellow team
    (b) 13–6 for the yellow team
    (c) 11–6 for the yellow team.

78. Since the Canadian Women's Champions have been given a bye into the following year's Tournament of Hearts, two teams have been repeat winners. They are
    (a) Sandra Schmirler and Connie Laliberte
    (b) Heather Houston and Sandra Peterson
    (c) Marilyn Bodogh and Alison Goring.

79. Of the six curlers named above, which one won the Tournament of Hearts for a second time eleven years after her first win?
    (a) Sandra Schmirler
    (b) Connie Laliberte
    (c) Marilyn Bodugh.

80. What husband and wife have each skipped teams that have won the Canadian Championships?
    (a) The Duguids
    (b) The Sparkes
    (c) The Richardsons.

81. Which two men's curling championship teams consisted of four brothers?
    (a) The Richardsons and the Watsons
    (b) The Richardsons and the Campbells
    (c) The Watsons and the Howards

Tales From the Rink

The Richardson family curling team, which won so many championships, was said to issue a standard challenge: "You can't throw a rock into the house if you allow us to be your sweepers."

Because they were excellent judges of rock weight, and such powerful sweepers, they would make a quick decision when the rock was released, and decide either to sweep it through the house, or let it die in front of the rings. Besides humbling a lot of good curlers who took up the challenge, we understand that they collected many a free drink and side bet.

82. What member of the 1998 U.S. men's Olympic curling team is a fifth-generation curler?
    (a) Tim Solin
    (b) Tim Somerville
    (c) John Gordon.

83. Which of the following key variables in the game of curling are not defined in the published rules?
    (a) The shape of the bottom of a rock.
    (b) The amount and nature of pebble put on the ice.
    (c) Both (a) and (b).

84. When did the first covered rink appear in Canada?
    (a) 1847
    (b) 1849
    (c) 1876.

85. What is the traditional greeting before and after every curling game?
    (a) Enjoy it, dude!
    (b) Good curling!
    (c) Have a good game!

86. When was the first North American curling club established?
    (a) 1791
    (b) 1807
    (c) 1825.

87. In what city was the first North American curling club established?
    (a) Toronto
    (b) Montreal
    (c) Ottawa.

88. Who is credited with introducing the slide delivery?
    (a) Ken Watson
    (b) Stan Austman
    (c) Ernie Richardson.

89. When the Scots and the Canadians first met at the 1959 Scotch Cup, the Scots were disgusted with a particular aspect of the Canadians' play, declaring "That's nae curling." What was it that bothered them about the Canadian version of the game?
    (a) The use of high-tech brushes
    (b) The takeout game
    (c) Both (a) and (b).

90. In what year was the first U.S. curling championship held?
    (a) 1957
    (b) 1959
    (c) 1963.

91. Who was the only skip to win both the Scotch Cup (in 1966) and the Silver Broom (in both 1968 and 1969)?
    (a) Ron Northcott
    (b) Don Duguid
    (c) Alf Phillips, Jr.

92. Who, in 1981, became the youngest skip to ever win a Brier?
    (a) Kerry Burtnyk
    (b) Pat Ryan
    (c) Eugene Hritzuk.

93. What curler lost in the Alberta playdowns in 1928, and then created a scandal by jumping the border and joining in on the Saskatchewan playdowns?
    (a) Joe Heartwell
    (b) Gordon Hudson
    (c) Bill Grant.

94. Which member of the Canadian Olympic men's curling team in Nagano lowered his pants at a news conference to show the Olympic rings tattooed on his buttock?
    (a) Paul Martin
    (b) Richard Hart
    (c) George Karrys.

95. How many ends are there in a game of curling in officiated play?
    (a) 20
    (b) 10
    (c) 8.

96. How many viewers tuned in to watch the women's finals during the Canadian Olympic trials?
    (a) 250,000
    (b) 500,000
    (c) 955,000.

97. Which country walked away with the first-ever gold medal in women's curling at the 1998 Winter Olympic Games in Nagano, Japan?
    (a) Canada
    (b) U.S.
    (c) Sweden.

98. Which country walked away with the first-ever gold medal in men's curling at the 1998 Winter Olympic Games in Nagano, Japan?
    (a) Canada
    (b) U.S.
    (c) Sweden.

99. How many curlers enjoy the sport world-wide?
    (a) 1.5 million
    (b) 1.2 million
    (c) 1.1 million.

100. What Saskatchewan curler made his way into the history books by sliding all the
way down a sheet of ice and placing his final stone on the button?
    (a) Stan Austman
    (b) Ken Watson
    (c) Garnet Campbell.

The Cheat Sheet

1. (b) Curling got its name because of the low murmuring sound a curling stone
makes as it makes its way down the ice.

2. (a) The famous Stirling Stone was found in the bottom of an old pond in
Scotland.

3. (b) Early curlers in Ontario and Quebec curled with metal irons rather than stones.

4. (b) Andrew Kay's company, based in Aryshire, Scotland, was the first to machine-
tool curling stones—something that made it possible to play a game of curling
with stones of equal weight.

5. (b) The first Grand Match was held in Scotland in 1846–47.

6. (c) Twenty-five percent of Saskatchewan adults curl.

7. (b) The Scotch Cup was sponsored by the Scotch Whisky Association.

8. (a) Canada and Scotland were the countries competing in the first Scotch Cup.

9. (a) There are 1200 curling clubs in Canada.

10. (b) Six million Canadians watched curling on TV during 1997.

11. (b) The audience viewing figures for the 1997 Brier and the 1997 NHL playoffs
were 1.44 million for the Brier and 1.36 million for the NHL playoffs.

12. (b) Eighty countries carried curling coverage during the Winter Games in Nagano.

13. (c) The Galloway Curling Club in British Columbia is notorious for having a
crooked run in its ice. Locals know how to "play the hump" to their advantage
by placing a rock next to the button in a way that makes it next to impossible
to remove.

14. (b) The biggest change to the world of curling during the 1960s was the switch
from corn brooms to push brooms (brushes).

15. (c) The 1989 Brier was held in Saskatoon, Saskatchewan.

16. (b) Ken Watson had his hopes of an eight-ender dashed by a stray ash from another player's cigar.

17. (b) Alfie Phillips, Jr. commandeered a bus so that he could drive himself back to
the hotel at the Perth, Scotland, world championships in 1967.

18. (c) It costs $200 for a team to enter the playdowns for the Brier.

19. (c) It costs $150 for a team to enter the playdowns for the Scott Tournament of Hearts.

20. (c) Forty-five thousand Canadian curlers enter the seniors' competition for curlers 50 and older each year.

21. (b) Marilyn Darte and Ed Werenich faced off in the Battle of the Sexes in 1986. Ed won.

22. (a) Ed Werenich was the Canadian curler who was delighted to receive 25 cases of Labatt's Blue beer—shipped at a cost of $1000—at the 1990 world championships in Sweden.

23. (b) When a Scottish skip wants his teammates to sweep he yells, "Soop! Soop!"

24. (b) John Cairnie is credited with creating the curling world's first artificial rink. He built an artificial "curling pond" on the grounds of his estate, Curling Hall, in 1827.

25. (c) There have been sixteen Scottish Grand Matches held in January, nine held in December, seven held in February, and one held in November.

26. (b) Curling teams are traditionally identified by the last name of the skip.

27. (a) The oldest continuously operating curling club in the United States is located in Milwaukee, Wisconsin. It was founded in 1845. The Orchard Lake Curling Club (near Detroit) was founded in 1832, and therefore holds the distinction of being the first curling club in the United States.

28. (a) Curling was first held as an Olympic demonstration sport in 1924.

29. (a) Wisconsin has the largest concentration of curlers. There are 4000 curlers in the state—roughly one-quarter of those found in the entire United States.

30. (c) Ireland does not belong to the World Curling Federation. Despite the passion for curling in nearby Scotland, curling has never really caught on in Ireland.

31. (b) U.S. Women's Olympic curlers Lisa Schoeneberg and Erika Brown knew each other long before they headed off to the 1998 Nagano Olympics because Lisa used to babysit Erika.

32. (a) Erika Brown used to practise curling with tissue boxes and ash trays when she was a child.

33. (c) A "burned" rock is one that was touched by a sweeper while it was traveling down the ice.

34. (c) The Silver Broom was sponsored by an airline.

35. (a) The winner of the skills competition held in conjunction with the Labatt Brier wins an automobile.

36. (a) The skip of the first Olympic women's curling champions was Sandra Schmirler of Canada.

37. (b) The curler known as "Fast Eddy" is Ed Lukowich.

38. (a) The curler nicknamed "the wrench" has the last name Werenich.

39. (c) Wayne Middaugh, Mike Harris, and Russ Howard are all golf professionals.

40. (a) The Somervilles are from the United States.

41. (c) Canadian women have won the World Curling Championship more than 50 percent of the time since 1979.

42. (b) The country that has the second most women's champions is Sweden.

43. (a) Canada has won the World Men's Curling Championship more than any other country.

44. (c) "Negative Ice" means that there is a slope to the ice and rocks curl in the opposite direction to that expected.

45. (b) Your lead misses his second shot where you called for an in-turn takeout. You hold the broom in the same location for your second's first rock, but this time you call for an out-turn takeout. This is because your lead is right-handed, and your second is left-handed.

46. (b) If a curler inadvertently uses a rock of the wrong color, once the rock comes to rest it is replaced with a rock of the correct color and the rock thrown in error is returned to the delivery end of the ice.

47. (c) If a curler falls coming out of the hack, but holds onto his rock so that it barely crosses the tee line, he forfeits his shot and is not allowed to rethrow.

48. (c) When a team is forced to play with three players due to the absence or injury of their fourth team member, the greatest number of rocks the skip is allowed to throw on each end is two. The lead and the second throw three rocks each.

49. (c) If the tee is covered by a rock, making it impossible to measure to see which rock is second, with both skips' agreement, the rock over the tee is removed and then rocks are measured in the normal way.

50. (b) When rocks are nearly the same distance from the tee, the rock will be considered closest if it has any part of the rock closest to the tee.

51. (c) A sweeper loses his slider and it hits the stone being swept, but does not disturb its path. Once the stone comes to rest, the opposing skip can have it taken out of play and move any rocks it disturbed back to their original positions or let the shot stand, but he cannot have the player replay the shot.

52. (c) All of the following factors reduce the amount a rock curls: (1) excessive spin; (2) higher speed; and (3) more sweeping.

53. (b) Some world-class tournaments do not allow a team to concede the game before a specified number of ends have been played, no matter how far behind they are in points. This is because the sponsors have prebooked a certain amount of TV time and would be left with nothing to fill the time slot.

143

54. (c) There are often numbers on rocks in addition to the color markings. This is so that each player always throws the same rocks, in case they behave slightly differently.

55. (b) A red stone breaks into two pieces on the last shot of an end and, after all stones have been played, the smallest piece is closest to the tee but the largest piece is farther from the tee than one yellow opposition stone. In this case, the yellow team counts one.

56. (b) You are playing on a sheet of ice that has no side boards, only lines in the ice. A rock is delivered such that part of the rock crosses the sideline, but it curls back clearing the line before reaching the house. The rock must be taken out of play as soon as it crosses the line.

57. (b) A matched set of rocks means that the rocks behave nearly identically in terms of the amount they curl and the distance they travel.

58. (c) In a ten-end game, the score is tied after nine ends. Reds have last rock in the tenth end, but nobody scores—the end is blanked. The red team gets last rock in the extra end.

59. (a) In a mixed team, if the skip is a woman, the lead is a man.

60. (a) A rock crosses the tee line and both skips want to sweep it. The skip of the team to which the rock belongs has first choice.

61. (c) Joe brings his lucky broom to the curling match. It is a family heirloom and he has used it for years. The official asks to see his broom and tells him he cannot use because the broom may put debris on the ice.

62. (b) A rock can be sitting outside the hog line and still be in play if it hit a rock that had hit a long guard.

63. (c) Both MacDonald Tobacco and Molson's have sponsored the Brier (the Canadian Men's Championship) at some point.

64. (a) Both Air Canada and the Ford Motor Company of Canada have sponsored the World Championships at some point.

65. (c) The Frances Brodie Trophy is given to recognize the women's World Curling Championships player who best demonstrates the spirit of curling. Brodie was a Scottish curling pioneer who helped to establish the first women's world championship in Perth, Scotland.

66. (b) Curling was first played as a demonstration sport in Chamonix, France.

67. (c) After your vice delivers his two rocks, your team discovers to its horror that there are three rocks left. Either the lead or the second forgot to throw one of her rocks! The skip delivers the next two rocks and then the lead throws the last rock.

68. (b) A team notices that the other team's sweeping appears to be far more effective

than their own. They decide to change the heads on the ends of their brushes when the end is completed. This is permitted under the rules.

69. (b) The only junior men's champion to skip more than once was Paul Gowsell.

70. (c) The greatest allowable circumference for a curling stone is 36 inches.

71. (c) When curling is played under officiated conditions and a time clock is used, the time clocks of both teams are stopped while a measurement is taken.

72. (c) A player is not permitted to rethrow the rock if he forgets to remove the protective cover from his slider and the rock just reaches the first hog line.

73. (b) The rock is not in play and must be removed.

74. (c) Minnesota had more than one team at the first Olympic Trials in both the men's and women's events.

75. (b) The ice width is different.

76. (a) A curler who is delivering a stone fails to put turn on his rock because the handle has come loose on his rock. He is not permitted to replay the shot because the handle didn't completely separate from the stone.

77. (a) In a ten-end tournament game, the red team is behind by a score of 9–6 at the end of nine ends. After six of the red team's rocks have been thrown, the red skip finds himself facing four of the yellow team's rocks in the rings, with no red stones, and so he concedes the game. The official score for the game is 9–6 for the yellow team because the stones thrown during the incomplete end are not counted in the final score.

78. (b) Since the Canadian Women's Champions have been given a bye into the following year's Tournament of Hearts, two women have been repeat winners— Heather Houston's team and Sandra Peterson's team.

79. (b) Connie Laliberte won the Tournament of Hearts for a second time eleven years after her first win.

80. (a) The Duguids have each skipped teams that have won the Canadian Championships.

81. (b) The Richardsons and the Campbells are two men's curling championship teams that consisted of four brothers.

82. (a) Tim Solin, a member of the 1998 U.S. men's Olympic curling team, is a fifth generation curler.

83. (c) The science of polishing and shaping the bottom of rocks is in the hands of the rock manufacturers and repair facilities. Ice makers control the amount and nature of pebble on the ice.

84. (a) The first covered rink appeared in Canada in 1847 (in Montreal).

85. (b) The traditional greeting before and after every curling game is "Good curling."

86. (b) The first North American curling club was established in 1807.

87. (b) The first North American curling club was established in Montreal.

88. (a) Kevin Watson is credited with introducing the slide delivery.

89. (b) The Scots were bothered by the Canadians' takeout game.

90. (a) The first U.S. curling championship was held in 1957.

91. (a) The only skip to win both the Scotch Cup (in 1966) and the Silver Broom (in both 1968 and 1969) was Ron Northcott.

92. (a) In 1981, Kerry Burtnyk became the youngest skip to ever win a Brier.

93. (a) Joe Heartwell was the curler who lost in the Alberta playdowns in 1928, and then created a scandal by jumping the border and joining in on the Saskatchewan playdowns.

94. (a) Paul Martin (a reserve member of the Canadian Olympic men's curling team in Nagano) lowered his pants at a news conference to show the press his Olympic rings tattoo.

95. (b) There are ten ends in an officiated game of curling.

96. (c) 955,000 viewers tuned in to watch the women's finals during the Canadian Olympic trials.

97. (a) Canada walked away with the first-ever gold medal in women's curling at the 1998 Winter Olympic Games in Nagano, Japan.

98. (c) Sweden walked away with the first-ever gold medal in men's curling at the 1998 Winter Olympic Games in Nagano, Japan.

99. (a) 1.5 million curlers enjoy the sport world-wide.

100. (a) Stan Austman made his way into the history books by sliding all the way down a sheet of ice and placing his final stone on the button.

So how did you do?

Here's how to interpret your score:

0–30%	You're a bona fide Idiot. (Don't try to show off your knowledge at the rink—and, whatever you do, don't tell anyone that you've read this book! It could be bad for sales.)
30–75%	There's hope for you. Tuck your Idiot's guide in your gym bag and read it between ends.
75%–100%	You're no Idiot—you're a curling connoisseur. See you at the rink!

Glossary

Backboards   The boards behind the hack at either end of the playing area.

Backing   Rocks behind a target rock or a target area that can either save a draw from traveling too far or make a rock difficult to remove.

Back Rings   The portion of the 8-foot and 12-foot rings near the back line.

Back-ring Weight   A stone thrown just hard enough to reach the back of the house.

Big End   Any end in which four or more stones count.

Biter   A rock that barely overhangs or touches the 12-foot ring.

Biting the Rings   Barely touching the rings.

Blank End   An end that is scoreless—either by accident or intentionally. In some cases, a skip will deliberately blank an end in order to retain last-rock advantage—and hopefully score more than one point—in the subsequent end.

Bonspiel   A curling tournament.

Borrow   The amount of left- or right-hand draw taken by a stone (Scottish curling term).

Breaking an Egg   Touching a stone lightly (Scottish curling term).

Broom   The instrument used to sweep the ice. The term "broom" is also used to refer to brushes, the sweeping implement of choice since the 1970s.

Bumper   The foam plastic or rubber backstop that rests against the backboards to protect them from fast-moving stones. Also a light tap-back of a rock that doesn't remove it.

Bunker   Uneven ice (Scottish curling term).

Burned Rock   A stone in motion that is touched by a member of the team delivering the rock and/or by any part of that person's equipment.

Burying a Stone   Placing a shot behind a guard or guards so that it is impossible to hit it directly.

Button   The area immediately surrounding the tee. The button is one foot in diameter.

Cash Spiel   A bonspiel played for money.

Center Guard   A stone that is in front of the house, either on or touching the center line.

Center Line   A line drawn from one hack to the other, passing through the tee at both ends of the ice.

Chap and Lie   To strike an opponent's rock lightly and leave one's own stone in play.

Chip   A shot that hits another stone lightly on the edge, moving it sideways. A chip is similar to a wick, but it's a more delicate maneuver.

Circles   The round scoring area, 12 feet in diameter, with concentric circles 1, 4, and 8 feet in diameter inside. Also called rings, house, or head.

Closing a Port   Blocking an opening between two stones so that a rock cannot pass between them and reach the house.

Cold Draw   A draw where there is no backing or rocks to wick in off.

Come Around   A draw shot that barely passes a guard and comes to rest behind it.

Coming Home   The final end of regulation play.

Corner Guard   A stone that is situated in front of the house, midway between the house and hog line, about two to three feet on either side of the center line.

Corner Freeze   A rock that comes to rest touching another rock on an angle to the center line.

Counter   A stone that is in a scoring position.

Crampit   An early form of the hack that consisted of a spiked metal sheet strapped to the foot.

Cross Handle   A stone where the handle is at right angles to the center line.

Cup   The concave portion of the bottom of the stone.

Curl   The rotating movement of a stone caused by turning the handle.

Delivery   The act of throwing a rock.

Delicate Weight   A very gentle hit.

Divider   A wooden partition that is frozen into the ice to separate adjacent sheets of ice from one another. Note: many rinks do not have dividers.

Dolly   Wooden skittle marking the tee (Scottish curling term).

Double   Removing two stones from play with one shot.

Dour ice   Ice that is not keen (Scottish curling term).

Draw   Although a draw is normally into the house, any rock where the speed will make it stop in the field of play without hitting another rock is a draw. Also the amount a stone moves sideways due to curl.

Draw Game   A game that focuses on the placement and guarding of your own rocks.

Draw Shot   A rock that is delivered so that it comes to rest in the spot indicated by the skip.

Draw Weight   The speed required for a rock to end up in the house.

Drive   To strike and move a rock (drive a rock through the house).

Drug Ice   Soft, damp, or slow ice (Scottish curling term).

Eight-ender   An end in which a team has scored the maximum possible number of points: eight.

End   A portion of the game, similar to an inning in baseball. An end is complete when all sixteen rocks (eight per team) have been thrown. A standard curling-club game is usually eight ends, or about two hours long. Championship games, on the other hand, are 10 ends or about 2.5 hours long.

Extra End   An additional end played to break a tie at the end of regulation play.

Fall   A slope on the ice that causes a rock to move in a direction opposite to that expected from the rotation of the handle. Also called a run-back or negative ice.

Fast Ice   Low-friction ice (little effort is required to have a rock travel the length of the ice.

Freebies   Shots that are so easy that even an Idiot should be able to make them!

Freeze   A draw that finishes touching or nearly touching another rock.

Front End   The lead and second player on a curling team.

Front Rings   The portion of the 8-foot and 12-foot rings in front of the tee line.

149

Frozen   Rocks that are touching one another.

Give Ice   An estimate by the skip of the amount of curl needed for the next shot. The skip places her broom at the point to which the curler should aim if her stone is to curl into the right position.

Goose Neck   The curved part of the handle of the curling stone that joins the grip to the center bolt.

Guard   A rock between the hog line and the house that is used to try to prevent the opposition from hitting a rock in the house.

Hack   The rubber starting block embedded in the ice from which the curler begins deliver of a stone. The name originates from the footholds that early curlers "hacked" into the ice.

Hack Weight   A takeout played with sufficient weight to reach the hack at the target end of the ice.

Hammer   The last rock in an end.

Head   The round scoring area, 12 feet in diameter, with concentric circles 1, 4, and 8 feet in diameter inside. Also known as house or circles.

Heavy   A stone that is delivered with more than the desired amount of weight or force.

Heavy Ice   Opposite of fast or keen ice. Heavy ice requires a stone to be thrown with more than normal weight in order to reach the house. Heavy ice is usually caused by a frosty ice surface or fresh pebble that makes the ice slow.

Hit   A rock intended to collide with another rock (as opposed to a draw).

Hit and Stay   A rock that hits out an opponent's rock but remains in play itself. If it hits so dead on that it remains exactly where it hit the opposing rock, it is called "hit and stick."

Hit the Broom   When a curler releases his rock on the correct aim line (at the skip's broom), he is said to have hit the broom.

Hog   A stone that stops short of the hog line.

Hog Line   A line located 21 feet from each tee. A rock must be released before the near hog line, and travel beyond the far hog line, or it will be removed from play.

Hogging a Rock   To fail to get a rock across the line at the far end of the ice, therefore causing it to be taken out of play.

House   The round scoring area, 12 feet in diameter, with concentric circles 1, 4, and 8 feet in diameter inside. Sometimes called the circles or the head.

Hurry   A command shouted by the skip to tell the sweepers to sweep quickly.

Ice   The allowance the skip makes for the rock to curl when he places his broom.

In-turn   A rock whose handle is rotated inward toward the body. An in-turn for a right-handed curler rotates clockwise while an in-turn for a left-handed curler rotates counter-clockwise.

In-wick   A stone that glances off the inside edge of another stone to gain a good position (Scottish curling term for wick-in).

Junk   When there are many stones in play (particularly in front of the house).

Keen Ice   When little effort is required to deliver the rock. Also known as fast ice.

Kuting   An old Scottish term for curling.

Last Rock   The last rock to be thrown in an end. A team that throws the last rock in an end is said to have the hammer or last-rock advantage.

Lead   The player who, alternating with the opponents' lead, delivers the first two rocks of each end.

Lie Shot   Having the stone nearest the tee.

Light   A stone that is delivered with less than the desired weight or force.

Long Guard   A guard near the hog line.

Lose Handle or Lose Turn   A stone that loses its initial rotating motion during its travel down the rink.

Mate   A term used in the Maritimes to describe the third or vice-skip. The third, alternating with the opponents' third, delivers the fifth and sixth rocks for his team; holds the broom for the skip, and assists the skip with game strategy.

Narrow   A rock delivered inside the intended line of delivery (between the skip's broom and the target).

Near Frozen   Rocks that are nearly touching one another.

Negative Ice   Ice where the uneven nature of the ice makes the rock curl in the opposite direction to that expected.

Non-uniform Ice   For various reasons (consistent level of ice, uniformity of pebble, temperature differences) the rock may behave differently in various parts of the ice (curl more or less or lose speed at a different rate). When these differences are significant, we have non-uniform ice.

Off the Broom   A stone that is not delivered on the line of the skip's broom.

On Line   A rock that follows the desired path.

On the Broom   A shot that started out on a line toward the skip's broom. If the skip misjudged the amount of curl required or if the weight of the rock is not correct, the shot can be on the broom but still a miss.

Out-turn   A rock whose handle is rotated outward or away from the body. An out-turn for a right-handed curler rotates counter-clockwise while an out-turn for a left-handed curler rotates clockwise.

Out-wick   Delivering a stone with enough weight that it would go through the house and stop behind the rings if it did not hit another rock.

Pat-lid or Pot-lid   A stone lying on the tee (Scottish curling term).

Pebble   The controlled roughness of the ice formed by a light spray of water that freezes on contact with the ice.

Peel   A takeout shot that removes a stone from play and rolls out of play itself.

Peel Weight   Sufficient weight to force both the rock being hit and the shooter to clear the ice.

Pick-up   Dirt or broom hairs that interfere with a stone's path (Scottish curling term).

Pinch the Broom   A delivery that is barely narrow of the skip's broom.

Playdown   A series of games in a curling competition that ultimately determines the winner. Similar to the play-offs in hockey.

Pocket   A cluster of stones forming a U-shape, or a modified U-shaped area in which a stone can be placed so that it is difficult to remove.

Points Game   A singles game whose purpose is to test accuracy in selected shots. One or two stones are set up in the house or close to it prior to play, and shots are then played to test drawing, wicking, raising, chipping, guarding, etc.

Port   An opening between two or more rocks that is wide enough to allow a stone to pass through.

Pull   The amount a stone moves sideways due to curl.

Quacking   Causing a stone to rock from side to side on its run up the rink (Scottish curling term).

Quiet Weight   A takeout delivered with just enough weight to knock an opposing stone out of the rings.

Raise   The action of bumping a stone from one position to another position.

Rings   The circles that make up the house.

Rink   A curling team that consists of four players: the skip, third (vice-skip), second, and lead. Also refers to the place where curling is played.

Rock   Stone.

Roll   The movement of a stone after it hits another stone off center.

Rub   A stone that barely grazes another.

Run   A portion of the ice surface where a delivered stone behaves in a manner different from what might normally be expected due to a ridge or valley in the ice.

Runner   A fast-moving stone.

Second   The player who, alternating with the opponent's second, delivers the third and fourth rocks for his team during each end.

Second Shot   The stone that is second-nearest to the tee.

Sheet   The 146-foot-long area of the ice on which the game is played.

Short   A stone that stops before reaching the desired position.

Short Guard   A guard near the house.

Shot   The stone that is nearest the tee during the play of an end (also known as shot rock). It may also refer to the playing of a stone (i.e., making a shot).

Shot Rock   The rock that is closest to the tee.

Skins Game   A curling game in which there is a prize for each end. (The prize carries over to the next end if no one wins.)

Skip   The player who, alternating with the other team's player, normally plays the last two rocks for his team in an end; and who is responsible for directing the strategy of the game.

Slide   The part of the delivery in which the curler slides partway down the ice.

Slider   A slippery device that is worn on the sliding foot during the delivery of a stone. Most specially made curling shoes have sliders built in.

Soop   To sweep (Scottish curling term).

Spiel   Bonspiel.

Split   Hitting a rock in front of the house on an angle so that both it and the shooter end up in the house.

Straight Handle   A stone that is unintentionally delivered with neither an in-turn nor an out-turn.

Straight Ice   Ice conditions that do not cause the stones to curl very much.

Steal   What happens when the team that does not have last rock scores one or more points.

Sweeping   Using a brush or broom to polish the ice in an effort to alter the action of the rock.

Swingy Ice   Ice conditions in which a rock draws more than normal.

Takeout   A type of shot that removes another rock from play.

Takeout Game   A game that focuses on removing your opponents' stones from play.

Takeout Weight   A rock with sufficient speed to drive an opponents' rock out of play, beyond the back line, is said to have takeout weight.

Tap-back   A very gentle hit.

Tee   The center point of the house.

Tee Line   A line passing through the tee at right angles to the center line. It marks the point beyond which an opposing stone may be swept.

Third   The player who, alternating with the opponent's third, delivers the fifth and sixth rocks for his team during each end; holds the broom for the skip; and assists the skip with game strategy. The third is sometimes called a vice-skip or mate.

Touched Stone   A stone in motion that is touched by a member of the team delivering the rock and/or any part of that person's equipment.

Vice-skip   The player who, alternating with the opponent's third, delivers the fifth and sixth rocks of each end; holds the broom for the skip; and assists the skip with game strategy. The vice-skip is sometimes called a third or mate.

Weight   The amount of force or speed on a rock as it makes its way down the ice.

Wick   A stone that gently strikes the edge of another stone and glances off at an angle.

Wick-in   A wick where a rock near the edge of the ice is bounced off in order to direct the shooter nearer to the button.

Wide   A stone that is delivered outside the line of the skip's brush (to the side of the skip's broom away from the target).

Wobbler   A stone that is delivered in such a way that it rocks from one side to another as it progresses.

Rules of Curling for General Play

Canadian Curling Association Rules of Play

Copyright by Canadian Curling Association. Reprinted with permission. To obtain an up-to-date copy of the rules or a copy of the rules for officiated and national championship play, please write to the Canadian Curling Association, Suite 511, 1600 James Naismith Drive, Gloucester, Ontario, K1B 5N4. Phone: (613) 748-5628; Fax: (613) 748-5713; email: cca@curling.ca; Web site: www.curling.ca

1. Application

    (1) The Rules of Curling for Officiated Play apply to any competition to which they are made applicable by the curling body having jurisdiction.

    (2) The Rules of Curling for General Play are not intended to be used in conjunction with officiating. If a curling body having jurisdiction over an event(s) wishes to make this rule book applicable to a specific competition(s) while also utilizing officials, they should also put in place a set of guidelines outlining the authority of the officials relative to the implementation of penalties.

    (3) If special rules are in effect, they shall take precedence over the general rules of curling.

2. Definitions

    (1) "competition" means a playdown involving any number of teams playing games to determine a winner.

    (2) "end" means the part of the game in which two opposing teams each deliver eight stones alternately and then determine the score.

(3) "CCA" means the Canadian Curling Association.

(4) "game" means play between two teams to determine a winner.

(5) "house" means the area within the outside circle at each end of the sheet.

(6) "sheet" means an area of ice marked in accordance with rule 3.

(7) "team" means three to four players playing together in accordance with rule 5 and may include the team alternate and coach as determined by the rules of the competition.

(8) "delivering team" means the team who is in control of the house and whose turn it is to deliver.

(9) "stone set in motion" means a stone in motion whose movement from a stationary position, in play, is caused by a delivered stone or another stone previously set in motion.

(10) "biting" means that the vertical projection of a stone is in contact with the line to which the biting refers.

3. Sheet

(1) The length of the sheet from backboard to backboard shall be 146 feet (44.501 meters). The width of the sheet from sideline to sideline shall be 14 feet 2 inches (4.318 meters). This area shall be delineated by lines drawn or dividers placed on the perimeter.

(2) At each end of the sheet there shall be three distinct lines drawn from sideline to sideline as follows:

(a) each tee line, one-half inch in width, shall be placed 16 feet (4.877 meters) from the backboard to the centre of the tee line and there shall be 114 feet (34.747 meters) from the centre of one tee line to the other tee line. The intersection of the tee line and the centre line is called the tee.

(b) each backline, one-half inch in width, shall be placed with its outer edge 6 feet 1/2 inch (1.842 meters) from the centre of the tee line so that the inner (circle side) edge just touches the outer edge of a circle 6 feet from the tee.

(c) each hogline, 4 inches (10.16 centimeters) in width, shall be placed with the inner (circle side) edge 21 feet (6.401 meters) from the centre of the tee line.

(3) With each tee as centre, there shall be drawn four concentric circles at each end with the outer edge of the outer circle having a radius of 6 feet (1.829 meters), the next circle 4 feet (1.219 meters), the next circle 2 feet (60.96 centimeters) and the inner circle 6 inches (15.24 centimeters).

(4) The centre line, one-half inch in width, shall be placed the length of the sheet through the centre of the tee lines to a point 12 feet (3.658 meters) behind each tee. At this point, lines of 1 foot 6 inches (45.72 centimeters) in length shall be

placed at right angles to the centre line and shall be known as the hack line. The inside (circle side) edge of the hack boards shall be placed on this hack line.

(5) The intersection of each tee line and each centre line shall be identified by an adjustable tee centre. The base portion should be securely anchored at the exact intersection of the tee line and centre line of each house, and the top portion should be capable of vertical adjustment to suit varying ice levels. The design of the tee centre shall be accepted by the CCA.

(6) The hack(s) used for delivery shall be of a style and size accepted by the CCA. The hack(s) shall be placed on the hack line in such a manner that the inside edge of the hack(s) is no further than 3 inches (7.62 centimeters) from the centre line. The hack(s) shall not exceed 8 inches (20.32 centimeters) in length.

(7) The diagram on pages 38 and 39 shows the proper layout of the sheet in accordance with the measurements in this section.

4. Stones

(1) Curling stones shall be of circular shape.

(2) No stone, including handle and bolt, shall be of greater weight than 44 lbs. (19.96 kilograms), have a greater circumference than 36 inches (91.44 centimeters) or be less than 4.5 inches (11.43 centimeters) in height measured between the bottom and top of the stone.

(3) Two sets of eight stones shall be provided for each sheet of play.

(4) A team member or coach shall not physically alter the running surface or weight of the assigned or selected game stones in any manner.

Interpretation: This includes the stones of the opposition as well as those of the player's team.

(5) If a stone is broken in play, a replacement stone shall be placed by the official where the largest fragment comes to rest. The inside edge of the replacement stone shall be placed in this same position as the inside edge of the largest fragment.

(6) A stone that rolls over in its course or comes to rest on its side or top shall be removed immediately from play.

(7) All 16 stones originally on the sheet at the start of the game must be delivered in every completed end. No interchange of stones or redelivery of previously delivered stones in that end may take place so that a stone is delivered for the second time.

Interpretation: The start of the game is established by the initiation of the delivery of the first stone of the game.

Penalty: If a team declares its own violation of Rule 4(7), the non-offending team may allow the play to stand or remove the stone just delivered from play and replace all affected stones as close as possible to their original position.

(8) If the handle comes off a stone during any of the four phases of the delivery, [see] Rule 8(1), the delivering team may allow the play to stand or redeliver the stone after all affected stones have been replaced as close as possible to their original positions and prior to the opposition delivering its next stone.

5. Teams

(1) Every team shall be composed of a minimum of four players as determined by the rules of the competition except as provided for in Rule 5(5).

(2) The teams opposing each other in a game shall toss a coin to determine which team leads in the first end, after which the winner of the preceding end leads. The winner of the toss has the choice between playing the first or second stone of the end. The team that plays the first stone of the end has choice of handle colour unless this is otherwise determined by the rules of competition. If special rules govern the championship, they shall take precedence.

(3) Each player on a four player team shall deliver two stones in each end alternately with his/her opponent.

(4) The delivery rotation declared by a team at the start of a game shall be followed throughout that game except as provided for in Rule 5(5) (6) or (7).

(5) (a) A team may play with three players if the rules of the competition so provide, with the first two players each delivering three stones in each end. It shall be referred to as a three player team. Under no circumstance may a team play with fewer than three players delivering stones.

Interpretation: A team shall include a minimum of two players from the original team and an alternate or player(s) from the players' pool if the rules of the competition so provide.

(b) A team that is missing a player(s) and has a team alternate may activate the team alternate.

(c) A team that is missing a player(s) and does not have a team alternate may access the players' pool if the rules of the competition so provide.

(d) An alternate player or player(s) from the players' pool who joins a team prior to the start of a game or between ends may play any position on the team. The team shall redeclare their delivery rotation at this time if required.

(e) If, during an end in play, a player(s) is unable to complete the delivery rotation declared by the team at the start of the game, the team may activate the team alternate or player(s) from the players' pool. An alternate player or player(s) from the player's pool who enters a game during an end shall replace the sidelined player(s) in the team's delivery rotation. At the beginning of the next end the alternate player or player(s) from the players' pool may play any position on the team and the team shall redeclare their delivery rotation at this time.

Interpretation: An alternate player or player(s) from the players' pool may only enter a game during an end if they deliver a stone(s) within the end.

(6) (a) A team that commences a game with three players and expects the fourth player to join the team during the game must establish the team's four player delivery rotation prior to commencing the game.

(b) A player who is late for a game may enter the game between ends or may enter an end already in progress providing he/she is able to deliver a stone(s) within the team's established delivery rotation. If an alternate or player(s) from the players' pool has been activated, the replaced team member(s) shall not join the team until the next game.

(c) A player who has left a game due to injury or illness may re-enter the game between ends or during an end already in progress providing he/she is able to deliver a stone(s) within the team's established delivery rotation. If an alternate player or player(s) from the players' pool has been activated, the replaced team member shall not rejoin the team until the next game.

Interpretation: A player may enter or re-enter a game during an end already in progress only if they deliver a stone(s) within the end.

(7) (a) If a player delivers his/her first stone of the end and due to injury or illness is unable to deliver his/her second stone of the end and the rules of the competition allow the team to continue play with three players, the following procedures shall be followed:

– If the lead player, the second player shall deliver the lead player's stone.

– If the second player, the lead player shall deliver the second player's stone.

– If the third player, the second player shall deliver the third player's stone.

– If the fourth player, the third player shall deliver the fourth player's stone.

(b) If due to injury or illness a player is unable to deliver both his/her stones during an end, and the rules of the competition allow the team to continue with three players, the following procedures shall be followed:

– If the lead player, the second player shall deliver both of the lead player's stones and one of the second player's stones, and the third player shall deliver one of the second player's stones and both of the third player's stones.

– If the second player, the lead player shall deliver the first of the second player's stones, and the third player shall deliver the second of the second player's stones and both of the third player's stones.

– If the third player, the second player shall deliver both of the third player's stones.

> – If the fourth player, the third player shall deliver both of the fourth player's stones.

Interpretation: Rule 5(7)(a) and 5(7)(b) only apply to the situation where injury or illness occurs during an end and the rules of the competition allow the team to continue with three players. If the player is unable to return to the game in the next end, Rule 5(5) shall be applied. If injury or illness occurs between ends, refer to Rule 5(5).

Penalty: If a team declares its own violation of Rule 5(4), (5), (6), or (7), the non-offending team may allow the play to stand or remove the stone just delivered from play and replace all affected stones as close as possible to their original position.

6. Skips

(1) The skip has the exclusive direction of the game for his/her team and shall deliver stones in each end except as provided for in Rule 5(7).

(2) Subject to Rule 5(4), the skip may play any position in the delivery rotation of his/her team. The player designated as skip shall remain in that capacity throughout the course of that game as provided for in Rule 5(6) and (7).

(3) When it is the skip's turn to deliver, he/she shall elect a teammate to act as skip. This player designated as vice-skip shall remain in that capacity throughout the course of that game. The vice-skip shall also assume the responsibilities of the skip when the skip is not on the playing surface.

Penalty: If a team declares its own violation of Rule 6 (1), (2) or (3), the non-offending team may allow the play to stand or remove the stone just delivered from play and replace all affected stones as close as possible to their original positions.

7. Position of Players

(1) Members of the non-delivering team:

(a) Only the skip and vice-skip may stand behind the tee line at the playing end when the opposing team is delivering a stone, and they shall yield choice of position to the delivering team. Both players shall be motionless with their brooms positioned in a manner not to interfere or distract the attention of the player who is in Phase 1, 2 or 3 of the curling delivery Rule 8(1).

(b) The player whose turn is next to deliver a stone may take a stationary position by the backboard at the delivering end and to the side of the sheet. The player must remain silent and motionless when the delivering team player is in Phase 1, 2 or 3 of the curling delivery Rule 8(1).

(c) The players not taking the positions 7(1)(a) or 7(1) (b) shall position themselves between the hoglines and to the extreme sides of the sheet when the opposing team is delivering a stone. The players positioned in this area shall remain in single file when the delivering team player is in phase 1, 2 or 3 of the curling delivery Rule 8(1).

(d) the non-delivering team members shall not take any position or cause such motion that would obstruct, interfere with or distract the delivering team.

Penalty: If a team declares its own violation of Rule 7(1)(a), (b), (c) or (d), the non-offending team may replace all affected stones as close as possible to their original position and re-deliver the stone prior to the opposition delivering their next stone.

(2) Members of the delivering team:

(a) Only the skip or vice-skip shall be positioned inside the hogline of the playing end while a stone is being delivered and shall have choice of position.

Penalty: If a team declares its own violation of Rule 7(2)(a), the non-offending team may allow the play to stand or remove the stone just delivered from play and replace all affected stones as close as possible to their original position.

8. Delivery

(1) There are four phases to the delivery of a curling stone:

(a) Phase 1: The delivery of a curling stone is deemed to be in the "preparation phase" at the instant the player whose turn it is next to deliver places a foot in the hack.

(b) Phase 2: The delivery of a curling stone is deemed to be in the "initiation phase" from the instant the player commences a movement of the stone (forward or backward) which results in its continual progression toward the nearer tee line.

(c) Phase 3: The delivery of a curling stone is deemed to be in the "delivery phase" from the instant delivery is initiated until the instant it has been released as defined in Rule 8(4).

(d) Phase 4: The delivery of a curling stone is deemed to be in the "delivered phase" from the instant it has been released, as defined in Rule 8(4) until it has come to rest at the opposite end from which it was released or is out of play, whichever shall first occur.

(2) Only right-handed deliveries shall be initiated from the hack located to the left of the centre line and only left-handed deliveries shall be initiated from the hack located to the right of the centre line. Both right-handed and left-handed deliveries may be initiated from a hack located on the centre line.

Interpretation: If a single moveable hack is in use it shall be positioned as required by the delivering team in accordance with Rule 3(6) and 8(2).

Penalty: If a team declares its own violation of Rule 8(2), the non-offending

161

team may allow the play to stand or remove the stone just delivered from play and replace all affected stones as close as possible to their original position.

(3) If a player wishes to redeliver a stone as a result of their own team's action, they may do so providing the stone has not been released from the player's hand and has not reached the nearer tee line.

Interpretation: A stone may be replayed if the player's body or equipment reaches the tee line providing the stone does not.

(4) In the delivery of a stone, the player shall release the handle before the stone reaches the nearer hogline.

Penalty: The delivered stone and all affected stones must come to rest before any action may take place. If a team declares its own violation of rule 8(4), the non-offending team may allow the play to stand or remove the stone just delivered from play and replace all affected stones as close as possible to their original position.

(5) If an extreme circumstance occurs during the delivery that distracts the thrower to a significant degree during Phase 1, 2, or 3 of delivery Rule 8(1), the stone may be redelivered prior to the opposition delivering their next stone.

(6) A player shall only commence the "initiation" phase of a curling delivery after the previous stone and any stones set in motion have come to rest or have passed the backline.

(7) Each player shall be ready to deliver when his/her turn comes.

(8) Delay of a game in progress by a player for any reason excluding accident or illness shall not exceed three minutes.

(9) If a player delivers a stone belonging to the opposing team, a stone belonging to his/her team shall be put in its place.

(10) (a) If a player delivers a stone out of proper rotation, the end shall continue and the delivery rotation shall continue to be in accordance with Rule 5(3), (4).

Interpretation: This includes the situation when the team with last stone throws first.

(b) If an error in delivery rotation causes a player on the same team to miss a turn, the player who has missed a turn shall deliver the last stone for his/her team in the end.

Interpretation: This rules applies to the situation when the second player delivers the lead player's second stone and other similar delivery rotation errors.

(11) If the opposing teams agree that a stone has been missed but are unable to determine which player missed his/her turn, the lead of the team that missed a turn shall play the last stone for his/her team in that end.

(12) (a) If a team delivers two stones in succession in the same end, the official shall remove the second stone to be played, replace any stone(s) displaced by the stone and the end shall continue. The delivery rotation of the offending team shall be altered for that end so that the player who delivered the second of the two stones delivered in succession shall deliver the last stone for his/her team in the end.

(b) If the non-offending team delivers a stone prior to the error in delivery rotation being detected, the end shall be continued. If the non-offending team has last stone they shall deliver the last two stones of the end in succession. If the non-offending team is the team who started the end without last stone they shall deliver the last stone of the end.

(13) If a player on a four player team delivers three stones in one end, except as provided for in Rules (7)(a) and (b), the end shall be continued and the fourth player on the offending team shall deliver one stone only in that end.

9. Touched Delivered Stone or Stones Set in Motion

(1) A delivered stone or stone set in motion shall not be touched by any player or that player's equipment nor shall he/she cause the stone to be touched by an opposing player or that player's equipment.

Interpretation: A stone which is released and retouched as part of a player's regular delivery is not considered a touched delivered stone provided the final contact with the stone is in accordance with Rule 8(4).

Penalty: The delivered stone or stone(s) set in motion and all affected stones shall come to rest before any action is taken. If a team declares its own violation of rule 9(1) the non-offending team may:

   (i) allow the play to stand;

   (ii) remove the touched delivered stone or stone(s) set in motion from play and replace all affected stones as close as possible to their original position; or

   (iii) place the touched delivered stone or stone(s) set in motion and all stones it would have affected where they would have come to rest had the violation not occurred.

(2) If a delivered stone was touched or caused to be touched by an external force, i.e., stone, broom or brush from another sheet, spectator, etc., the player shall be allowed to redeliver the stone. If the touched stone has displaced other stones, they shall be replaced as close as possible to their original positions to the satisfaction of both teams.

10. Displaced Stationary Stones

(1) A stationary stone shall not be displaced by a player or that player's equipment

nor shall a player cause a stone to be displaced by an opposing player or that player's equipment.

Penalty—Situation #1: If a team declares its own violation of Rule 10(1), the non-offending team shall replace the displaced stone(s) as close as possible to its original position.

Interpretation: If there is any question as to which stone(s) was closer to the tee, the displaced stone(s) shall be positioned in favour of the non-offending team. If the displacement occurs after delivery of the final stone of the end is initiated and prior to agreement of the score, Rule 13(9) shall apply.

Penalty—Situation #2: If a violation of Rule 10(1) occurs and the displaced stationary stone would have altered the course of a delivered stone or stone set in motion, the non-offending team may:

   (i) allow the play to stand;

  (ii) remove the stone just delivered or stone set in motion from play and replace all affected stones as close as possible to their original positions; or

 (iii) place the stone just delivered or stone set in motion and all stones it would have affected where they would have come to rest had the violation not occurred.

    Interpretation: If there is any question as to which stone(s) would have been closer to the tee had the violation not occurred, the stone(s) that would have been affected by the delivered stone or stone set in motion shall be positioned in favour of the non-offending team.

(2) A stationary stone shall not be displaced by a delivered stone or stone(s) set in motion that deflects from a divider or a stationary stone on an adjacent sheet. This is the responsibility of the delivering team.

Penalty: If a violation of Rule 10(2) occurs the non-offending team shall replace the affected stone(s) as close as possible to its original position.

Interpretation: If there is any question as to which stone(s) was closer to the tee or would have been closer to the tee had the violation not occurred, the displaced stone(s) or stone(s) in motion shall be positioned in favour of the non-offending team. If the displacement occurred at the conclusion of play in an end and prior to agreement of the score, Rule 13(9) shall apply.

(3) If the stones are displaced during an end in a way other than stated in the preceding rules, the official shall determine, in consultation with the teams, the positions to which the stones are to be returned. If the teams cannot agree on the original position of the displaced stones relative to which was closer to the tee, the end shall be replayed. If the displacement occurred at the conclusion of play in an end and prior to agreement of the score, Rule 13(10) shall apply.

11. Sweeping/Brushing

   (1) (a) Between the tee lines, all members of the delivering team may sweep/brush any of their team's stones that have been delivered or set in motion by their team's delivered stone.

      (b) Only the skip or vice-skip of the non-delivering team may sweep/brush their team's stone(s) after it is set in motion by a stone of the delivering team.

   (2) Behind the tee line, only one player from each team may sweep/brush at one time. This may be the skip or vice-skip of either team or the lead or second of the delivering team.

      Interpretation: The only time a lead or second of the delivering team may sweep/brush behind the tee line is when sweeping/brushing his/her team's delivered stone or any stone set in motion by his/her team's delivered stone.

   (3) Behind the tee line, each team shall have first privilege of sweeping/brushing its own stone. If the choice is not to sweep/brush, that team shall not obstruct or prevent its opponent from sweeping/brushing the stone.

   (4) An opponent's stone shall not be swept/brushed until it reaches the farther tee line and shall only be swept/brushed behind the tee line.

      Penalty: If a team declares its own violation of Rule 11(1), (2), (3) or (4), the non-offending team may allow the play to stand or place the stone and all stones it would have affected where they would have come to rest had the sweeping violation not occurred.

   (5) (a) The sweeping/brushing motion shall be from side to side.

      (b) The sweeping/brushing motion shall not leave any debris in front of a delivered stone or stone set in motion

      (c) The final sweeping/brushing motion shall finish to either side of the delivered stone or stone set in motion.

12. Method of Play—To be determined by the curling body having jurisdiction—Free Guard Zone Rule Option

   (1) The area between the hogline and tee line excluding the house shall be the free guard zone.

      Interpretation: A stone which comes to rest touching or in front of the hogline after making contact with a stone in the free guard zone is considered to be in the free guard zone. A stone which comes to rest outside the rings but touching the tee line is not in the free guard zone.

   (2) After delivery of each of the first two stones of an end it is the responsibility of the skip of the team who is about to deliver to ensure agreement with the opposing skip as to whether or not the stone just delivered has come to rest in the free

guard zone. If they cannot agree, they may make the determination by using the six foot measuring stick. If the position of another stone hinders the use of the six foot measure they may reposition this stone, complete the measurement and replace the stone to its original position.

(3) Any stationary stone(s) located within the free guard zone shall not be removed from play until after the third stone of the end has been delivered and all stones have come to rest or are out of play.

Interpretation: This includes the delivering team's stones. A delivered third stone of an end may hit a stone in the free guard zone onto a stone not in the free guard zone providing the original free guard zone stone remains in play. If the original free guard zone stone is removed from play, penalty situation #1 shall apply.

Situation #1: If a stone(s) in the free guard zone is removed from play prior to the delivery of the fourth stone of the end, the non-offending team may allow the play to stand or remove the stone just delivered from play and replace the displaced stationary stone(s) as close as possible to its original position.

Situation #2: If the delivered third stone of an end initially hits a stone not in the free guard zone and as a result a stone in the free guard zone is removed from play, the non-offending team may allow the play to stand or remove the stone just delivered from play and replace the stone removed from the free guard zone as close as possible to its original position. The stone that was initially hit shall remain where it finally comes to rest.

Situation #3: If the delivered third stone of an end simultaneously hits a stone not in the free guard zone and a stone in the free guard zone and as a result the stone in the free guard zone is removed from play, the rule shall be applied as if the stone not in the free guard zone was hit initially (see situation #2). If the teams cannot agree the delivering team shall be given the benefit of the doubt.

(4) In all other respects the normal rules of play shall apply.

13. Stones in Play and Scoring

(1) A game shall be of such length or duration as is stated in the rules governing the competition.

(2) A stone that does not come to rest inside the inner edge (circle side) of the farther hogline shall be removed from play immediately except where it has struck another stone lying in play.

Interpretation: A stone which crosses the hogline but, when stopping, spins such that it comes to rest biting the hogline, is considered "out of play".

(3) A stone coming to rest beyond the outer edge of the backline shall be immediately removed from play.

Interpretation: A stone which crosses the backline but, when stopping, spins such that it comes to rest biting the backline, is considered "in play".

(4) A stone that touches a sideline, hits a divider or comes to rest biting a sideline shall be removed immediately from play.

(5) A game shall be decided by a majority of points.

(6) Each stone that is eligible to be counted is within 6 feet (1.83 meters) of the tee.

(7) A team scores one point for each stone that is closer to the tee than any stone of the opposing team.

(8) An end shall be decided when the skips or vice-skips in charge of the house at the time agree upon the score for the end.

(9) If a stone which may have affected the points scored in an end is displaced prior to the skips or vice-skips deciding the score, the team causing the displacement shall forfeit the point(s) involved.

(10) Should an individual other than the two teams or their coaches displace or cause the displacement of a stone(s) prior to agreement of the score or a measure being determined, the following shall apply:

   (a) Preceding the final end;

      (i) If the displaced stone(s) would have determined who won an end, the end shall be replayed.

      (ii) If a team secured a point(s) and the displaced stone(s) would have determined if an additional point(s) is scored, that team shall have the option of replaying the end or keeping the point(s) already secured and proceeding to the next end.

   (b) In the final end:

      (i) If the game is tied and the displaced stone(s) would have determined which team won the game the end shall be replayed.

      (ii) If the displaced stone(s) would have determined if the game was tied or lost by the team that was behind in points, that team shall have the option of replaying the end or keeping the point(s) they had already secured and playing an additional end without last rock.

      (iii) If the team that was behind in points had already secured sufficient points to tie the game, and the displaced stone(s) would have determined if they won the game, that team shall have the option of replaying the end or keeping the point(s) already secured and playing an additional end, with last rock being determined by a single draw to the tee with sweeping/brushing. The team who was ahead in points when the end began shall have the choice of drawing first or last.

(iv) If the displaced stone(s) would have determined if the game was lost, tied or won, the team that was down in points shall have the option of replaying the end or keeping the point(s) already secured if any and playing an additional end, with last rock being determined by a single draw to the tee with sweeping/brushing. The team who was ahead in points when the end began shall have the choice of drawing first or last.

Interpretation: Rule 13(10)(b)(iv) applies to the following types of situations:

– A team is one down going home and measuring two of their stones to determine if they have lost, tied or won the game.

– A team is two down going home counting one and measuring two of their stones to determine if they have lost, tied or won the game.

(11) If after regulation play the score is tied, play shall be continued without changing the rotation of play (end the stones are thrown to) for such additional end or ends as may be required to decide the winning team.

14. Measuring

(1) Measurements shall be taken from the tee to the closest part of the stone.

Interpretation: Because stones may vary in width, measurements may not be taken from the tee to the farthest part of a stone.

(2) No physical device to aid visual observation may be used in measuring prior to the last stone delivered in the end coming to rest except as provided for in Free Guard Zone (Rule 12).

(3) Decisions on whether a stone is in or out of play are visual (no accepted measuring device). If the opposing teams cannot agree, they may consult a non-partisan third party.

(4) If two or more stones are so close to the tee that a measuring device cannot be used, the stones shall be declared tied and only stones closer to the tee shall be counted in the end otherwise the end shall be considered blank.

15. Equipment

(1) A player shall not use footwear or equipment that may damage or affect the playing quality of the ice surface. Examples: excessive debris from a corn/straw broom, shedding brushes, faulty slider.

(2) At the start of each game, each curler shall declare what type of sweeping/brushing device they shall be using for the duration of the game (brush, synthetic straw style broom or corn/straw broom). Players may change or exchange brushes, brush heads and synthetic straw style brooms during a game. Players shall use the same corn/straw broom for the duration of the game and shall not exchange a corn/straw broom with another player. If a broom or brush is broken during a game it shall be replaced by the same type of sweeping/brushing device.

16. Postponement

    (1) If for any reason a game is postponed to another time, the game shall continue from the last completed end.

    (2) If a team is unable to commence play at a designated time, it shall be assessed a penalty of one point and one end shall be considered played for the first five minutes the team does not commence play unless otherwise stated by the rules governing the competition. One penalty point shall be assessed and one end shall be considered played for each additional five minutes the team does not commence play unless otherwise stated by the rules governing the competition When the game commences, the non-offending team shall be given the choice of last rock or colour of handle unless otherwise stated by the rules governing the competition. After 30 minutes have elapsed the non-offending team shall be declared the winner unless otherwise stated by the rules governing the competition.

17. Special Considerations

    If any exceptions to the preceding rules are necessary to accommodate players with physical disabilities, appropriate adjustments are considered acceptable.

18. Miscellaneous

    Should any situation occur that is not covered by the rules, the decision shall be made in accordance with equity.

United States Curling Association Rules of Play

USCA Edition—Club and Bonspiel Use

Copyright by United States Curling Association. Reprinted with permission. These rules were accurate at the time this book went to press. To obtain an up-to-date copy of the rules, please contact the United States Curling Association, 1100 CenterPoint Drive, Box 866, Stevens Point, WI 54481. Phone: (715) 344-1199; Fax: (715) 344-2279; email: usacurl@coredcs.com; Web site: www.usacurl.org

1. Definitions

    In these rules, umpires' rulings, and other official documents of the United States Curling Association and its officers:

    (a) "competition" means a playdown by any number of teams playing games to determine a winner;

    (b) "end" means that part of a game in which the two opposing teams each deliver eight stones alternately and then determine the score;

    (c) where five players are registered, these five players have equal standing and may be used at any time in accordance with the rules, at the discretion of the skip or coach;

(d) "USCA" means the United States Curling Association;

(e) "game" means play between two teams to determine a winner;

(f) "house" means the area within the outside circle at each end of the rink;

(g) "match" means play between two or more teams on one side against an equal number of teams on the other side to determine a winning side by the total number of shots or games;

(h) "rink" means an area of ice marked in accordance with Rule 3.

2. Application

These rules apply to games in USCA-member leagues, bonspiels or other competitions that do not lead to USCA National Championships.

3. Rink

(1) When possible, the rink shall be drawn on the ice in accordance with the diagram below.

(2) Two rubber hacks of a style and size approved by the USCA shall be placed on the line with the inside edge of each hack 7.62 cm (3 inches) from the center line on opposite sides of the center line. The length of the hack shall not exceed 20.32 (8 inches). The rubber of the hack shall be attached firmly to wood or other suitable material and the hack shall be recessed into the ice as much as is practical, but no more than 5.04 cm (2 inches) in depth. There shall be no obstruction behind the hack structure.

The U.S. ice

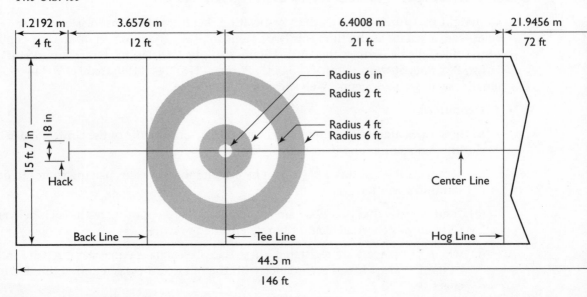

(3) The back edge of the back line shall be at the outer edge of the outer circle where the center line crosses the back line. The 6-foot measure should be exactly at the outermost marking.

4. Stones

(1) Curling stones shall be of circular shape.

(2) No stone, including handle and bolt, shall be of greater weight than 19.96 kg (44 lbs.) or of greater circumference than 91.44 cm (36 inches) or of less height than 11.43 cm (4.5 inches).

(3) If a stone is broken in play a replacement stone shall be placed where the largest fragment came to rest. The end in play and the game shall be completed using the replacement stone.

(4) A stone that rolls over in its course or comes to rest on its side or top shall be removed immediately from play.

(5) Where the handle of a stone quits the stone in delivery, the player is entitled to replay the stone, if the delivering team so desires. The handle must be completely separated from the stone.

(6) A stone that does not clear the farther hog line shall be removed immediately from play except where it has struck another stone lying in play.

(7) A stone which comes to rest beyond and lying clear of the back line shall be removed from play immediately.

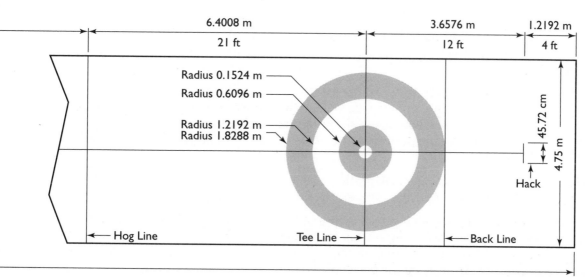

Conversion: 1 foot = .3048 metres

(8) A stone that hits a side board or touches a side line shall be removed immediately from play.

(9) No stone(s) shall be measured by instrument until the last stone of the end has come to rest except by the umpire, when requested by a skip, to decide whether or not a stone is in play, or whether or not a stone is in the house when the "Free Guard Zone" system of play is being used. If the position of the rocks in the house makes it impossible to use the 6-foot measuring device to decide whether a stone is in play at the 6 o'clock position, the umpire will do this visually and his/her decision will be final.

(10) All sixteen stones assigned to a given sheet shall be delivered at each end unless the players in charge of the house have agreed upon a score for the end or the game has been conceded.

5. Teams

(1) At the start of a competition every team shall be composed of four players, each player playing two stones and playing each stone alternately with his/her opponent.

(2) No player shall use footwear or equipment that may damage the surface of the ice.

(3) The rotation of play established in the first end shall be observed throughout the game.

(4) Prior to the game, the opposing third players shall determine by lot which team shall lead at the first end after which the winner of the preceding end shall lead.

(5) Where a player is unable to continue to play in a game or to play at the start of a game, his/her skip may:

(a) finish the game then in progress and start any subsequent game with the remaining players, in which case the first two players shall throw three stones each; or

(b) bring in a qualified substitute for the game then in progress at the beginning of the next end, or at the start of any subsequent game. A qualified substitute is a person who meets the criteria for that competition. Any substitute must play in the position of the replaced player when entering a game in progress.

(c) commence the game with three players because one player is late, and the late player may enter the game in the next end, in his/her normal position.

(6) A player who has left a game because of illness, accident or other extenuating circumstances may rejoin his/her team at any time during any game in the competition, provided the rotation of play for the end in progress is not altered. If a substitute was selected the player may rejoin his/her team for the game.

(7) No team shall substitute for more than one of the original players in a competition (or one male and one female in mixed competition). However, any number of substitutes for that one player (or couple in mixed) is allowed.

6. Skips

   (1) The skip has the exclusive direction of the game for his/her team.

   (2) Subject to rule 5(3), the skip may play in any position in his/her team that he/she chooses.

   (3) When it is the skip's turn to play the acting skip shall take charge of the house. The acting skip shall be the only player beside the skip allowed in the house when the opposition is throwing.

7. Position of Players

   (1) Only skips and acting skips in charge of the house for the time being may stand within the house and the skip of the playing team has the choice of place and shall not be obstructed by the other skip, but behind the tee line the privileges of both in regard to sweeping are equal.

   (2) The players, other than the skip and acting skip, shall not stand behind the house, but shall place themselves along the side of the rink between the hog lines, except when sweeping or about to deliver a stone. Non-delivering team members shall not take a position or cause such motion that would obstruct, interfere with or distract the delivering team.

8. Delivery

   (1) Right-handed players shall play from the hack on the left of the center line and left-handed players from the hack on the right of the center line. Any stone delivered from the wrong hack shall be removed from play immediately.

   (2) In the delivery of the stone, the stone shall be clearly released from the hand before the stone reaches the nearer hog line. If the player fails to so release the stone, it shall be removed from play immediately by the playing team. If the stone has struck another stone, the played stone shall be removed from play by the playing team and any displaced stone shall be replaced as nearly as possible where it originally lay to the satisfaction of the opposing skip.

   (3) Any hog-line infraction, agreed upon by both skips or at the direction of an observing umpire, if present, shall result in the stone being removed by the offending team. Any displaced stones shall be repositioned by the non-offending team. Benefit to either team is not a factor.

   (4) A stone that has not been released from the player's hand and that has not reached the nearer tee line may be returned to the hack and re-delivered.

   (5) Each player shall be ready to deliver his/her stone when his/her turn comes, and shall not take an unreasonable time to play.

(6) Where a player delivers a stone belonging to the opposing team, a stone belonging to his/her team shall be put in its place.

(7) Where a player delivers a stone out of proper rotation it shall be removed from play immediately by the playing team and returned to the player to be delivered in proper rotation, but when the mistake is not discovered until after the stone has come to rest or struck another stone, the end shall be continued as if the mistake had not occurred, and the missed stone shall be delivered by the player missing his/her turn as the last stone for his/her team in that end.

(8) Where the skips agree that a stone has been missed but are unable to agree as to which player missed his/her turn, the lead of the team that made the mistake shall play the last stone for his/her team in that end.

(9) Where two stones of a team are delivered in succession in the same end, the opposing skip shall remove the stone played by mistake, replace to his/her satisfaction any stone displaced by the stone played by mistake, and continue the end as if the mistake had not occurred, and the player who delivered the stone played by mistake shall re-deliver it as the last stone for his/her team in that end. Should the infraction not be discovered until after further rocks have been played, the end shall be replayed.

(10) Where a player delivers three stones in one end, the end shall be continued as if the mistake had not occurred and the fourth player of the team that made the mistake shall deliver one stone only in that end.

9. Sweeping

   (1) Between the tee lines, a running stone, or stone(s) set in motion by a running stone, may be swept by any one or more of the team to which it belongs. Any stone in motion is a running stone. A stationary stone must be set in motion before it can be swept.

   (2) Between the tee lines, no player shall sweep an opponent's stone.

   (3) Behind the tee line, if the delivering team's choice is not to sweep, they shall not obstruct or prevent the opponent from sweeping the stone.

   (4) Behind the tee line, only one player from each team may sweep at any one time. This may be the skip or acting skip from either team. Only the player in charge of the house shall be allowed to sweep behind the tee line, and shall not start to sweep an opponent's stone before the stone reaches the line.

      (a) The acting skip does not assume charge of the house until the skip leaves to throw his/her first stone, and then remains in charge.

      (b) If the skip throws other than fourth stones, he/she shall resume control of the house when his/her second stone, and any other stone whose movement has been generated by that stone, has come to rest.

174

(5) (a) The sweeping motion, which shall be from side to side, shall leave no debris in front of the running stone and shall finish to either side of the stones.

   (b) The sweepers and their equipment must be seen to be clear of the stone at all times.

   (c) Penalty: If a team draws an infraction and the stone involved is their own it shall be removed from play. However, if the stone involved belongs to the opposition, the opposition shall direct the repositioning of the stone to where they consider it would have come to rest had it not been infracted. If, in the opinion of the non-offending skip, repositioning of the stone would benefit the offending team, it may be left where it came to rest.

10. Touched Running Stones

   (1) If a running stone is touched by any of the playing team or by his/her equipment, the touched stone shall be removed from play immediately by that team. However, if in the opinion of the opposing skip, removal of the stone would be beneficial to the offending team, then he/she may place the stone as nearly as possible to the position where he/she considers it would have come to rest had it not been touched. He/she may also reposition any stone or stones that would have been displaced had the running stone not been touched and been allowed to continue. For an opposing skip to reposition any potentially displaced stones, the infraction must have occurred inside the hog line at the playing end.

   (2) If a running stone is touched by any of the opposing team or by his/her equipment, the stone shall be placed where the skip of the team to which it belongs considers it would have come to rest if it had not been touched.

   (3) If the position of any stone is altered by a touched stone, the skip opposed to the team at fault may elect:

      (a) to remove the touched stone and replace all other altered stones to the position where he/she considers they originally lay; or

      (b) to leave the touched stone and all altered stones where they came to rest.

11. Displaced Stationary Stones

   (1) If a stone which would have altered the course of a running stone is displaced by the playing team, the running stone shall be allowed to come to rest and may be left there or removed from play immediately at the discretion of the opposing skip:

      (a) If the running stone is removed from play then all displaced stones shall be placed where the opposing skip considers they originally lay.

      (b) If the running stone is left where it came to rest, then displaced stones must remain where they came to rest.

(2) A stationary stone which is displaced and has no effect on the outcome of the running stone shall be replaced where it originally lay, by the opposing skip.

12. Scoring

(1) Games shall be decided by a majority of shots and a team scores one shot for each stone that is nearer the tee than any stone of the opposing team.

(2) Every stone that is within 1.83 meters (6) feet of the tee is eligible to be counted. The 6-foot measuring device shall be the sole instrument used to determine whether a stone is in the house, at the conclusion of the end, subject to Rule 4(9).

(3) Measurements shall be taken from the tee to the nearest part of the stone.

(4) An end shall be considered as decided when the skips or acting skips in charge of the house at the time agree upon the score for that end. Should any stone(s) be displaced before agreement has been reached, the non-offending team shall receive the benefit which may have accrued from a measurement. Should an umpire displace a stone when measuring one of the stones involved in the measurement, the stones shall be considered a tie.

(5) If two or more stones are so close to the tee that it is impossible to use a measuring device to determine the scoring stone, the determination shall be made visually by the umpire. If no decision can be made, the end shall be scored as a blank end.

13. Umpire

(1) The umpire has the general supervision of all games to which he/she is assigned.

(2) The umpire shall determine any matter in dispute between opposing skips, whether or not the matter is covered in the rules.

14. Postponement

If for any reason a game is postponed to another time, or a game is suspended, the game will continue at the point the game was suspended.

The Hottest Curling Sites on the Web

Canadian Curling Association

www.curling.ca

The site contains detailed information on high-level competitive play: the Labatt Brier, the Scott Tournament of Hearts, the World Curling Championships, the World Junior Championships, and so on. The site also contains a comprehensive list of provincial and regional curling associations, information on the Business of Curling program (a club marketing and management program), and links galore.

Curling History Page

home.istar.ca/~rockroll/curling.html

This is the place for trivia buffs and other curling enthusiasts who want to know who won what when. The site is overflowing with stats on winners at the Canadian, American, and World championship level.

Curling Home Page

www.curling.com

This site contains links to curling clubs, curling associations, and late-breaking curling news.

Ed White's Curling Poems

www.cocula.com/users/selkins/cp95.htm

You won't find many Web sites devoted to curling poems. In fact, we'd be willing to bet that this is the only one out there.

Front Ender's Union

www.cyberus.ca/~linseman/history.html

Tired of being treated like a second-class citizen because you play front end? This site celebrates the important role that is played by the lead and the second. According to the information posted on the site, the Front Ender's Union was established during a "post-round-robin, pool-side siesta" (!) following the 1993 Ontario Blue Light Tankard in Trenton, Ontario. The rest, as they say, is history.

In The Hack

www.inthehack.com

This site contains coverage of major curling events and gives you the opportunity to purchase curling apparel and other related merchandise.

International Curling Information Network Group (ICING)

icing.org

The Mother of all curling Web sites, the International Curling Information Network Group is a Web site devoted to providing comprehensive coverage of every conceivable aspect of the sport. You'll find information on the game of curling (history, description, rules, and equipment), links to curling organizations and clubs around the world, television schedules, leads on bonspiels, advice from coaches and trainers, curling graphics, humor, pools and trivia, information about curling supplies, and much more.

John Murphy's Home Page

www.geocities.com/Colosseum/9424

Created by a curling coach, this Web site contains the most comprehensive set of curling links you'll find anywhere. Bookmark it and use it as your launching pad to information on curling associations, championships, supplies, software, media coverage, statistics, clubs, and much more.

Shot Rock Bonspiel Finder

www.bonspiel.com

As the name indicates, this site allows you to search for bonspiel information by date, location, and so on.

SLAM! Curling

www.canoe.ca/SlamCurling/home.html

This is the place to turn throughout the curling season for up-to-date results on competitive play.

TSN Curling Page

www.tsn.ca/curling

In addition to listings on upcoming curling games on television, you'll find background information on the sport; links to events, associations, and clubs; a glossary of curling terms; and a list of Curling Hall of Famers. You can even use the live chat forum to talk about the game with other curlers and wannabe curlers.

Turner Curling Museum

www.compusmart.ab.ca/nplooy/turner.htm

This site contains information about the Turner Curling Museum in Weyburn, Saskatchewan–a collection of curling memorabilia from around the world. According to the Web site, the Museum is home to 18,000 curling pins, 75 curling stones (weighing between 17 and 62 pounds apiece), 300 curling books (soon to be 301, we hope!), and much more.

United States Curling Association

www.usacurl.org

In addition to providing a lot of detailed information on the services offered by the United States Curling Association, this site also contains information on the history of the sport, strategy, and high-level competitive play. There are also a number of useful links.

World Curling Federation

www.curling.org

The World Curling Federation Web site contains information on the programs and services offered by the Federation, a useful handbook for beginners, and a copy of the Federation's rules of competition.

Curling Products and Services

Curling Equipment

Alpine Curling
W4819 Greenbush Road
Monroe, Wisconsin 53566
Phone: (608) 325-6365
Email: icemaker@alpinecurling.com
Web site: www.alpinecurling.com
Alpine Curling sells such curling supplies as brushes, shoes, sliders, and rink and ice equipment.

Asham Curling Supplies
700 McPhillips Street
Winnipeg, MB
R2X 2H5
Phone: (204) 589-6321
Fax: (204) 947-3290
Email: asham@asham.com
Web site: www.asham.com
This company sells shoes, sliders, performance soles, and a range of accessories, including gloves, curling pants, and the Housetalk Board—a miniature curling rink that can be used when plotting strategy.

Canada Curling Stone Co.
1895 Blue Heron Drive
Unit 1
London, Ontario
N6H 5M8
Phone: (519) 474-1339
Fax: (519) 474-3591
Email: kveale@thecurlingstore.on.ca
Web site: www.thecurlingstore.on.ca
The company carries a range of curling supplies and giftware items.

Curlbec Inc.
1810–55th Ave
Lachine, Quebec
Phone: (514) 631-3751 or (800) 567-7757
Fax (514) 631-2909
Email: webmaster@quesoft.com
Web site: www.curlbec.com
Curlbec Inc. is a major supplier of curling merchandise in Canada.

Curling Depot
175 Essa Road
Barrie, Ontario
L4N 3L2
Phone/Fax: (705) 727-0087
Email: curldepo@bconnex.net
Web site: www.bconnex.net/~curldepo/index.htm
This company sells shoes, brushes, clothing, and other curling-related goods.

Furgale Industries
324 Lizzie Street
Winnipeg, Manitoba
R3A 0Y7
Phone: 1 (800) 665-0506 or (204) 949-4200
Web site: www.8-ender.com/8-ender/index.html
Furgale Industries manufactures curling brushes made of hog's hair, horse hair, and synthetic materials.

Goldline Store—Mississauga
7295 Rapistan Court
Mississauga, Ontario
L5N 5Z4
(905) 826-5250

Goldline Store—Scarborough
50**6** Ellesmere Road
Scarborough, Ontario
M1R 4Z3
(416) 750-7685
Order desk phone: (905) 826-5250
Order desk fax: (905) 826-0969
Email: store@goldline.on.ca
Web site: www.netaccess.on.ca/~psmith/icing/goldline/1997-98/cover.htm
Goldline operates retail stores in Mississauga and Scarborough, but also accepts on-line, telephone, or fax orders. The company sells curling clothing, shoes, gloves, sliders, brooms and brushes, and much more.

John Michael's Collection of Curling Pins and Jewellery
99 Coe Hill Drive, Unit 117
Toronto, Ontario.
M6S 3E4
Phone/Fax: (416) 766-6057
Email: curling@pathcom.com
Web site: www.pathcom.com/~curling
Curling pins are hot commodities at bonspiels and other get-togethers. This company sells pins and other types of jewellery that feature such curling paraphernalia as rocks and brooms. Both pewter and costume jewellery are available.

McGowan Curling Aids
4819 Park Avenue
Terrace, British Columbia
V8G 1W3
Phone/Fax: (250) 635-2234
This company sells curling aids that allow curlers with physical disabilities to play the game without bending over.

Olson Curling Manufacturing and Supplies Ltd.
10555-116 Street
Edmonton, Alberta, T5H 3L8
Phone: (403) 425-8646 or (800) 661-2492
Fax: (403) 425-9555
Email: olson@oanet.com
Web site: www.olsoncurling.com
Olsen manufactures and/or supplies such curling-related merchandise as brooms, gloves, ice-making equipment, shoes, sliders, and more.

Steve's Curling Supplies
5010 Ironwood Drive
Madison,Wisconsin 53716
Phone: (608) 222-1691
Orders: (800) 227-CURL (U.S. only)
Email: dianecurl@aol.com
Web site: www.abcon.com/stevescurling/index.html
Steve's Curling Supplies is operated by Steve Brown, coach of the U.S. Women's
Olympic curling team and father of Erika Brown, one of the members of the team. The
company sells an assortment of curling-related products: brushes, shoes, books, cloth-
ing, and everything else imaginable.

Wright Ice Pro Shop
Box 71
Qualicum Beach, British Columbia
V9K 1S7
Phone: (250) 752-6162
Fax: (250) 752-6641
Email: wright@nanaimo.ark.com
Web site: nanaimo.ark.com/~wright
As well as selling a variety of curling supplies, this site provides some interesting infor-
mation on the art of icemaking. There's your chance to learn something while you
shop.

Curling Software

Curling Information System
Web site: ourworld.compuserve.com:80/homepages/Csaager
The Curling Information System allows coaches and players to analyze each player's
strengths and weaknesses. (Don't even think about pirating the software—the software
developers make a point of mentioning that making additional copies of the product is
prohibited and "against the Spirit of Curling"!)

CurlStat Software
Web site: www.top.net/rozar/curlstat.html
CurlStat is a software program designed to be used by coaches who wish to track the
performance of individual players over the course of a game.

Schedule Wizard—Sports League Scheduling Software
Timeless Technologies
Belfast Post Office
Prince Edward Island
C0A 1A0
(888) 846-3832; (800) 207-0026; or (902) 659-2000
Fax: (902) 659-2003
Email: sales@timelesstech.com
Web site: www.timelesstech.com/html/schedulewizard.html
As the name implies, this software package is designed to take some of the drudgery
out of setting up the schedule for a bonspiel.

WinCurl 2.01 for Windows
Ivany Software
197 Jubilee Rd.
Bridewater, Nova Scotia.
B4V 3G5
Email: ivanysw@istar.ca
Web site: home.iSTAR.ca/~ivanysw
The manufacturers of this product describe it as "a game, simulator, and training aid
for the sport of curling.")

Curling Publications

Sweep! Curling's Magazine
12–6655 Kitimat Road
Mississauga, Ontario
L5N 6J4
Phone: (905) 542-0539
Fax: (905) 567-8920
Email: sweep@inthehack.com/sweep
Web site: www.inthehackcom/sweep
Sweep! is published six times per year (October through April). Subscription rates are as
follows: $20 for one year or $35 for two years within Canada; $25 (U.S. funds) for one
year or $44 (U.S. funds) for two years within the U.S.; and $46 (Canadian funds) for
one year or $81 (Canadian funds) for two years elsewhere. Club rates are available.

Canadian Curling News
99 Bronte Road
Suite 813
Oakville, Ontario
L6L 3B7
Phone/Fax: (905) 827-3839
Web site: www.curlingnews.com
Canadian Curling News is a newspaper that is published six times per year during the curling season. Subscription rates are as follows: $23.54 for one year or $41.73 for two years within Canada; $22 (U.S. funds) for one year or $39 (U.S. funds) for two years within the U.S.; and $50 (Canadian funds) for one year or $89 (Canadian funds) for two years to Scotland, Europe, Scandinavia, Japan, Australia, and New Zealand.

Curling Camp

WOW! Special Event Management Inc.
24 Harriet Street
Penetanguishene, Ontario
L9M 1K9
Phone: (705) 549-8975
Fax: (705) 549-4429
Email: wow@csolve.net
WOW! Special Event Management Inc. organizes Hot Shots Fantasy Curling Camps—a series of three-day clinics featuring video training, strategy sessions, and curling instruction from world champion curlers. The $559 fee includes a souvenir curling jacket.

Recommended Reading

Curling: The Basics Reviewed. Ottawa, Ontario: Canadian Curling Association, 1995.

Lukowich, Ed. *Curling to Win.* Toronto: McGraw-Hill Ryerson Limited, 1986.

Lukowich, Ed. *The Curling Book.* Saskatoon: Western Producer Prairie Books, 1981.

Lukowich, Ed. *The Joy of Curling.* Scarborough: McGraw-Hill Ryerson Limited, 1990.

Murray, W.H. *The Curling Companion.* Don Mills: Collins Publishers, 1981.

Richardson, Ernie, McKee, Joyce and Maxwell, Doug. *Curling.* Toronto: Thomas Allen Limited, 1962.

Richardson, Ernie. *Ernie Richardson's Curling: Techniques and Strategy.* Toronto: McClelland and Stewart Limited, 1973.

Smith, David B. *Curling: An Illustrated History.* Edinburgh: John Donald Publishers Ltd., 1981.

Sonmor, Jean. *Burned by the Rock: Inside the World of Men's Championship Curling.* Toronto: Macmillan Canada, 1991.

Stevenson, John A. *Curling in Ontario 1846–1946.* Toronto: The Ryerson Press, 1950.

Watson, Ken. *Ken Watson on Curling.* Toronto: The Copp Clark Publishing Company, 1950.

Weeks, Bob. *The Brier: The History of Canada's Most Celebrated Curling Championship.* Toronto: Macmillan Canada, 1995.

Directory of Curling Organizations

National and International Organizations

Canadian Curling Association
Suite 511, 1600 James Naismith Drive
Gloucester, Ontario
K1B 5N4
Phone: (613) 748-5628
Fax: (613) 748-5713
Email: cca@curling.ca
Web site: www.curling.ca

United States Curling Association
1100 CenterPoint Drive
Box 866
Stevens Point, WI
54481
Phone: (715) 344-1199
Fax: (715) 344-2279
Email: usacurl@coredcs.com
Web site: www.usacurl.org

Anne Robertson
President
U.S. Women's Curling Association
2238A Bluemound Road
Waukesha, WI
53186
Phone: (414) 968-9778
Fax: (414) 798-0602

World Curling Federation
81 Great King Street
Edinburgh, Scotland
EH3 6RN
Phone: 44-131-556-4884
Fax: 44-131-556-9400

Provincial Organizations

Yukon

Gordon Moffatt
President
Yukon Curling Association
40 Finch Crescent
Whitehorse, Yukon
Y1A 5X5
Phone: (403) 633-3236
Fax: (403) 668-7696

Darryl Bray
Secretary
Yukon Curling Association
P.O. Box 6091
Whitehorse, Yukon
Y1A 5L7
Phone: (403) 668-7121

Northwest Territories

Maureen Miller
President
Northwest Territories Curling Association
13 Horton Crescent
Yellowknife, Northwest Territories
X1A 3B8
Phone: (403) 873-6239

Jim Sosiak
Secretary
Northwest Territories Curling Association
107 Wilkinson Crescent
Yellowknife, Northwest Territories
X1A 3V1
Phone: (403) 669-9209
Fax: (403) 669-4193

British Columbia

Grant Young
President
British Columbia Interior Curling
    Association
375 Nina Place
Kamloops, British Columbia
V2C 6B7
Phone: (250) 573-3149
Fax: (250) 573-2211

Neil King
Secretary
British Columbia Interior Curling
    Association
539 Williams Crescent
Prince George, British Columbia
V2N 1Y2
Phone: (250) 561-1215
Fax: (250) 561-1703

Janice Mori
President
British Columbia Ladies' Curling
    Association,
7909 Cunliffe Road
Vernon, British Columbia
V1B 1T4
Phone: (250) 545-6221
Fax: (250) 545-5964

Liz Goldenberg
Secretary
British Columbia Ladies' Curling
    Association
287 Seymour River Place
North Vancouver, British Columbia
V7H lS6
Phone: (604) 924-2475
Fax: (604) 718-6305

Wayne Brown
President
Pacific Coast Curling Association
603 Yambury Road
Qualicum, British Columbia
V9K 1C5
Phone: (250) 752-5142
Fax: (250) 752-8035

Gordon Brown
Secretary
Pacific Coast Curling Association
1246 Esquimalt Road
Suite 103
Victoria, British Columbia
V9A 3N8
Phone: (604) 652-8020
Fax: (604) 384-9435

Graham Prouse
President
Peace Curling Association
P.O. Box 2391
Fort Nelson, British Columbia
V0C 1R0
Phone: (604) 774-2401
Fax: (604) 774-4450

Alberta

Roger Hohm
President
Alberta Curling Federation
2120 10A Street
Coaldale, Alberta
T1M 1T6
Phone: (403) 345-6459
Fax: (403) 223-3396

Kathy Odegard
Secretary
Alberta Curling Federation
11759 Groat Road
Edmonton, Alberta
T5M 3K6
Phone: (403) 453-8557
Fax: (403) 453-8553

Cindy Klemchuk
Secretary
Peace Curling Association
P.O. Box 265
Grand Prairie, Alberta
T8V 3A4
Phone: (403) 532-4782; (800) 565-0171
Fax: (403) 538-2485

Darrel Sutton
President
Northern Alberta Curling Association
9440 49th Street, Suite 110
Edmonton, Alberta
T6B 2M9
Phone: (403) 467-9003
(NACA Phone) (403) 440-4270
(NACA Fax) (403) 463-4519

Marylynn Morris
Secretary
Northern Alberta Curling Association
9440 49th Street, Suite 110
Edmonton, Alberta
T6B 2M9
Phone: (403) 467-6547
(NACA Phone) (403) 440-4270
(NACA Fax) (403) 463-4519

Don Petlak
President
Southern Alberta Curling Association
519 High View Point
High River, Alberta
T1V 1P1
Phone: (403) 652-2518
Fax: (403) 652-6951

Glenda MacLean
Secretary
Southern Alberta Curling Association
2408 20th Avenue S.W., Suite 101
Calgary, Alberta
T3C 0K6
Phone: (403) 295-3765
Fax: (403) 246-9349

Saskatchewan

Dennis Pomeroy
President
Saskatchewan Curling Association
2205 Victoria Avenue
Regina, Saskatchewan
S4P 0S4
Phone: (306) 783-4271
Fax: (306) 783-9110

Don Bacon
Executive Director
Saskatchewan Curling Association
2205 Victoria Avenue
Regina, Saskatchewan
S4P 0S4
Phone: (306) 545-5565
Fax: (306) 525-4009

Manitoba

Ken Parfeniuk
President
Manitoba Curling Association
1274 Magnus Avenue
Winnipeg, Manitoba
R2X 0N8
Phone: (204) 582-1214

Ian Staniloff
Executive Director
Manitoba Curling Association/Manitoba
    Ladies' Curling Association
200 Main Street, Suite 208
Winnipeg, Manitoba
R3C 4M2
Phone: (204) 925-5723
Fax: (204) 925-5720

Nancy Rummery
President
Manitoba Ladies' Curling Association
381 Westwood Drive, Suite 79
Winnipeg, Manitoba
R3K 1G4
Phone: (204) 489-4864
Fax: (204) 925-5720

Ontario

Fred Temple
President
Ontario Curling Association
25 Bythia Street
Orangeville, Ontario
L9W 2S2
Phone: (519) 941-3696
Fax: (519) 941-9031

John McCrae
General Manager
Ontario Curling Association
1400 Bayly Street
Office Mall 2, #2B
Pickering, Ontario
L1W 3R2
Phone: (905) 571-5364
Fax: (905) 831-1083
Web site: web.idirect.com/~ontcurl

Carol Doeske
General Manager
Ontario Ladies' Curling Association
5 Scarfe Gardens
Brantford, Ontario
N3T 6B2
Phone: (519) 758-9490
Fax: (519) 759-1033
Email: peter.droeske@sympatico.ca
Web site: web.idirect.com/~ontcurl

Janette Thwaites
General Manager
Ontario Ladies' Curling Association
36 Isabel Street
St. Thomas, Ontario
N5R 3J7
Phone: (519) 633-5323
Fax: (519) 633-0659

W.H. Everitt
President
Northern Ontario Curling Association
P.O. Box 961
Blind River, Ontario
P0R 1B0
Phone: (705) 356-7706

Dr. Clyde Opaleychuk
Secretary
Northern Ontario Curling Association
154 Durham Street
Sudbury, Ontario
P3E 3M7
Phone: (705) 688-2594
Fax: (705) 673-2248

Leslie Uhlig
President
Northern Ontario Women's Curling
    Association
88 Parkshore Drive
Sault Ste. Marie, Ontario
P6A 6B3
Phone: (705) 945-9284
Fax: (705) 949-6583

Lauri Graham
Secretary
Northern Ontario Women's Curling
    Association
127 Johnson Avenue
Sault Ste. Marie, Ontario
P6C 2V4
Phone: (705) 946-2174

Rob Gordon
President
Temiskaming & Northern Ontario Curling
    Association
P.O. Box 676
Haileybury, Ontario
P0J 1K0
Phone: (705) 672-2476
Fax: (705) 672-2451

Joe Gubbels
Secretary
Temiskaming & Northern Ontario Curling
    Association
P.O. Box 381
Schumacher, Ontario
P0N 1G0
Phone: (705) 264-7437
Fax: (705) 268-1928

William Charlebois
President
Northwestern Ontario Curling Association
275 West Christina Street
Thunder Bay, Ontario
P7E 4P5
Phone: (807) 577-9424
Fax: (807) 577-5707

Peter McCallum
Secretary
Northwestern Ontario Curling Association
433 Catherine Street
Thunder Bay, Ontario
P7E 1K9
Phone: (807) 622-8254
Fax: (807) 626-9622

191

Ray Thiboutot
President
Canadian Branch, Royal Caledonian
    Curling Club
4505 David Drive
Elizabethtown, Ontario
K6T 1A4
Phone: (613) 342-4431
Fax: (613) 342-2316

Quebec

Claude Fortin
President
Quebec Curling Association
7525 rue Doucet
Charlesbourg, Quebec
G1H 5M9
Phone: (418) 626-9013
Fax: (418) 739-3457

Claude Bergeron
Secretary
Quebec Curling Association
268, de la Corniche
Saint-Nicolas, Quebec
G0S 2Z0
(Phone/Fax) (418) 831-2680

Gaston Letendre
Secretary
Canadian Branch, Royal Caledonian
    Curling Club
785, boul. Provencher
Brossard, Quebec
J4W 1Y5
Phone: (514) 466-7385; (800) 452-1654
Fax: (514) 466-2568
Email: cbranch@total.net

Elly Meyer
President
Quebec Ladies' Curling Association
106 Ventnor
Pointe Claire, Quebec
H9S 4E2
Phone: (514) 694-6543
Fax: (514) 694-3122

Elaine de Ryk
Secretary
Quebec Ladies' Curling Association
1084 Legault
Greenfield Park, Quebec
J4V 3C4
Phone: (514) 445-7300

Andree Benoit
President
Northwestern Quebec Curling Association
144 Vaillancourt
Sullivan, Quebec
J0Y 2N0
Phone: (819) 824-4205
Fax: (819) 825-4008

Claude Noel
Secretary
Northwestern Quebec Curling Association
281, 3e rue est
Amos, Quebec
J9T 2A7
Phone: (819) 732-2089
Fax: (819) 732-1617

New Brunswick

Beth Sullivan
President
New Brunswick Curling Association
670 Brunswick Avenue
Bathurst, New Brunswick
E2A 1W3
Phone: (506) 548-3882
Fax: (506) 546-1011

Lynn MacKenzie
Executive Director
New Brunswick Curling Association
24 Lakewood Drive
Moncton, New Brunswick
E1E 3L7
Phone: (506) 855-9766
(NBCA Phone) (506) 854-9143
(NBCA Fax) (506) 388-5708

Nova Scotia

Greg Thorbourne
President
Nova Scotia Branch, Royal Caledonian
    Curling Club
P.O. Box 1270
Liverpool, Nova Scotia
B0T 1K0
Phone: (902) 354-4143
Fax: (902) 354-5206

Simone MacKenzie
Development Co-ordinator/Secretary
Nova Scotia Branch, Royal Caledonian
    Curling Club/ Nova Scotia Ladies'
    Curling Association
P.O. Box 3010 South
5516 Spring Garden Road
Halifax, Nova Scotia
B3J 3G6
Phone: (902) 425-5450 Ex. 345
Fax: (902) 425-5606
Email: nscurl@sportns.ns.ca

Gail Brown
President
Nova Scotia Ladies' Curling Association
54 Raven Road
R.R. 2
Truro, Nova Scotia
B2N 5E5
Phone: (902) 895-2635
Fax: (902) 425-5606

Prince Edward Island

Dawn MacFadyen
President
Prince Edward Island Curling Association
Borden, R.R. 1
Augustine Cove, Prince Edward Island
C0B 1X0
Phone: (902) 855-2711
Fax: (902) 437-6397

Jim Trainor
Secretary
Prince Edward Island Curling Association
5 Callbeck Crescent
Charlottetown, Prince Edward Island
C1A 9B4
Phone: (902) 628-1949

Newfoundland

Joyce Narduzzi
President
Newfoundland & Labrador Curling
    Association
611 Caribou Crescent
Labrador City, Labrador
A2V 1P8
Phone: (709) 944-3192

Eugene Trickett
Secretary
Newfoundland & Labrador Curling
    Association
P.O. Box 21238
St. John's, Newfoundland
A1A 5B2
(Phone/Fax) (709) 722-1156

193

The Winners' Circle

Note that championship names change throughout the years and have been listed under the name that applied at the time.

World Champions (Men's)

Ford World Men's Champions

1998	Canada	Wayne Middaugh, Graeme McCarrell, Ian Tetley, Scott Bailey
1997	Sweden	Peter Lindholm, Tomas Nordin, Magnus Swartling, Peter Narup
1996	Canada	Jeff Stoughton, Ken Tresoor, Gary Vanderberghe, Steve Gould
1995	Canada	Kerry Burtnyk, Jeff Ryan, Rob Meakin, Keith Fenton

World Curling Champions

1994	Canada	Rick Folk, Pat Ryan, Bert Gretzinger, Gerry Richard
1993	Canada	Russ Howard, Glenn Howard, Wayne Middaugh, Peter Corner
1992	Switzerland	Marcus Eggler, Frederic Jean, Stefan Hofer, Bjorn Schroder
1991	Scotland	David Smith, Graeme Connal, Peter Smith, David Hay
1990	Canada	Ed Werenich, John Kawaja, Ian Tetley, Pat Perroud
1989	Canada	Pat Ryan, Randy Ferbey, Don Walchuk, Don McKenzie
1988	Norway	Eigil Ramsfjell, Sjur Loen, Morten Sogaard, Bo Bakke
1987	Canada	Russ Howard, Glenn Howard, Tim Belcourt, Kent Carstairs

1986   Canada   Ed Lukowich, John Ferguson, Neil Houston, Brent Syme

Air Canada Silver Broom Champions

1985   Canada   Al Hackner, Rick Lang, Ian Tetley, Pat Perroud

1984   Norway   Eigil Ramsfjell, Sjur Loen, Gunnar Meland, Bo Bakke

1983   Canada   Ed Werenich, Paul Savage, John Kawaja, Neil Harrison

1982   Canada   Al Hackner, Rick Lang, Bob Nichol, Bruce Kennedy

1981   Switzerland   Jurg Tanner, Jurg Hornisberger, Patrick Loertscher, Franz Tanner

1980   Canada   Rick Folk, Ron Mills, Tom Wilson, Jim Wilson

1979   Norway   Kristian Soerum, Morten Soerum, Eigil Ramsfjell, Gunner Meland

1978   U.S.A.   Bob Nichols, Bill Strum, Tom Locken, Bob Christman

1977   Sweden   Ragner Kamp, Hakan Rudstrom. Bjorn Rudstrom, Christer Martensson

1976   U.S.A.   Bruce Roberts, Joe Roberts, Gary Kleffman, Jerry Scott

1975   Switzerland   Otto Danieli, Roland Schneider, Rolf Gautschi, Ueli Mulli

1974   U.S.A.   Bud Somerville, Bob Nichols, Bill Strum, Tom Locken

1973   Sweden   Kjell Oscarius, Bengt Oscarius, Tom Schaeffer, Boa Carlman

1972   Canada   Orest Meleschuck, Dave Romano, John Hanesiak, Pat Hailley

1971   Canada   Don Duguid, Rod Hunter, Jim Pettapiece, Bryan Wood

1970   Canada   Don Duguid, Rod Hunter, Jim Pettapiece, Bryan Wood

1969   Canada   Ron Northcott, Dave Gerlach, Bernie Sparks, Fred Storey

1968   Canada   Ron Northcott, Jimmy Shields, Bernie Sparks, Fred Storey

Scotch Cup Champions

1967   Scotland   Chuck Hay, John Bryden, Alan Glen, David Howie

1966   Canada   Ron Northcott, George Fink, Bernie Sparkes, Fred Storey

1965   U.S.A.   Bud Somerville, Bill Strum, Al Gagne, Tom Wright

1964   Canada   Lyall Dagg, Leo Hebert, Fred Britton, Barry Naimark

1963   Canada   Ernie Richardson, Arnold Richardson, Garnet Richardson, Mel Perry

1962   Canada   Ernie Richardson, Arnold Richardson, Garnet Richardson, Wes Richardson

195

1961	Canada	Hector Gervais, Ray Werner, Vic Raymer, Wally Ursuliak
1960	Canada	Ernie Richardson, Arnold Richardson, Garnet Richardson, Wes Richardson
1959	Canada	Ernie Richardson, Arnold Richardson, Garnet Richardson, Wes Richardson

World Champions (Ladies)

Ford World Women's Champions

1998	Sweden	Elisabet Gustafson, Katarina Nyberg, Louise Marmont, Elisabeth Perrson
1997	Canada	Sandra Schmirler, Jan Betker, Joan McCusker, Marcia Gudereit
1996	Canada	Marilyn Bodogh, Kim Gellard, Corie Beveridge, Jane Hooper-Perroud
1995	Sweden	Elizabet Gustafson, Katarina Nyberg, Louise Marmont, Elizabeth Persson
1994	Canada	Sandra Peterson, Jan Betker, Joan McCusker, Marcia Gudereit
1993	Canada	Sandra Peterson, Jan Betker, Joan McCusker, Marcia Gudereit
1992	Sweden	Elisabet Johanssen, Katarina Nyberg, Louise Marmont, Elisabeth Persson
1991	Norway	Dordi Nordby, Hanne Pettersen, Mette Halvorsen, Anne Jotun
1990	Norway	Dordi Nordby, Hanne Pettersen, Mette Halvorsen, Anne Jotun
1989	Canada	Heather Houston, Lorraine Lang, Diane Adams, Tracy Kennedy
1988	Germany	Andrea Schopp, Almut Scholl, Monika Wagner, Suzanne Fink
1987	Canada	Pat Sanders, Georgina Hawkes, Louise Herlinveaux, Deb Massullo
1986	Canada	Marilyn Darte, Kathy McEdwards, Chris Jurgenson, Jan Augustyn
1985	Canada	Linda Moore, Lindsay Sparkes, Debbie Jones, Laurie Carney
1984	Canada	Connie Laliberte, Chris More, Corinne Peters, Janet Arnott
1983	Switzerland	Erika Mueller, Barbara Meyer, Barbara Meier, Christina Wirz
1982	Denmark	Marianne Jorgenson, Helena Blach, Astrid Birnbaum, Jette Olsen
1981	Sweden	Elisabeth Hogstrom, Carina Olsson, Birgitta Sewick, Karin Sjogran

| 1980 | Canada | Marj Mitchell, Nancy Kerr, Shirley McKendry, Wendy Leach |
| 1979 | Switzerland | Gaby Casanova, Rosie Manger, Linda Thommen, Betty Bourguin |

World Champions (Junior Men's)

Karcher World Junior Men's Champions

1998	Canada	John Morris, Craig Saville, Andy Ormsby, Brent Laing
1997	Switzerland	Ralph Stockli, Michael Boesiger, Pascal Sieber, Clemens Oberwiler
1996	Scotland	James Dryburgh, Ross Barnet, Ronald Brewster, David Murdoch
1995	Scotland	Tom Brewster, Paul Westwood, Ronald Brewster, Steven Still
1994	Canada	Colin Davidson, Kelly Mittelstadt, Scott Pfeiffer, Sean Morris
1993	Scotland	Craig Wilson, Neil Murdoch, Ricky Burnett, Craig Strawhorn
1992	Switzerland	Stefan Heilmann,Christoph Grossenbacher Lucian Jenzer, Roger Wyss
1991	Scotland	Alan MacDougall, James Dryburgh, Fraser MacGregor, Colin Beckett
1990	Switzerland	Stefan Traub, Andreas Oestreich, Markus Widmer, Roland Muessler
1989	Sweden	Peter Lindholm, Magnus Swartling, Owe Ljundahl, Peter Narup
1988	Canada	Jim Sullivan, Charles Sullivan, Craig Burgess, Dan Alderman
1987	Scotland	Douglas Dryburgh, Philip Wilson, Lindsay Clark, Billy Andrew
1986	Scotland	David Aitken, Robin Halliday, Peter Smith, Harry Reilly
1985	Canada	Bob Ursel, Brent Mendella, Gerald Chick, Mike Ursel
1984	U.S.A.	Al Edwards, Mark Larson,Dewey Basley, Kurt Disher
1983	Canada	John Base, Bruce Webster, Dave McAnerney, Jim Donahoe
1982	Sweden	Soren Grahn, Niklas Jarund, Henrik Holmberg, Anders Svennerstedt
1981	Scotland	Peter Wilson, Jim Cannon, Roger McIntyre, John Parker
1980	Scotland	Andrew McQuistin, Norman Brown, Hugh Aitken, Dick Adams
1979	U.S.A.	Don Barcome, Randy Darling, Bobby Stalker, Earl Barcome
1978	Canada	Paul Gowsell, John Ferguson, Doug McFarlane, Kelly Stearne

1977	Canada	Bill Jenkins, John Scales, Sandy Stewart, Alan Mayhew
1976	Canada	Paul Gowsell, Neil Houston, Glen Jackson, Kelly Stearne
1975	Sweden	Jan Ullsten, Mats Nyberg, Ander Grahn, Bo Soderstrom

World Champions (Junior Ladies)

Karcher World Junior Women's Champions

1998	Canada	Melissa McClure, Nancy Toner, Brigitte McClure, Bethany Toner
1997	Scotland	Julia Ewart, Michele Sivera, Mhairi Ferguson, Lynn Cameron
1996	Canada	Heather Godberson, Carmen Whyte, Kristie Moore, Terelyn Bloor
1995	Canada	Kelly McKenzie, Joanne Fillion, Carlene Muth, Sasha Bergner
1994	Canada	Kim Gellard, Corie Beveridge, Lisa Savage, Sandy Graham
1993	Scotland	Kirsty Hay, Gillian Barr, Joanna Pegg, Louise Wilkie
1992	Scotland	Gillian Barr, Claire Milne, Janice Wait, Nikki Mauchline
1991	Sweden	Eva Eriksson, Marla Soderkvist, Asa Eriksson, Elisabeth Brito
1990	Scotland	Kirsty Addison, Karen Addison, Joanna Pegg, Laura Scott
1989	Canada	LaDawn Funk, Sandy Symyrozum, Cindy Larsen, Laurelle Funk
1988	Canada	Julie Sutton, Judy Wood, Susan Auty, Marla Geiger

Canadian Champions (Men's)

Labatt Brier Champions

1998	Ontario	Wayne Middaugh, Graeme McCarrell, Ian Tetley, Scott Bailey
1997	Alberta	Kevin Martin, Don Walchuk, Rudy Ramcharan, Don Bartlett
1996	Manitoba	Jeff Stoughton, Ken Tresoor, Garry Vanderberghe, Steve Gould
1995	Manitoba	Kerry Burtnyk, Jeff Ryan, Rob Meakin, Keith Fenton
1994	British Columbia	Rick Folk, Pat Ryan, Bert Gretzinger, Gerry Richard
1993	Ontario	Russ Howard, Glenn Howard, Wayne Middaugh, Peter Corner
1992	Manitoba	Vic Peters, Dan Carey, Chris Neufeld, Don Rudd
1991	Alberta	Kevin Martin, Kevin Park, Dan Petryk, Don Bartlett
1990	Ontario	Ed Werenich, John Kawaja, Ian Tetley, Pat Perroud

1989	Alberta	Pat Ryan, Randy Ferbey, Don Walchuk, Don McKenzie
1988	Alberta	Pat Ryan, Randy Ferbey, Don Walchuk, Don McKenzie
1987	Ontario	Russ Howard, Glenn Howard, Tim Belcourt, Kent Carstairs
1986	Alberta	Ed Lukowich, John Ferguson, Neil Houston, Brent Syme
1985	Northern Ontario	Al Hackner, Rick Lang, Ian Tetley, Pat Perroud
1984	Manitoba	Mike Riley, Brian Toews, John Helston, Russ Wookey
1983	Ontario	Ed Werenich, Paul Savage, John Kawaja, Neil Harrison
1982	Northern Ontario	Al Hackner, Rick Lang, Bob Nicol, Bruce Kennedy
1981	Manitoba	Kerry Burtynk, Mark Olson, Jim Spencer, Ron Kammerlock
1980	Saskatchewan	Rick Folk, Ron Mills, Tom Wilson, Jim Wilson

Macdonald Brier Champions

1979	Manitoba	Barry Fry, Bill Carey, Gord Sparkes, Bryan Wood
1978	Alberta	Ed Lukowich, Mike Chernoff, Dale Johnston, Ron Schindle
1977	Quebec	Jim Ursel, Art Lobel, Don Aitken, Brian Ross
1976	Newfoundland	Jack MacDuff, Toby McDonald, Doug Hudson, Ken Templeton
1975	Northern Ontario	Bill Tetley, Rick Lang, Bill Hodgson, Peter Hnatiw
1974	Alberta	Hec Gervais, Ron Anton, Warren Hansen, Darrel Sutton
1973	Saskatchewan	Harvey Mazinke, Bill Martin, George Achtymichuk, Dan Klippenstein
1972	Manitoba	Orest Meleschuk, Dave Romano, John Hanesiak, Pat Hailley
1971	Manitoba	Don Duguid, Rod Hunter, Jim Pettapiece, Bryan Wood
1970	Manitoba	Don Duguid, Rod Hunter, Jim Pettapiece, Bryan Wood
1969	Alberta	Ron Northcott, Dave Gerlach, Bernie Sparkes, Fred Storey
1968	Alberta	Ron Northcott, Jim Shields, Bernie Sparkes, Fred Storey
1967	Ontario	Alf Phillips Jr., John Ross, Ron Manning, Keith Reilly
1966	Alberta	Ron Northcott, George Fink, Bernie Sparkes, Fred Storey
1965	Manitoba	Terry Braunstein, Don Duguid, Ron Braunstein, Ray Turnbull

1964	British Columbia	Lyall Dagg, Leo Hebert, Fred Britton, Barry Naimark
1963	Saskatchewan	Ernie Richardson, Arnold Richardson, Garnet Richardson, Mel Perry
1962	Saskatchewan	Ernie Richardson, Arnold Richardson, Garnet Richardson, Wes Richardson
1961	Alberta	Hec Gervais, Ron Anton, Ray Werner, Wally Ursuliak
1960	Saskatchewan	Ernie Richardson, Arnold Richardson, Garnet Richardson, Wes Richardson
1959	Saskatchewan	Ernie Richardson, Arnold Richardson, Garnet Richardson, Wes Richardson
1958	Alberta	Matt Baldwin, Jack Geddes, Gordon Haynes, Bill Price
1957	Alberta	Matt Baldwin, Gordon Haynes, Art Kleinmeyer, Bill Price
1956	Manitoba	Billy Walsh, Al Langlois, Cy White, Andy McWilliams
1955	Saskatchewan	Garnet Campbell, Don Campbell, Glen Campbell, Lloyd Campbell
1954	Alberta	Matt Baldwin, Glen Gray, Pete Ferry, Jim Collins
1953	Manitoba	Ab Gowanlock, Jim Williams, Art Pollon, Russ Jackman
1952	Manitoba	Billy Walsh, Al Langlois, Andy McWilliams, John Watson
1951	Nova Scotia	Don Oyler, George Hanson, Fred Dyke, Wally Knock
1950	Northern Ontario	Tom Ramsay, Len Williamson, Bill Weston, Bill Kenny
1949	Manitoba	Ken Watson, Grant Watson, Lyle Dyker, Charles Read
1948	British Columbia	Frenchy D'Amour, Bob McGhie, Fred Wendell, Jim Mark
1947	Manitoba	Jimmy Welsh, Alex Welsh, Jack Reid, Harry Monk
1946	Alberta	Bill Rose, Bart Swelin, Austin Smith, George Crooks

Championships not played from 1943 to 1945.

1942	Manitoba	Ken Watson, Grant Watson, Charlie Scrymgeour, Jim Grant
1941	Alberta	Howard Palmer, Jack LeBeau, Art Gooder, Clare Webb
1940	Manitoba	Howard Wood, Ernie Pollard, Howard Wood Jr., Roy Enman
1939	Ontario	Bert Hall, Perry Hall, Ernie Parkes, Cam Seagram

1938	Manitoba	Ab Gowanlock, Bung Cartmell, Bill McKnight, Tom McKnight
1937	Alberta	Cliff Manahan, Wes Robinson, Ross Manahan, Lloyd McIntyre
1936	Manitoba	Ken Watson, Grant Watson, Marvin McIntyre, Charles Kerr
1935	Ontario	Gordon Campbell, Don Campbell, Gord Coates, Duncan Campbell
1934	Manitoba	Leo Johnson, Lorne Stewart, Linc Johnson, Marno Frederickson
1933	Alberta	Cliff Manahan, Harold Deeton, Harold Wolfe, Bert Ross
1932	Manitoba	Jimmy Congalton, Howard Wood, Bill Noble, Harry Mawhinney
1931	Manitoba	Bob Gourlay, Ernie Pollard, Arnold Lockerbie, Ray Stewart
1930	Manitoba	Howard Wood, Jimmy Congalton, Victor Wood, Lionel Wood
1929	Manitoba	Gordon Hudson, Don Rollo, Ron Singbusch, Bill Grant
1928	Manitoba	Gordon Hudson, Sam Penwarden, Ron Singbusch, Bill Grant
1927	Nova Scotia	Murray Macneill, Al MacInnes, Cliff Torey, Jim Donahoe

Canadian Champions (Ladies)

Scott Tournament of Hearts Champions

1998	Alberta	Cathy Borst, Heather Godberson, Brenda Bohmer, Kate Horne
1997	Saskatchewan	Sandra Schmirler, Jan Betker, Joan McCusker, Marcia Gudereit
1996	Ontario	Marilyn Bodogh, Kim Gellard, Corie Beveridge, Jane Hooper Perroud
1995	Manitoba	Connie Laliberte, Cathy Overton, Cathy Gauthier, Janet Arnott
1994	Team Canada	Sandra Peterson, Jan Betker, Joan McCusker, Marcia Gudereit
1993	Saskatchewan	Sandra Peterson, Jan Betker, Joan McCusker, Marcia Gudereit
1992	Manitoba	Connie Laliberte, Laurie Allen, Cathy Gauthier, Janet Arnott
1991	British Columbia	Julie Sutton, Jodie Sutton, Melissa Soligo, Karri Willms
1990	Ontario	Alison Goring, Kristin Turcotte, Andrea Lawes, Cheryl McPherson

201

1989	Team Canada	Heather Houston, Lorraine Lang, Diane Adams, Tracy Kennedy
1988	Ontario	Heather Houston, Lorraine Lang, Diane Adams, Tracy Kennedy
1987	British Columbia	Pat Sanders, Georgina Hawkes, Louise Herlinveaux, Deb Massullo
1986	Ontario	Marilyn Darte, Kathy McEdwards, Chris Jurgenson, Jan Augustyn
1985	British Columbia	Linda Moore, Lindsay Sparkes, Debbie Jones, Laurie Carney
1984	Manitoba	Connie Laliberte, Chris More, Corinne Peters, Janet Arnott
1983	Nova Scotia	Penny LaRocque, Sharon Horne, Cathy Caudle, Pam Sanford
1982	Nova Scotia	Colleen Jones, Kay Smith, Monica Jones, Barbara Jones-Gordon

Canadian Ladies Curling Association Champions

| 1981 | Alberta | Susan Seitz, Judy Erickson, Myrna McKay, Betty McCracken |
| 1980 | Saskatchewan | Marj Mitchell, Nancy Kerr, Shirley McKendry, Wendy Leach |

Macdonald Lassie Champions

1979	British Columbia	Lindsay Sparkes, Dawn Knowles, Robin Wilson, Lorraine Bowles
1978	Manitoba	Cathy Pidzarko, Chris Pidzarko, Iris Armstrong, Patti Vanderkerckhove
1977	Alberta	Myrna McQuarrie, Rita Tarnava, Barb Davis, Jane Rempel
1976	British Columbia	Lindsay Davie, Dawn Knowles, Robin Klassen, Lorraine Bowles
1975	Quebec	Lee Tobin, Marilyn McNeil, Michelle Garneau, Laurie Ross
1974	Saskatchewan	Emily Farnham, Linda Saunders, Pat McBeath, Donna Collins
1973	Saskatchewan	Vera Pezer, Sheila Rowan, Joyce McKee, Lenore Morrison
1972	Saskatchewan	Vera Pezer, Sheila Rowan, Joyce McKee, Lenore Morrison

Canadian Ladies Curling Association Champions

| 1971 | Saskatchewan | Vera Pezer, Sheila Rowan, Joyce McKee, Lenore Morrison |

1970	Saskatchewan	Dorenda Schoenhals, Cheryl Stirton, Linda Burnham, Joan Anderson
1969	Saskatchewan	Joyce McKee, Vera Pezer, Lenore Morrison, Jennifer Falk
1968	Alberta	Hazel Jamieson, Gail Lee, Jackie Spencer, June Coyle

Diamond "D" Champions

1967	Manitoba	Betty Duguid, Joan Ingram, Laurie Bradawaski, Dot Rose
1966	Alberta	Gail Lee, Hazel Jamieson, Sharon Harrington, June Coyle
1965	Manitoba	Peggy Casselman, Val Taylor, Pat MacDonald, Pat Scott
1964	British Columbia	Ina Hansen, Ada Calles, Isabel Leith, May Shaw
1963	New Brunswick	Mabel DeWare, Harriet Strattan, Forbis Stevenson, Marjorie Fraser
1962	British Columbia	Ina Hansen, Ada Callas, Isabel Leith, May Shaw
1961	Saskatchewan	Joyce McKee, Sylvia Fedoruk, Barbara MacNevin, Rosa McFee

Canadian Champions (Junior Men's)

Maple Leaf Junior Men's Champions

1998	Ontario	John Morris, Craig Savill, Andy Ormsby, Brent Laing
1997	Alberta	Ryan Keane, Scott Pfeifer, Blayne Iskiw, Peter Heck
1996	Northern Ontario	Jeff Currie, Greg Given, Andrew Mikkelsen, Tyler Oinonen

Canadian Junior Men's Champions

| 1995 | Manitoba | Chris Galbraith, Scott Cripps, Brent Barrett, Bryan Galbraith |

Pepsi Junior Men's Champions

1994	Alberta	Colin Davison, Kelly Mittelstadt, Scott Pfeifer, Sean Morris
1993	Nova Scotia	Shawn Adams, Ben Blanchard, Joh Philip, Robert MacArthur
1992	Quebec	Michel Ferland, Marco Berthelot, Steve Beaudry, Steve Guetre
1991	Northern Ontario	Jason Repay, Aaron Skillen, Scott McCallum, Trevor Clifford

1990	Ontario	Noel Herron, Robert Brewer, Steve Small, Richard Polk
1989	British Columbia	Dean Joanisse, David Nantes, Tim Coomes, Jef Pilon
1988	British Columbia	Mike Wood, Mike Bradley, Todd Troyer, Greg Hawkes
1987	New Brunswick	Jim Sullivan, Charlie Sullivan, Craig Burgess, Dan Alderman
1986	Manitoba	Hugh McFadyen, Jon Mead, Normal Gould, John Lange
1985	Alberta	Kevin Martin, Richard Feeney, Daniel Petryk, Michael Berger
1984	Manitoba	Bob Ursel, Brent Mendella, Gerald Chick, Mike Ursel
1983	Saskatchewan	Jamie Schneider, Danny Ferner, Steven Leippi, Kelly Vollman
1982	Ontario	John Base, Bruce Webster, Dave McAnerney, Jim Donahoe
1981	Manitoba	Mert Thompsett, Bill McTavish, Joel Gagne, Mike Friesen
1980	Quebec	Denis Marchand, Denis Cecil, Yves Barrette, Larry Phillips
1979	Manitoba	Mert Thompsett, Lyle Derry, Joel Gagne, Mike Friesen
1978	Alberta	Darren Fish, Lorne Barker, Murray Ursulak, Barry Barker
1977	Alberta	Paul Gowsell, John Ferguson, Doug MacFarlane, Kelly Stearne
1976	Prince Edward Island	Bill Jenkins, John Scales, Sandy Stewart, Alan Mayhew

Pepsi Schoolboy Champions

1975	Alberta	Paul Gowsell, Neil Houston, Glen Jackson, Kelly Stearne
1974	Alberta	Rob King, Brad Hannah, Bill Fowlis, Chris King
1973	Ontario	Mark McDonald, Lloyd Emmerson, Phillip Tomsett, Jon Clare
1972	Alberta	Lawrence Niven, Rick Niven, Jim Ross, Ted Poblawski
1971	Saskatchewan	Greg Montgomery, Don Despins, Jeff Montgomery, Rod Verboom
1970	New Brunswick	Ronald Ferguson, Garth Jardine, Brian Henderson, Cyril Sutherland
1969	Saskatchewan	Robert Miller, Roger Rask, Lloyd Helm, William Aug
1968	Ontario	William Hope, Bruce Lord, Brian Domney, Dennis Gardiner
1967	Alberta	Stanley Trout, Doug Dobry, Allan Kullay, Donald Douglas

1966	Alberta	Brian Howes, Blair Pallesen, John Thompson, Chris Robinson
1965	Saskatchewan	Dan Fink, Ken Runtz, Ron Jacques, Larry Lechner
1964	Northern Ontario	Bob Ash, Bill Ash, Gerry Armstrong, Fred Prier
1963	Alberta	Wayne Saboe, Ron Hampton, Rick Aldridge, Mick Adams
1962	Saskatchewan	Mike Lukowich, Ed Lukowich, Doug McLeod, David Moore
1961	British Columbia	Jerry Caughlin, Jack Cox, Mike Shippitt, David Jones
1960	Alberta	Tommy Kroeger, Jack Isaman, Ron Nelson, Murray Sorenson
1959	Alberta	John Trout, Bruce Walker, Dave Woods, Allen Sharpe
1958	Northern Ontario	Tom Tod, Neil McLeod, Patrick Moran, David Allin

Victor Sifton Trophy Champions

1957	Ontario	Ian Johnson, Peter Galsworthy, Dave Robinson, Mike Jackson
1956	Saskatchewan	Bob Hawkins, Ted Clarke, Bruce Beveridge, Dave Williams
1955	Saskatchewan	Bayne Secord, Stan Austman, Merv Mann, Gary Stevenson
1954	Saskatchewan	Bayne Secord, Don Snider, Stan Austman, Don Brownell
1953	Ontario	Bob Walker, Duncan Brodie, Claire Peocock, George MacGregor
1952	Saskatchewan	Gary Thode, Gary Cooper, Doug Conn, Roy Hufsmith
1951	Saskatchewan	Gary Thode, Gary Cooper, Orest Hyrniuk, Roy Hufsmith
1950	Saskatchewan	Bill Clark, Gary Carlson, Ian Innes, Harold Grassie

Canadian Champions (Junior Women's)

Maple Leaf Junior Women's Champions

1998	New Brunswick	Melissa McClure, Nancy Toner, Brigitte McClure, Bethany Toner
1997	Nova Scotia	Meredith Doyle, Beth Roach, Tara Hamer, Candice MacLean
1996	Alberta	Heather Godberson, Carmen Whyte, Kristie Moore, Terelyn Bloor

Canadian Junior Women's Champions

| 1995 | Manitoba | Kelly MacKenzie, Joanne Fillion, Carlene Muth, Sasha Bergner |

Pepsi Junior Women's Champions

1994	Manitoba	Jennifer Jones, Trisha Baldwin, Jill Officer, Dana Malanchuk
1993	Ontario	Kim Gellard, Corie Beveridge, Lisa Savage, Sandy Graham
1992	Saskatchewan	Amber Holland, Cindy Street, Tracy Beach, Angela Street
1991	New Brunswick	Heather Smith, Denis Cormier, Suzanne LeBlanc, Lesley Hicks
1990	Saskatchewan	Atina Ford, Darlene Kidd, Leslie Beck, Cindy Ford
1989	Manitoba	Cathy Overton, Tracy Baldwin, Carol Harvey, Tracy Bush
1988	Alberta	LeDawn Funk, Sandy Symyrozum, Cindy Larsen, Laurelle Funk
1987	British Columbia	Julie Sutton, Judy Wood, Susan Auty, Marla Geiger
1986	British Columbia	Jodie Sutton, Julie Sutton, Dawn Rubner, Chris Thompson
1985	Saskatchewan	Kimberley Armbruster, Sheila Calcutt, Wanda Figitt, Lorraine Krupski
1984	Manitoba	Darcy Kirkness, Barb Kirkness, Janet Harvey, Barbara Fetch
1983	Ontario	Alison Goring, Kristin Holman, Cheryl McPherson, Lynda Armstrong
1982	British Columbia	Sandra Plut, Sandra Rainey, Leigh Fraser, Debra Fowles
1981	Manitoba	Karen Fallis, Karen Tresoor, Caroline Hunter, Lynn Fallis
1980	Nova Scotia	Kay Smith, Krista Gatchell, Cathy Caudle, Peggy Wilson

Canadian Girls Champions

1979	Saskatchewan	Denise Wilson, July Walker, Dianne Choquette, Shannon Olafson
1978	Alberta	Cathy King, Brenda Oko, Maureen Olsen, Diane Bowes
1977	Alberta	Cathy King, Robin Ursuliak, Maureen Olsen, Mary Kay James
1976	Saskatchewan	Colleen Rudd, Carol Rudd, Julie Burke, Lori Glenn

1975	Saskatchewan	Patricia Crimp, Colleen Rudd, Judy Sefton, Merrill Greabeiel
1974	Manitoba	Chris Pidzarko, Cathy Pidzarko, Patti Vanderkerckhove, Barbara Rudolph
1973	Saskatchewan	Janet Crimp, Carol Davis, Chris Gervais, Susan Carney
1972	Manitoba	Chris Pidzarko, Cathy Pidzarko, Beth Brunsden, Barbara Rudolph
1971	Alberta	Shelby McKenzie, Marlene Pargeter, Arlene Hrdlicka, Debbie Goliss

United States

National Champions (Men's)

1998	Stevens Point, WI	Paul Pustovar, Dave Violette, Greg Wilson, Cory Ward
1997	Langdon, ND	Craig Disher, Kevin Kakela, Joel Jacobson, Paul Peterson
1996	Superior, WI	Tim Somerville, Mike Schneeberger, Myles Brundidge, John Gordon
1995	Superior, WI	Tim Somerville, Mike Schneeberger, Myles Brundidge, John Gordon
1994	Bemidji, MN	Scott Baird, Pete Fenson, Mark Haluptzok, Tim Johnson
1993	Bemidji, MN	Scott Baird, Pete Fenson, Mark Haluptzok, Tim Johnson
1992	Seattle, WA	Doug Jones, Jason Larway, Joel Larway, Tom Violette
1991	Madison, WI	Steve Brown, Paul Pustovar, George Godfrey, Wally Henry and Mike Fraboni
1990	Seattle, WA	Bard Nordlund, Doug Jones, Murphy Tomlinson, Tom Violette
1989	Seattle, WA	Jim Vukich, Curt Fish, Bard Nordlund & Jason Lanway, James Pleasants
1988	Seattle, WA	Doug Jones, Bard Nordlund, Murphy Tomlinson, Mike Grennan
1987	Seattle, WA	Jim Vukich, Ron Sharpe, George Pepelnjak, Gary Joraanstad
1986	Madison, WI	Steve Brown, Wally Henry, George Godfrey, Richard Maskel
1985	Wilmette, IL	Tim Wright, John Jahant, Jim Wilson, Russ Armstrong
1984	Hibbing, MN	Joe Roberts, Bruce Roberts, Gary Kleffman, Jerry Scott

1983	Colo. Springs, CO	Don Cooper, Jerry Van Brunt, Jr., Bill Shipstad, Jack McNelly
1982	Madison, WI	Steve Brown, Ed Sheffield, Huns Gustrowsky, George Godfrey
1981	Superior, WI	Bob Nichols, Bud Somerville, Bob Christman, Robert Buchanan
1980	Hibbing, MN	Paul Pustover, John Jankila, Gary Kleffman, Jerry Scott
1979	Bemidji, MN	Scott Baird, Dan Haluptzok, Mark Haluptzok, Bob Fenson
1978	Superior, WI	Bob Nichols, Bill Strum, Tom Locken, Bob Christman
1977	Hibbing, MN	Bruce Roberts, Paul Pustovar, Gary Kleffman, Jerry Scott
1976	Hibbing, MN	Bruce Roberts, Joe Roberts, Gary Kleffman, Jerry Scott
1975	Seattle, WA	Ed Risling, Charles Lundgren, Gary Schnee, Dave Tellvik
1974	Superior, WI	Bud Somerville, Bob Nichols, Bill Strum, Tom Locken
1973	Winchester, MA	Charles Reeves, Doug Carlson, Henry Shean, Barry Blanchard
1972	Grafton, ND	Robert Labonte, Frank Aasand, John Aasand, Ray Morgan
1971	Edmore, ND	Dale Dalziel, Dennis Melland, Clark Sampson, Rodney Melland
1970	Grafton, ND	Art Tallackson, Glenn Gilleshammer, Ray Holt, Trueman Thompson
1969	Superior, WI	Bud Somerville, Bill Strum, Franklin Bradshaw, Gene Oveson
1968	Superior, WI	Bud Somerville, Bill Strum, Al Gagne, Tom Wright
1967	Seattle,WA	Bruce Roberts, Tom Fitzpatrick, John Wright, Doug Walker
1966	Fargo, ND	Bruce Roberts, Joe Zbacnik, Gerry Toutant, Mike O'Leary
1965	Superior, WI	Bud Somerville, Bill Strum, Al Gagne, Tom Wright
1964	Duluth, MN	Robert Magie, Jr., Bert Payne, Russell Barber, Britton Payne
1963	Detroit, MI	Mike Slyziuk, Nelson Brown, Ernest Slyziuk, Walter Hubchik
1962	Hibbing, MN	Dick Brown, Terry Kleffman, Fran Kleffman, Nick Jerulle
1961	Seattle, WA	Frank Crealock, Ken Sherwood, John Jamieson, Bud McCartney
1960	Grafton, ND	Orvil Gilleshammer, Glenn Gilleshammer, Wilmer Collette, Donald Labonte
1959	Hibbing, MN	Dick Brown, Terry Kleffman, Fran Kleffman, Nick Jerulle

| 1958 | Detroit, MI | Mike Slyziuk, Douglas Fisk, Ernest Slyziuk, Merritt Knowlson |
| 1957 | Hibbing, MN | Harold Lauber, Louis Lauber, Peter Beasy, Matt Berklich |

National Champions (Women's)

1998	Wilmette, IL	Kari Erickson, Lori Kreklau, Stacey Liapis, Ann Swisshelm
1997	Arlington, WI	Patti Lank, Analissa Johnson, Joni Cotten, Tracy Sachtjen
1996	Madison, WI	Lisa Schoeneberg, Erika Brown, Lori Mountford, Allison Darragh and Debby Henry
1995	Madison, WI	Lisa Schoeneberg, Erika Brown, Lori Mountford, Marcia Tillisch and Allison Darragh
1994	Denver, CO	Bev Behnke, Dawna Bennett, Susan Anscheutz, Pam Finch
1993	Denver, CO	Bev Behnke, Dawna Bennett, Susan Anschuetz, Pam Finch
1992	Madison, WI	Lisa Schoeneberg, Amy Wright, Lori Mountford, Jill Jones
1991	Houston, TX	Maymar Gemmell, Judy Johnston, Janet Hunter, Brenda Jancic
1990	Denver, CO	Bev Behnke, Dawna Bennett, Susan Anschuetz, Pam Finch
1989	Rolla, ND	Jan Lagasse, Janie Kakela, Cooky Bertsch, Eileen Mickelson
1988	Seattle, WA	Nancy Langley, Nancy Pearson, Leslie Frosch, Mary Hobson
1987	Seattle, WA	Sharon Good, Joan Fish, Beth Bronger-Jones, Aija Edwards
1986	St. Paul, MN	Gerry Tilden, Linda Barneson, Barb Polski, Barb Gutzmer
1985	Fairbanks, AK	Bev Birklid, Peggy Martin, Jerry Evans, Katrina Sharp
1984	Duluth, MN	Amy Hatten, Terry Leksell, Karen Leksell, Kelly Sieger
1983	Seattle, WA	Nancy Langley, Dolores Campbell, Nancy Wallace, Leslie Frosch
1982	Oak Park, IL	Ruth Schwenker, Stephanie Flynn, Donna Purkey, Kathleen Wilson
1981	Seattle, WA	Nancy Langley, Carol Dahl, Leslie Frosch, Nancy P. Wallace
1980	Seattle, WA	Sharon Kozai, Joan Fish, Betty Kozai, Aija Edwards
1979	Seattle, WA	Nancy Langley, Dolores Wallace, Leslie Frosch, Nancy Wallace
1978	Wausau, WI	Sandy Robarge, Elaine Collins, Jo Shannon, Virginia Morrison

| 1977 | Hastings, NY | Margaret Smith, Cynthia Smith, Jackie Grant, Eve Switzer |

National Champions (Junior Men's)

1998	Omaha, NE	Andy Rosa, Steve Jaixen, Kevin Jordan, Chris Becher
1997	Bemidji, MN	Matt Stevens, Craig Brown, Bob Liapis, Jeremy Fogelson
1996	Seattle, WA	Travis Way, Troy Schroeder, Owen Bunstein, Brandon Way
1995	Centerville, WI	Mike Peplinski, Craig Brown, Ryan Braudt, Cory Ward
1994	Centerville, WI	Mike Peplinski, Craig Brown, Ryan Braudt, Cory Ward
1993	Hibbing, MN	Garrett Paine, Kevin Kosel, Danny Hadrava, Joel Koski
1992	Bemidji, MN	Eric Fenson, Shawn Rojeski, Kevin Bergstrom, Ted McCann
1991	Bemidji, MN	Eric Fenson, Shawn Rojeski, Kevin Bergstrom, Ted McCann
1990	Poynette, WI	Kurt Marquardt, Jeff Falk, Dan Thurston, Mike Thurston
1989	Poynette, WI	Kurt Marquardt, Jeff Falk, Dan Thurston, Mike Thurston
1988	Poynette, WI	Will Marquardt, Jim Falk, Jeff Falk, Kurt Marquardt
1987	Grafton, ND	Darren Kress, Bret Davis, Duane McGregor, Connor Oihus
1986	Cavalier, ND	Scott Brown, Darin Holt, Perry Hillman, Darren Kress
1985	Seattle, WA	Rodger Schnee, Kelly Yalowicki, Shane Way, Mark Lundgren
1984	Rolla, ND	Al Edwards, Mark Larson, Dewey Basley, Kurt Discher
1983	Rolla, ND	Al Edwards, Mark Larson, Kenny Mickelson, Dana Westemeier
1982	Seattle, WA	Dale Risling, Milt Best, Rob Foster, Jim Foster
1981	Seattle, WA	Ted Purvis, Dale Risling, Milt Best, Dean Risling
1980	Devils Lake, ND	Scott Dalziel, Todd Dalziel, Scott Gerrard, Paul Thompson
1979	Grand Forks, ND	Don Barcome, Randy Darling, Bobby Stalker, Earl Barcome
1978	Seattle, WA	Jeff Tomlinson, Tom Purvis, Curt Fish, Marc McCartney
1977	Grand Forks, ND	Don Barcome, Dale Mueller, Gary Mueller, Earl Barcome
1976	Grand Forks, ND	Don Barcome, Dale Mueller, Earl Barcome, Gary Mueller
1975	Hibbing, MN	Steve Penecello, Rick Novak, Ben Gareski, Ken Baehr

| 1974 | Hibbing, MN | Gary Kleffman, Jerry Scott, Rick Novak, Ben Gardeski |

National Champions (Junior Women's)

1998	Bemidji, MN	Hope Schmitt, Nikki Baird, Katie Schmitt, Teresa Bahr
1997	Bemidji, MN	Risa O'Connell, Amy Becher, Natalie Simenson, Missi O'Connell
1996	Omaha, NE	Amy Becher, Theresa Faltesek, Monica Carlson, Heather Miller
1995	Bemidji, MN	Risa O'Connell, Missi O'Connell, Natalie Simenson, Alison Naylor
1994	Madison, WI	Erika Brown, Debby Henry, Stacey Liapis and Allison Darragh, Analissa Johnson
1993	Bemidji, MN	Erika Brown, Kari Liapis Erickson, Stacey Liapis, Debbie Henry
1992	Bemidji, MN	Erika Brown, Kari Liapis, Stacey Liapis, Bobbie Breyen and Debbie Henry
1991	Madison, WI	Erika Brown, Jill Jones, Shellie Holerud, Debbie Henry
1990	Bemidji, MN	Kari Liapis, Staci Liapis, Heidi Rollheiser, Bobbie Breyen
1989	Lodi, WI	Erika Brown, Tracy Zeman, Shellie Holerud, Jill Jones
1988	Lodi, WI	Tracy Zeman, Erika Brown, Marni Vaningan, Shellie Holerud
1987	Lodi, WI	Tracy Zeman, Pam Goetz, Shellie Holerud, Lori Meyers

Canadian Curling Hall of Fame (Men)

Aitken, Donald J.	1979	
Allan, J.W.	1974	Inaugural provincial association president
Anderson, Dr. A.F.	1976	CCA past president, 1940–41
Angus, A.F.	1974	Inaugural provincial association president
Anton, Ronald M.	1975	Two-time Brier winner
Argue, Horace F.	1974	Inaugural provincial association president
Armstrong, James E.	1976	CCA past president, 1946–47
Armstrong, Dr. James	1990	
Auger, Henri	1974	Inaugural provincial association president
Avery, Francis (Frank)	1974	

Balderston, Norman	1988	
Baldwin, Matthew M.	1973	Three-time Brier-winning skip
Belcourt, Timothy	1991	
Bennett, Hon. Gordon L.	1976	CCA past president, 1966–67
Boreham, H. Bruce	1975	
Bourne, Earl E.G.	1976	CCA past president 1961–62
Boyd, Earl	1974	Inaugural provincial association president
Boyd, H.E.	1974	Inaugural provincial association president
Boyd, Ralph S.	1989	CCA past president, 1985–86
Boyd, W. Cecil	1976	CCA past president, 1954–55
Buxton, Noel R.	1987	
Cameron, Douglas A.	1974	Seven-time Brier competitor
Cameron, George J.	1973	
Cameron, R.W. (Bert)	1975	
Campbell, Hon. Brig. Colin A.	1973	CCA past president, 1947–48
Campbell, Glen M.	1974	Six-time Brier competitor
Campbell, Gordon	1975	
Campbell, Dr. Maurice	1976	CCA past president, 1970–71
Campbell, Hon. Thane A.	1974	CCA past president, 1941–42
Campbell, W. Garnet	1974	Ten-time Brier competitor
Carstairs, Kent	1991	
Carter, Harry P.	1976	CCA past president, 1968–69
Congalton, James	1975	Two-time Brier winner
Cowan, Walter B.	1976	CCA past president, 1959–60
Cream, Robert C.	1976	
Culliton, Hon. Edward M.	1974	
Currie, D. William	1976	CCA past president, 1973–74
Deacon, Keith	1974	Inaugural provincial association president

Delmage, Al. R.	1991	
Dillon, George V.	1974	Eight-time Brier competitor
Dillon, Robert F.	1974	Seven-time Brier competitor
Donahoe, James E.	1973	First Brier winner
Donahue, Hon Sen. Richard A.	1976	CCA past president, 1955–56
Duguid, Donald G.	1974	Three-time Brier winner
Dutton, John	1976	CCA past president, 1956–57
England, J. Irl	1976	CCA past president, 1972–73
Ferbey, Randy	1993 1995	Two-time Brier winner
Ferguson, John	1992	
Fisher, Thomas R.	1986	CCA past president, 1981–82
Folk, Richard D. (Rick)	1985	
Fortier, H.C. (Rene)	1974	
Fox, Gordon	1994	
Gatchell, William	1995	
Geary, Reginald H.	1979	
Gervais, Hector J.	1975	Two-time Brier winner
Good, William (Sr.)	1992	
Gooder, Edwin	1982	
Gow, Hon. Peter	1974	Inaugural provincial association president
Gowanlock, Albert (Ab)	1975	Two-time Brier winner
Grant, William A.	1975	Two-time Brier winner
Gray, Maj. Thomas	1977	
Gunn, John	1987	
Gunnlaugson, Lloyd H.	1989	
Gurowka, Joseph A.	1989 1993	CCA past president 1988–89
Hackner, Allan A.	1988 1992	Two-time Brier winner
Haig, Hon. Sen. John T.	1973	

Hall, Perry G.	1974	Six-time Brier competitor
Harper, Geo. M. (Scotty)	1974	
Harrison, Neil	1991	
Harstone, Ross, G.L.	1974	
Haynes, J. Gordon	1975	Two-time Brier winner
Heartwell, Robert J.	1990	
Hobbs, Walter	1977	
Houston, Neil	1992	
Howard, Glenn	1991	
Howard, Russell	1991	
Hudson, Gordon M.	1974	Two-time Brier winner; CCA past president, 1949–50
Hunter Roderick G.M.	1974	Two-time Brier winner
Jackson, Niven M.	1976	CCA past president, 1951–52
Kawaja, John	1991	
Kennedy, Bruce	1988	
Keys, John E.	1979	
Kingsmith, Raymond A.	1986 1994	CCA past president, 1983–84
Lamb, Arthur N.	1979	
Lang, Richard P. (Rick)	1988 1992	Three-time Brier winner
Langlois, Allan D.	1975	Two-time Brier winer
Leaman, William	1977	CCA past president, 1975–76
Lewis, Donald E.	1989	
Lobel, Arthur L.	1979	
Low, William	1974	Inaugural provincial association president
Lucas, Frederick J.	1974	
Lukowich, Edward	1992	
Lumsden, William E.	1976	CCA past president, 1967–68
Lyall, Lt. Col. Peter D.L.	1973	
Mabey, Harold L. (Sr.)	1975	

Macdonald, Dr. Wendell L.	1975 1977	
MacGowan, Alan N	1976	CCA past president, 1960–61
MacInnes, J. Alfred	1973	First Brier winner
MacKay, Elbridge	1976	CCA past president, 1938–39
MacKay, William J.	1975	
MacKenzie, Donald	1993	
MacKinnon, Daniel D.	1974	Inaugural provincial association president
MacLeod, Donald R.	1990	CCA past president, 1990
Macneill, Murray	1973	First Brier winner
Magrath, W.J.	1974	Inaugural provincial association president
Malcolm, John S.	1974	
Manahan, Clifford R.	1975	Two-time Brier winner
Mather, J.B.	1974	Inaugural provincial association president
Maxwell, Douglas D.	1996	
Mazinke, Harvey G.	1989	CCA past president, 1987–88
McArthur, J.B.	1974	Inaugural provincial association president
McEwen, Cameron	1977	
McGibney, Doug (Buzz)	1978	
McGrath, Larry	1987	
McGraw, Thomas	1977	
McNeice, Burd S.	1979	
McWilliams, Andrew	1975	Two-time Brier winner
Millham, Herbert C.	1986 1992	CCA past president, 1977–78
Mills, Ronald A.	1985	
Mitton, Lorne	1995	CCA past president, 1994–95
Moss, John	1993	
Murchison, Clifford A.L.	1981	
Muzika, Jerry J.	1988	CCA past president, 1986–87
Ness, R. Bruce	1975	

215

Nicol, Robert B.	1988	
Norgan, George W. (Bill)	1976	CCA past president, 1942–46
Northcott, Ronald C.	1973	Three-time Brier-winning skip
O'Brien, Frank	1979	
Oleson, Stanley	1992	CCA past president, 1992–93
Olson, L.E. (Bud)	1976	CCA past president, 1974–75
Opaleychuk, Dr. Clyde R.	1986	CCA past president, 1984–85
Parish, A. William	1974	
Parkhill, Albert J.	1976	CCA past president, 1969–70
Pattee, James G. (Ted)	1975	CCA past president, 1962–63
Perroud, Patrick	1995	Two-time Brier winner
Perry, Capt. Charles	1977	
Pettapiece, James K.	1974	Two-time Brier winner
Pickering, Robert H.	1974	
Piercey, William F.	1975	
Pollard, Ernest	1975	Two-time Brier winner
Rankine, H. Fielding	1976	CCA past president, 1952–53
Rennie, Thomas H.	1973	
Richardson, Arnold W.	1973	Four-time Brier winner
Richardson, Carleton S.	1974	
Richardson, Ernest M.	1973	Four-time Brier winner
Richardson, Garnet S. (Sam)	1973	Four-time Brier winner
Richardson, Wesley H.	1973	Three-time Brier winner
Rockwell, Norman P.	1978	
Rothchild, Samuel	1975	CCA past president, 1957–58
Ryan, Patrick	1993	
	1994	Three-time Brier winner
Samson, Olivier	1978	
Sargent, Frank F.	1974	Inaugural provincial association president; CCA past president, 1965–66

Savage, A. Paul	1988	
Sinclair, John A.	1974	Inaugural provincial association president
Singbusch, Ronald	1975	Two-time Brier winner
Skinner, F. Arthur	1976	CCA past president, 1964–65
Smart, James	1974	Inaugural provincial association president
Smith, David C.	1978	CCA past president, 1976–77
Smith, Sir Donald	1973	
Smith, Emmett M.	1974	Inaugural provincial association president; CCA past president, 1953–54
Sparkes, Bernard L.	1974	Three-time Brier winner
Squarebriggs, John D.	1978	
Steeves, Dr. Edward	1991	Executive Honor Roll (CCA past president, 1989–91
Stent, Frank M.	1986	CCA past president, 1979–80
Stephenson, A.E.	1974	Inaugural provincial association president
Stewart, David Macdonald	1974	
Stewart, T. Howard	1973	
Stewart, Walter M.	1973	
Stone, Reginald E.	1974	
Stone, Roy H.	1974	
Storey, Frederick L.	1973	Three-time Brier winner
Syme, Brent	1992	
Tarlton, A.Ross	1982	
Thibodeau, Nicholas J.	1975	
Thompson, G. Clifton	1986	CCA past president, 1978–79
Thompson, T. Gordon	1976	CCA past president 1971–72
Topping, Richard T.	1976	CCA past president 1963–64
Torey, Clifford L.	1973	First Brier winner
Tracy, William R.	1982	
Travers, Thomas	1974	Inaugural provincial association president
Trites, Evan A.	1985	

Turnbull, Raymond	1993	
Tyre, James	1974	Inaugural provincial association president
Ursel, James W.	1979	
Walchuk, Donald J.	1993	
	1995	Three-time Brier winner
Walker, David	1977	
Walsh, William J.	1975	Two-time Brier winner
Walters, Cyril F.	1986	CCA past president, 1982–83
Watson, Grant G.	1974	Three-time Brier winner
Watson, J. Kenneth	1973	Three-time Brier-winning skip
Watt, Cecil M.	1986	CCA past president, 1980–81
Webb, Horace P.	1975	
Weldon, Kenneth B.	1982	
Welsh, James Oddie	1983	
Werenich, Edward	1988	
Weyman, Hugh E. (Jim)	1974	
Willis, Errick F.	1974	
Wilson, Archibald E.	1976	CCA past president, 1958–59
Wilson, James R.	1985	
Wilson, Thomas R.	1985	
Wood, Bryan D.	1974	Three-time Brier winner
Wood, D.J. Howard (Sr.)	1974	Three-time Brier winner

Canadian Curling Hall of Fame (Women)

Adams, Diane	1994	
Ball, Caroline	1985	
	1986	CLCA past president, 1980–81
Bartlett, Sylvia Ann (SueAnn)	1987	
Barraclough, Marilyn	1990	CLCA past president, 1988–89
Bergasse, Morag	1986	

Bray, Shirley	1991	
Calles, Ada	1976	
Clift, Kathleen (Kay)	1986	CLCA past president, 1970–71
Corby-Moore, Edith	1976	CLCA past president, 1977–78
Cragg, Pauline M.	1986	CLCA past president, 1962–63
Crosbie, Elsie	1988	CLCA past president, 1986–87
Delisle, Noreen	1986	CLCA past president, 1982–83
DeWare, Sen. Mabel	1986 1986	CLCA past president, 1977–78
Dillon, Catherine	1995	
Dockendroff, Marion	1986	Inaugural provincial association president; CLCA past president, 1972–73
Dwyer, Patricia	1992	
Elliiott, Jessie	1980	
Farnham, Emily B.	1993	
Fedoruk, Hon. Sylvia	1986	CLCA past president, 1971–72
Foster, Barbara	1991	CLCA past president 1989–90
Greenwood, Jill	1996	Three-time Canadian senior champion
Hansen, Ina	1976	
Hebb, Ann	1976	Inaugural provincial association president; CLCA past president, 1964–65
Hill, Darlene	1987	
Houston, Heather	1994	
Jamieson, Hazel I.	1982	
Johnson, Clara	1976	Inaugural provincial association president
Johnston, Katherine	1976	Inaugural provincial association president
Jones, Colleen P.	1989	
Jones-Walker, Debbie	1991	
Kaufman, June	1989	
Kennedy, Tracy	1994	
Kerr, Eva	1986	CLCA past president, 1981–82

Kerr, F. Marjorie	1986	CLCA past president, 1973–74
Knox, Sharon	1986	CLCA past president, 1983–84
Konkin, Irene	1987	
Krahn, Evelyn	1989	
	1994	CCA past president, 1993–94
Lang, Lorraine	1993	
	1994	
LaRocque, Penny	1989	
Light, Ina	1990	
Linkletter, Betty	1976	Inaugural provincial association president
Little, Shirley	1989	
Lytle, Velma M.	1976	Inaugural provincial association president
Macdonald, Elizabeth	1990	
MacLean, Aileen	1987	CLCA past president, 1985–86
MacMurray, Mary	1976	Inaugural provincial association president
MacRae, Dorothy (Dot)	1989	CLCA past president, 1987–88
Manley, Hadie	1990	
Martin, Flora	1979	
McKee, Joyce	1975	Five-time Canadian champion
	1976	
McLuckie, Lura	1978	
	1986	CLCA past president, 1967–68
Merry, Janet E.	1983	
	1986	CLCA past president, 1976–77
Messum, Edna	1993	
Mews, Olive	1976	Inaugural provincial association president
Moore, Linda	1991	
Morash, Shirley	1996	CCA past president, 1995–96
More, Christine M.	1988	
Morrison, Lenore (Lee)	1976	
Myers, Joyce	1989	
New, Dorothy D.	1986	CLCA past president, 1979–80

Nicholson, Mary-Anne	1992	CCA past president, 1991–92
Pezer, Dr. Vera	1976 1976	Three-time Canadian champion
Piers, Peggy	1984	
Pike, Violet	1983	
Porter, Muriel	1976	Inaugural provincial association president
Proulx, Rita C.	1976 1986 1987	Inaugural provincial association president CLCA past president, 1978–79
Roper, Barbara	1976	Inaugural provincial association president
Rowan, Sheila	1976	
Rowlands, Marion	1976	Inaugural provincial association president
Roy, Adeline M.R.	1977	
Segsworth, Mabel Dalton	1976	Inaugural provincial association president
Sinclair, Marjorie H.	1976	CLCA past president, 1963–64
Smith, Yvonne	1996	Three-time Canadian senior champion
Snowden, Jean	1982	CLCA past president, 1969–70
Sparkes, Lindsay E.	1988	
Thompson, Dorothy	1978	
Tipping, Edith	1986	CLCA past president, 1984–85
Tobin, Lee	1979	
Turner, Thora	1980	
Valentine, Margaret E.	1986	CLCA past president, 1965–66
Vandekerckhove (Vande) Patti	1989	
Wallace, Jo	1986	CLCA past president, 1968–69
Watson, Islay (Ila)	1976	Inaugural provincial association president
Watt, Hazel	1986	CLCA past president, 1960–61
Whalley, Joan	1981 1986	CLCA past president, 1975–76
Whitehead, Elma-Mae	1989	Inaugural provincial association president

Widdifield, Twyla	1989	
Wooley, Emily	1975	
Wood, Nora	1979	
Youngson, Muriel	1986	CLCA past president, 1961–62

U.S. Hall of Fame

Barcome, Dr. Donald	1994	
Befra, Frank	1998	
Brown, Ann	1993	
Brown, J. Nelson	1991	
Brown, Steve	1998	
Childs, Ted	1988	
Christman, Bob	1995	
Cobb, Art	1989	
Gagne, Al	1994	1965 World Champion
Gilleshammer, Orvil	1992	
Harris, Glenn	1988	
Kleffman, Gary	1994	1976 World Champion
Lauber, Harold	1997	
Locken, Tom	1994	
Marshall, Harvey	1989	
McBain, Hughston	1988	
McKay, Don	1988	
Nichols, Bob	1990	
Rickards, Norman	1991	
Roberts, Bruce	1988	
	1994	1976 World Champion
Roberts, Joe	1994	1976 World Champion
Roth, Mrs. Bernie	1996	
Scott, Jerry	1994	1976 World Champion
Sherwood, Ken	1997	

Slyziuk, Ernest	1996	
Slyziuk, Mike	1990	
Somerville, Bud	1984	
	1994	1965 World Champion
Stephens, Jim	1995	
Strum, Bill	1989	
	1994	1965 World Champion
Van Ess, Mary	1991	
Wright, Tom	1994	1965 World Champion

Index